Institutes of the
Christian Religion
Book I

- John Calvin -

ISBN:1631740202

Table of Contents:

INTRODUCTION
By The Rev. John Murray, M.A., Th.M.

The publication in English of another edition of the *opus magnum* of Christian theology is an event fraught with much encouragement. Notwithstanding the decadence so patent in our present-day world and particularly in the realm of Christian thought and life, the publishers have confidence that there is sufficient interest to warrant such an undertaking. If this faith is justified we have reason for thanksgiving to God. For what would be a better harbinger of another Reformation than widespread recourse to the earnest and sober study of the Word of God which would be evinced by the readiness carefully to peruse *The Institutes of the Christian Religion*.

Dr. B. B. Warfield in his admirable article, "On the Literary History of the *Institutes*," has condensed for us the appraisal accorded Calvin's work by the critics who have been most competent to judge. Among these tributes none expresses more adequately, and none with comparable terseness, the appraisal which is Calvin's due than that of the learned Joseph Scaliger, "Solus inter theologos Calvinus."

It would be a presumptuous undertaking to try to set forth all the reasons why Calvin holds that position of eminence in the history of Christian theology. By the grace and in the overruling providence of God there was the convergence of multiple factors, and all of these it would be impossible to trace in their various interrelations and interactions. One of these, however, calls for special mention. Calvin was an exegete and biblical theologian of the first rank. No other one factor comparably served to equip Calvin for the successful prosecution of his greatest work which in 1559 received its definitive edition.

The attitude to Scripture entertained by Calvin and the principles which guided him in its exposition are nowhere stated with more simplicity and fervor than in the Epistle Dedicatory to his first commentary, the commentary on the epistle to the Romans. "Such veneration," he says, "we ought indeed to entertain for the Word of God, that we ought not to pervert it in the least degree by varying expositions; for its majesty is diminished, I know not how much, especially when not expounded with great discretion and with great sobriety. And if it be deemed a great wickedness to contaminate any thing that is dedicated to God, he surely cannot be endured, who, with impure, or even with unprepared hands, will handle that very thing, which of all things is the most sacred on earth. It is therefore an audacity, closely allied to a sacrilege, rashly to turn Scripture in any way we please, and to indulge our fancies as in sport; which has been done by many in former times" (English Translation, Grand Rapids, 1947, p. 27).

It was Calvin preeminently who set the pattern for the exercise of that sobriety which guards the science of exegesis against those distortions and perversions to which allegorizing methods are ever prone to subject the interpretation and application of Scripture. The debt we owe to Calvin in establishing sound canons of interpretation and in thus directing the future course of exegetical study is incalculable. It is only to be lamented that too frequently the preaching of Protestant and even Reformed communions has not been sufficiently grounded in the hermeneutical principles which Calvin so nobly exemplified.

One feature of Calvin's exegetical work is his concern for the analogy of Scripture. He is always careful to take account of the unity and harmony of Scripture teaching. His expositions are not therefore afflicted with the vice of expounding particular passages without respect to the teaching of Scripture elsewhere and without respect to the

2

system of truth set forth in the Word of God. His exegesis, in a word, is theologically oriented. It is this quality that lies close to that which was *par excellence* his genius.

However highly we assess Calvin's exegetical talent and product, his eminence as an exegete must not be allowed to overshadow what was, after all, his greatest gift. He was *par excellence* a theologian. It was his systematizing genius preeminently that equipped him for the prosecution and completion of his masterpiece.

When we say that he was *par excellence* a theologian we must dissociate from our use of this word every notion that is suggestive of the purely speculative. No one has ever fulminated with more passion and eloquence against "vacuous and meteoric speculation" than has Calvin. And no one has ever been more keenly conscious that the theologian's task was the humble and, at the same time, truly noble one of being a disciple of the Scripture. "No man," he declares, "can have the least knowledge of true and sound doctrine without having been a disciple of the Scripture. Hence originates all true wisdom, when we embrace with reverence the testimony which God hath been pleased therein to deliver concerning himself. For obedience is the source, not only of an absolutely perfect and complete faith, but of all right knowledge of God" (*Inst.* 1, 6, 2). In the words of William Cunningham: "In theology there is, of course, no room for originality properly so called, for its whole materials are contained in the actual statements of God's word; and he is the greatest and best theologian who has most accurately apprehended the meaning of the statements of Scripture—who, by comparing and combining them, has most fully and correctly brought out the whole mind of God on all the topics on which the Scriptures give us information—who classifies and digests the truths of Scripture in the way best fitted to commend them to the apprehension and acceptance of men—and who can most clearly and forcibly bring out their scriptural evidence, and most skillfully and effectively defend them against the assaults of adversaries . . . Calvin was far above the weakness of aiming at the invention of novelties in theology, or of wishing to be regarded as the discoverer of new opinions" (*The Reformers and the Theology of the Reformation*, Edinburgh, 1866, p. 296). As we bring even elementary understanding to bear upon our reading of the *Institutes* we shall immediately discover the profound sense of the majesty of God, veneration for the Word of God, and the jealous care for faithful exposition and systematization which were marked features of the author. And because of this we shall find the *Institutes* to be suffused with the warmth of godly fear. The *Institutes* is not only the classic of Christian theology; it is also a model of Christian devotion. For what Calvin sought to foster was that "pure and genuine religion" which consists in "faith united with the serious fear of God, such fear as may embrace voluntary reverence and draw along with it legitimate worship such as is prescribed in the law" (*Inst.* 1, 2, 2).

The present edition is from the translation made by Henry Beveridge in 1845 for the Calvin Translation Society. The reader may be assured that the translation faithfully reflects the teaching of Calvin but must also bear in mind that no translation can perfectly convey the thought of the original. It may also be added that a more adequate translation of Calvin's *Institutes* into English is a real *desideratum*. In fulfilling this need the translator or translators would perform the greatest service if the work of translation were supplemented by footnotes in which at crucial points, where translation is difficult or most accurate translation im- possible, the Latin text would be reproduced and comment made on its more exact import. Furthermore, footnotes which would supply the reader with references to other places in Calvin's writings where he deals with the same subject would be an invaluable help to students of Calvin and to the cause of truth. Admittedly such work requires linguistic skill of the highest order, thorough knowledge of Calvin's writings, and deep sympathy with his theology. It would also involve prodigious labour. We may hope that the seed being sown by the present venture may bear fruit some day in such a harvest.

John Murray,
Professor of Systematic Theology, Westminster Theological Seminary. Philadelphia, Penna.

THE ORIGINAL TRANSLATOR'S PREFACE.
PREFIXED TO THE FOURTH EDITION 1581 AND REPRINTED VERBATIM IN ALL THE SUBSEQUENT EDITIONS.
THOMAS NORTON, THE TRANSLATOR TO THE READER.

Good reader, here is now offered you, the fourth time printed in English, M. Calvin's book of the Institution of Christian Religion; a book of great labour to the author, and of great profit to the Church of God. M. Calvin first wrote it when he was a young man, a book of small volume, and since that season he has at sundry times published it with new increases, still protesting at every edition himself to be one of those *qui scribendo proficiunt, et proficiendo scribunt*, which with their writing do grow in profiting, and with their profiting do proceed in writing. At length having, in many [of] his other works, traveled about exposition of sundry books of the Scriptures, and in the same finding occasion to discourse of sundry common-places and matters of doctrine, which being handled according to the occasions of the text that were offered him, and not in any other method, were not so ready for the reader's use, he therefore entered into this purpose to enlarge this book of Institutions, and therein to treat of all those titles and commonplaces largely, with this intent, that whensoever any occasion fell in his other books to treat of any such cause, he would not newly amplify his books of commentaries and expositions therewith, but refer his reader wholly to this storehouse and treasure of that sort of divine learning. As age and weakness grew upon him, so he hastened his labour; and, according to his petition to God, he in manner ended his life with his work, for he lived not long after.

So great a jewel was meet to be made most beneficial, that is to say, applied to most common use. Therefore, in the very beginning of the Queen's Majesty's most blessed reign, I translated it out of Latin into English for the commodity of the Church of Christ, at the special request of my dear friends of worthy memory, Reginald Wolfe and Edward Whitchurch, the one her Majesty's printer for the Hebrew, Greek, and Latin tongues, the other her Highness' printer of the books of Common Prayer. I performed my work in the house of my said friend, Edward Whitchurch, a man well known of upright heart and dealing, an ancient zealous gospeller, as plain and true a friend as ever I knew living, and as desirous to do anything to common good, especially by the advancement of true religion.

At my said first edition of this book, I considered how the author thereof had of long time purposely laboured to write the same most exactly, and to pack great plenty of matter in small room of words; yea, and those so circumspectly and precisely ordered, to avoid the cavillations of such as for enmity to the truth therein contained would gladly seek and abuse all advantages which might be found by any oversight in penning of it, that the sentences were thereby become so full as nothing might well be added without idle superfluity, and again so highly pared, that nothing could be diminished without taking away some necessary substance of matter therein expressed. This manner of writing, beside the peculiar terms of arts and figures, and the difficulty of the matters themselves, being throughout interlaced with the school men's controversies, made a great hardness in the author's own book, in that tongue wherein otherwise he is both plentiful and easy, insomuch that it sufficeth not to read him once, unless you can be content to read in vain. This consideration encumbered me with great doubtfulness for the whole order and frame of my translation. If I should follow the words, I saw that of necessity the hardness in the translation must needs be greater than was in the tongue wherein it was originally written. If I should leave the course of words, and grant myself liberty after the natural manner of my own tongue, to say that in English which I conceived to be his meaning in Latin, I plainly perceived how hardly I might escape error, and on the other side, in this matter of faith and religion, how perilous it was to err. For I durst not presume to warrant myself to have his meaning without his words. And they that wet what it is to translate well and faithfully, especially in matters of religion, do know that not the only grammatical construction of words sufficeth, but the very building and order to observe all advantages of vehemence or grace, by placing or accent of words, maketh much to the true setting forth of a writer's mind.

In the end, I rested upon this determination, to follow the words so near as the phrase of the English tongue would suffer me. Which purpose I so performed, that if the English book were printed in such paper and letter as the Latin is, it should not exceed the Latin in quantity. Whereby, beside all other commodities that a faithful translation of so good a work may bring, this one benefit is moreover provided for such as are desirous to attain some knowledge of the Latin tongue (which is, at this time, to be wished in many of those men for whose profession this book most fitly serveth), that they shall not find any more English than shall suffice to construe the Latin withal, except in such few places where the great difference of the phrases of the languages enforced me: so that, comparing the one with the other, they shall both profit in good matter, and furnish themselves with under- standing of that speech, wherein the greatest treasures of knowledge are disclosed.

In the doing hereof, I did not only trust mine own wit or ability, but examined my whole doing from sentence to sentence throughout the whole book with conference and overlooking of such learned men, as my translation being allowed by their Judgment, I did both satisfy mine own conscience that I had done truly, and their approving of it might be a good warrant to the reader that nothing should herein be delivered him but sound, unmingled, and un-corrupted doctrine, even in such sort as the author himself had first framed it. All that I wrote, the grave, learned, and virtuous man, M. David Whitehead (whom I name with honourable remembrance), did, among others, compare with the Latin, examining every sentence throughout the whole book. Beside all this, I privately required many, and generally all men with whom I ever had any talk of this matter, that if they found anything either not truly translated, or not plainly Englished, they would inform me thereof, promising either to satisfy them or to amend it. Since which time, I have not been advertised by any man of anything which they would require to be altered. Neither had I myself, by reason of my profession, being otherwise occupied, any leisure to peruse it. And that is the cause, why not only at the second and third time, but also at this impression, you have no change at all in the work, but altogether as it was before.

Indeed, I perceived many men well-minded and studious of this book, to require a table for their ease and furtherance. Their honest desire I have fulfilled in the second edition, and have added thereto a plentiful table, which is also here inserted, which I have translated out of the Latin, wherein the principal matters discoursed in this book are named by their due titles in order of alphabet, and under every title is set forth a brief sum of the whole doctrine taught in this book concerning the matter belonging to that title or common-place; and therewith is added the book, chapter, and section or division of the chapter, where the same doctrine is more largely expressed and proved. And for the readier finding thereof, I have caused the number of the chapters to be set upon every leaf in the book, and quoted the sections also by their due numbers with the usual figures of algorism. And now at this last publishing, my friends, by whose charge it is now newly imprinted in a Roman letter and smaller volume, with divers other Tables which, since my second edition, were gathered by M. Marlorate, to be translated and here added for your benefit.

Moreover, whereas in the first edition the evil manner of my scribbling hand, the inter- lining of my copy, and some other causes well known among workmen of that faculty, made very many faults to pass the printer, I have, in the second impression, caused the book to be composed by the printed copy, and corrected by the written; whereby it must needs be that it was much more truly done than the other was, as I myself do know above three hundred faults amended. And now at this last printing, the composing after a printed copy bringeth some ease, and the diligence used about the correction having been right faithfully looked unto, it cannot be but much more truly set forth. This also is performed, that the volume being smaller, with a letter fair and legible, it is of more easy price, that it may be of more common use, and so to more large communicating of so great a treasure to those that desire Christian knowledge for instruction of their faith, and guiding of their duties. Thus, on the printer's behalf and mine, your ease and commodity (good readers) provided for. Now resteth your own diligence, for your own profit, in studying it.

To spend many words in commending the work itself were needless; yet thus much I think, I may both not unruly and not vainly say, that though many great learned men have written books of common-places of our religion, as Melancthon, Sarcerius, and others, whose works are very good and profitable to the Church of God, yet by the consenting Judgment of those that understand the same, there is none to be compared to this work of Calvin, both for his substantial sufficiency of doctrine, the sound declaration of truth in articles of our religion, the large and learned confirmation of the same, and the most deep and strong confutation of all old and new heresies; so that (the Holy Scriptures excepted) this is one of the most profitable books for all students of Christian divinity. Wherein (good readers), as I am glad for the glory of God, and for your benefit, that you may have this profit of my travel, so I beseech you let me have this use of your gentleness, that my doings may be construed to such good end as I have meant them; and that if any thing mislike you by reason of hardness, or any other cause that may seem to be my default, you will not forthwith condemn the work, but read it after; in which doing you will find (as many have confessed to me that they have found by experience) that those things which at the first reading shall displease you for hardness, shall be found so easy as so hard matter would suffer, and, for the most part, more easy than some other phrase which should with greater looseness and smoother sliding away deceive your understanding. I confess, indeed, it is not finely and pleasantly written, nor carrieth with it such delightful grace of speech as some great wise men have bestowed upon some foolisher things, yet it containeth sound truth set forth with faithful plainness, without wrong done to the author's meaning; and so, if you accept and use it, you shall not fail to have great profit thereby, and I shall think my labour very well employed.

Thomas Norton.

PREFATORY ADDRESS
TO HIS MOST CHRISTIAN MAJESTY, THE MOST MIGHTY AND ILLUSTRIOUS MONARCH, FRANCIS, KING OF THE FRENCH, HIS SOVEREIGN; JOHN CALVIN PRAYS PEACE AND SALVATION IN CHRIST.

Sire,—When I first engaged in this work, nothing was farther from my thoughts than to write what should afterwards be presented to your Majesty. My intention was only to furnish a kind of rudiments, by which those who feel some interest in religion might be trained to true godliness. And I toiled at the task chiefly for the sake of my countrymen the French, multitudes of whom I perceived to be hungering and thirsting after Christ, while very few seemed to have been duly imbued with even a slender knowledge of him. That this was the object which I had in view is apparent from the work itself, which is written in a simple and elementary form adapted for instruction.

But when I perceived that the fury of certain bad men had risen to such a height in your realm, that there was no place in it for sound doctrine, I thought it might be of service if I were in the same work both to give instruction to my countrymen, and also lay before your Majesty a Confession, from which you may learn what the doctrine is that so inflames the rage of those madmen who are this day, with fire and sword, troubling your kingdom. For I fear not to declare, that what I have here given may be regarded as a summary of the very doctrine which, they vociferate, ought to be punished with confiscation, exile, imprisonment, and flames, as well as exterminated by land and sea.

I am aware, indeed, how, in order to render our cause as hateful to your Majesty as possible, they have filled your ears and mind with atrocious insinuations; but you will be pleased, of your clemency, to reflect, that neither in word nor deed could there be any innocence, were it sufficient merely to accuse. When any one, with the view of exciting prejudice, observes that this doctrine, of which I am endeavouring to give your Majesty an account, has been condemned by the suffrages of all the estates, and was long ago stabbed again and again by partial sentences of courts of law, he undoubtedly says nothing more than that it has sometimes been violently oppressed by the power and faction of adversaries, and sometimes fraudulently and insidiously overwhelmed by lies, cavils, and calumny. While a cause is unheard, it is violence to pass sanguinary sentences against it; it is fraud to charge it, contrary to its deserts, with sedition and mischief.

That no one may suppose we are unjust in thus complaining, you yourself, most illustrious Sovereign, can bear us witness with what lying calumnies it is daily traduced in your presence, as aiming at nothing else than to wrest the sceptres of kings out of their hands, to overturn all tribunals and seats of justice, to subvert all order and government, to disturb the peace and quiet of society, to abolish all laws, destroy the distinctions of rank and property, and, in short, turn all things upside down. And yet, that which you hear is but the smallest portion of what is said; for among the common people are disseminated certain horrible insinuations—insinuations which, if well founded, would justify the whole world in condemning the doctrine with its authors to a thousand fires and gibbets. Who can wonder that the popular hatred is inflamed against it, when credit is given to those most iniquitous accusations? See, why all ranks unite with one accord in condemning our persons and our doctrine!

Carried away by this feeling, those who sit in judgment merely give utterance to the prejudices which they have imbibed at home, and think they have duly performed their part if they do not order punishment to be inflicted on any one until convicted, either on his own confession, or on legal evidence. But of what crime convicted? "Of that condemned doctrine," is the answer. But with what justice condemned? The very essence of the defence was, not to abjure the doctrine itself, but to maintain its truth. On this subject, however, not a whisper is allowed!

Justice, then, most invincible Sovereign, entitles me to demand that you will undertake a thorough investigation of this cause, which has hitherto been tossed about in any kind of way, and handled in the most irregular manner, without any order of law, and with passionate heat rather than judicial gravity.

Let it not be imagined that I am here framing my own private defence, with the view of obtaining a safe return to my native land. Though I cherish towards it the feelings which become me as a man, still, as matters now are, I can be absent from it without regret. The cause which I plead is the common cause of all the godly, and therefore the very cause of Christ—a cause which, throughout your realm, now lies, as it were, in despair, torn and trampled upon in all kinds of ways, and that more through the tyranny of certain Pharisees than any sanction from yourself. But it matters not to inquire how the thing is done; the fact that it is done cannot be denied. For so far have the wicked prevailed, that the truth of Christ, if not utterly routed and dispersed, lurks as if it were ignobly buried; while the poor Church, either wasted by cruel slaughter or driven into exile, or intimidated and terror—struck, scarcely ventures to breathe. Still her enemies press on with their wonted rage and fury over the ruins which they have made, strenuously assaulting the wall, which is already giving way. Meanwhile, no man comes forth to offer his protection

14

against such furies. Any who would be thought most favourable to the truth, merely talk of pardoning the error and imprudence of ignorant men For so those modest personages speak; giving the name of *error and imprudence* to that which they know to be the infallible truth of God, and of *ignorant men* to those whose intellect they see that Christ has not despised, seeing he has deigned to intrust them with the mysteries of his heavenly wisdom. Thus all are ashamed of the Gospel.

Your duty, most serene Prince, is, not to shut either your ears or mind against a cause involving such mighty interests as these: how the glory of God is to be maintained on the earth inviolate, how the truth of God is to preserve its dignity, how the kingdom of Christ is to continue amongst us compact and secure. The cause is worthy of your ear, worthy of your investigation, worthy of your throne.

The characteristic of a true sovereign is, to acknowledge that, in the administration of his kingdom, he is a minister of God. He who does not make his reign subservient to the divine glory, acts the part not of a king, but a robber. He, moreover, deceives himself who anticipates long prosperity to any kingdom which is not ruled by the sceptre of God, that is, by his divine word. For the heavenly oracle is infallible which has declared, that "where there is no vision the people perish" (Prov. 29:18).

Let not a contemptuous idea of our insignificance dissuade you from the investigation of this cause. We, indeed, are perfectly conscious how poor and abject we are: in the presence of God we are miserable sinners, and in the sight of men most despised—we are (if you will) the mere dregs and off—scourings of the world, or worse, if worse can be named: so that before God there remains nothing of which we can glory save only his mercy, by which, without any merit of our own, we are admitted to the hope of eternal salvation:6 and before men not even this much remains, since we can glory only in our infirmity, a thing which, in the estimation of men, it is the greatest ignominy even tacitly to confess. But our doctrine must stand sublime above all the glory of the world, and invincible by all its power, because it is not ours, but that of the living God and his Anointed, whom the Father has appointed King, that he may rule from sea to sea, and from the rivers even to the ends of the earth; and so rule as to smite the whole earth and its strength of iron and brass, its splendour of gold and silver, with the mere rod of his mouth, and break them in pieces like a potter's vessel; according to the magnificent predictions of the prophets respecting his kingdom (Dan. 2:34; Isaiah 11:4; Psalm 2:9).

Our adversaries, indeed, clamorously maintain that our appeal to the word of God is a mere pretext,—that we are, in fact, its worst corrupters. How far this is not only malicious calumny, but also shameless effrontery, you will be able to decide, of your own knowledge, by reading our Confession. Here, however, it may be necessary to make some observations which may dispose, or at least assist, you to read and study it with attention.

When Paul declared that all prophecy ought to be according to the analogy of faith (Rom. 12:6), he laid down the surest rule for determining the meaning of Scripture. Let our doctrine be tested by this rule and our victory is secure. For what accords better and more aptly with faith than to acknowledge ourselves divested of all virtue that we may be clothed by God, devoid of all goodness that we may be filled by Him, the slaves of sin that he may give us freedom, blind that he may enlighten, lame that he may cure, and feeble that he may sustain us; to strip ourselves of all ground of glorying that he alone may shine forth glorious, and we be glorified in him? When these things, and others to the same effect, are said by us, they interpose, and querulously complain, that in this way we overturn some blind light of nature, fancied preparatives, free will, and works meritorious of eternal salvation, with their own supererogations also; because they cannot bear that the entire praise and glory of all goodness, virtue, justice, and wisdom, should remain with God. But we read not of any having been blamed for drinking too much of the fountain of living water; on the contrary, those are severely reprimanded who "have hewed them out cisterns, broken cisterns, that can hold no water" (Jer. 2:13). Again, what more agreeable to faith than to feel assured that God is a propitious Father when Christ is acknowledged as a brother and propitiator, than confidently to expect all prosperity and gladness from Him, whose ineffable love towards us was such that He "spared not his own Son, but delivered him up for us all" (Rom. 8:32), than to rest in the sure hope of salvation and eternal life whenever Christ, in whom such treasures are hid, is conceived to have been given by the Father? Here they attack us, and loudly maintain that this sure confidence is not free from arrogance and presumption. But as nothing is to be presumed of ourselves, so all things are to be presumed of God; nor are we stript of vainglory for any other reason than that we may learn to glory in the Lord. Why go farther? Take but a cursory view, most valiant King, of all the parts of our cause, and count us of all wicked men the most iniquitous, if you do not discover plainly, that "therefore we both labour and suffer reproach because we trust in the living God" (1 Tim. 4:10); because we believe it to be "life eternal" to know "the only true God, and Jesus Christ," whom he has sent (John 17:3). For this hope some of us are in bonds, some beaten with rods, some made a gazing—stock, some proscribed, some most cruelly tortured, some obliged to flee; we are all pressed with straits, loaded with dire execrations, lacerated by slanders, and treated with the greatest indignity.

Look now to our adversaries (I mean the priesthood, at whose beck and pleasure others ply their enmity against us), and consider with me for a little by what zeal they are actuated. The true religion which is delivered in the Scriptures, and which all ought to hold, they readily permit both themselves and others to be ignorant of, to neglect and despise; and they deem it of little moment what each man believes concerning God and Christ, or disbelieves, provided he submits to the judgment of the Church with what they call implicit faith; nor are they greatly concerned though they should see the glow of God dishonoured by open blasphemies, provided not a finger is raised against the primacy of the Apostolic See and the authority of holy mother Church. Why, then, do they war for the mass, purgatory, pilgrimage, and similar follies, with such fierceness and acerbity, that though they cannot prove one of them from the word of God, they deny godliness can be safe without faith in these things—faith drawn out, if I may so express it, to its utmost stretch? Why? just because their belly is their God, and their kitchen their religion; and they believe, that if these were away they would not only not be Christians, but not even men. For although some wallow in luxury, and others feed on slender crusts, still they all live by the same pot, which without that fuel might not only cool, but altogether freeze. He, accordingly, who is most anxious about his stomach, proves the fiercest champion of his faith. In short, the object on which all to a man are bent, is to keep their kingdom safe or their belly filled; not one gives even the smallest sign of sincere zeal.

Nevertheless, they cease not to assail our doctrine, and to accuse and defame it in what terms they may, in order to render it either hated or suspected. They call it new, and of recent birth; they carp at it as doubtful and uncertain; they bid us tell by what miracles it has been confirmed; they ask if it be fair to receive it against the consent of so many holy Fathers and the most ancient custom; they urge us to confess either that it is schismatical in giving battle to the Church, or that the Church must have been without life during the many centuries in which nothing of the kind was heard. Lastly, they say there is little need of argument, for its quality may be known by its fruits, namely, the large number of sects, the many seditious disturbances, and the great licentiousness which it has produced. No doubt, it is a very easy matter for them, in presence of an ignorant and credulous multitude, to insult over an un- defended cause; but were an opportunity of mutual discussion afforded, that acrimony which they now pour out upon us in frothy torrents, with as much license as impunity, would assuredly boil dry.

1. First, in calling it new, they are exceedingly injurious to God, whose sacred word deserved not to be charged with novelty. To them, indeed, I very little doubt it is new, as Christ is new, and the Gospel new; but those who are acquainted with the old saying of Paul, that Christ Jesus "died for our sins, and rose again for our justification" (Rom. 4:25), will not detect any novelty in us. That it long lay buried and unknown is the guilty consequence of man's impiety; but now when, by the kindness of God, it is restored to us, it ought to resume its antiquity just as the returning citizen resumes his rights.

2. It is owing to the same ignorance that they hold it to be doubtful and uncertain; for this is the very thing of which the Lord complains by his prophet, "The ox knoweth his owner, and the ass his master's crib; but Israel doth not know, my people doth not consider" (Isaiah 1:3). But however they may sport with its uncertainty, had they to seal their own doctrine with their blood, and at the expense of life, it would be seen what value they put upon it. Very different is our confidence—a confidence which is not appalled by the terrors of death, and therefore not even by the judgment—seat of God.

3. In demanding miracles from us, they act dishonestly; for we have not coined some new gospel, but retain the very one the truth of which is confirmed by all the miracles which Christ and the apostles ever wrought. But they have

a peculiarity which we have not—they can confirm their faith by constant miracles down to the present day! Way rather, they allege miracles which might produce wavering in minds otherwise well disposed; they are so frivolous and ridiculous, so vain and false. But were they even exceedingly wonderful, they could have no effect against the truth of God, whose name ought to be hallowed always, and everywhere, whether by miracles, or by the natural course of events. The deception would perhaps be more specious if Scripture did not admonish us of the legitimate end and use of miracles. Mark tells us (Mark 16:20) that the signs which followed the preaching of the apostles were wrought in confirmation of it; so Luke also relates that the Lord "gave testimony to the word of his grace, and granted signs and wonders to be done" by the hands of the apostles (Acts 14:3). Very much to the same effect are those words of the apostle, that salvation by a preached gospel was confirmed, "The Lord bearing witness with signs and wonders, and with divers miracles" (Heb. 2:4). Those things which we are told are seals of the gospel, shall we pervert to the subversion of the gospel? What was destined only to confirm the truth, shall we misapply to the confirmation of lies? The proper course, therefore, is, in the first instance, to ascertain and examine the doctrine which is said by the Evangelist to precede; then after it has been proved, but not till then, it may receive confirmation from miracles. But the mark of sound doctrine given by our Saviour himself is its tendency to promote the glory not of men, but of God (John 7:18; 8:50). Our Saviour having declared this to be test of doctrine, we are in error if we regard as miraculous, works which are used for any other purpose than to magnify the name of God. And it becomes us to remember that Satan has his miracles, which, although they are tricks rather than true wonders, are still such as to delude the ignorant and unwary. Magicians and enchanters have always been famous for miracles, and

miracles of an astonishing description have given support
to idolatry: these, however, do not make us converts to the
superstitions either of magicians or idolaters. In old times,
too, the Donatists used their power of working miracles as
a battering-ram, with which they shook the simplicity of the
common people. We now give to our opponents the answer
which Augustine then gave to the Donatists (in Joan. Tract.
23), "The Lord put us on our guard against those wonder—
workers, when he foretold that false prophets would arise,
who, by lying signs and divers wonders, would, if it were
possible, deceive the very elect" (Mt. 24:24). Paul, too,
gave warning that the reign of antichrist would be "withall
power, and signs, and lying wonders" (2 Thess. 2:9).

But our opponents tell us that their miracles are
wrought not by idols, not by sorcerers, not by false
prophets, but by saints: as if we did not know it to be one of
Satan's wiles to transform himself "into an angel of
light" (2 Cor. 11:14). The Egyptians, in whose
neighbourhood Jeremiah was buried, anciently sacrificed
and paid other divine honours to him (Hieron. in Praef.
Jerem). Did they not make an idolatrous abuse of the holy
prophet of God? and yet, in recompense for so venerating
his tomb, they thought14 that they were cured of the bite of
serpents. What, then, shall we say but that it has been, and
always will be, a most just punishment of God, to send on
those who do not receive the truth in the love of it, "strong
delusion, that they should believe a lie"? (2 Thess. 2:11).
We, then, have no lack of miracles, sure miracles, that
cannot be gainsaid; but those to which our opponents lay
claim are mere delusions of Satan, inasmuch as they draw
off the people from the true worship of God to vanity.

4. It is a calumny to represent us as opposed to the
Fathers (I mean the ancient writers of a purer age), as if the
Fathers were supporters of their impiety. Were the contest
to be decided by such authority (to speak in the most
moderate terms), the better part of the victory would be

ours. While there is much that is admirable and wise in the writings of those Fathers, and while in some things it has fared with them as with ordinary men; these pious sons, forsooth, with the peculiar acuteness of intellect, and judgment, and soul, which belongs to them, adore only their slips and errors, while those things which are well said they either overlook, or disguise, or corrupt; so that it may be truly said their only care has been to gather dross among gold. Then, with dishonest clamour, they assail us as enemies and despisers of the Fathers. So far are we from despising them, that if this were the proper place, it would give us no trouble to support the greater part of the doctrines which we now hold by their suffrages. Still, in studying their writings, we have endeavoured to remember (1 Cor. 3:21-23; see also Augustin. Ep. 28), that all things are ours, to serve, not lord it over us, but that we axe Christ's only, and must obey him in all things without exception. He who does not draw this distinction will not have any fixed principles in religion; for those holy men were ignorant of many things, are often opposed to each other, and are sometimes at variance with themselves.

It is not without cause (remark our opponents) we are thus warned by Solomon, "Remove not the ancient landmarks which thy fathers have set" (Prov. 22:28). But the same rule applies not to the measuring of fields and the obedience of faith. The rule applicable to the latter is, "Forget also thine own people, and thy father's house" (Ps. 45:10). But if they are so fond of allegory, why do they not understand the apostles, rather than any other class of Fathers, to be meant by those whose landmarks it is unlawful to remove? This is the interpretation of Jerome, whose words they have quoted in their canons. But as regards those to whom they apply the passage, if they wish the landmarks to be fixed, why do they, whenever it suits their purpose, so freely overleap them?

Among the Fathers there were two, the one of whom said, "Our God neither eats nor drinks, and therefore has no need of chalices and salvers;" and the other "Sacred rites do not require gold, and things which are not bought with gold, please not by gold." They step beyond the boundary, therefore, when in sacred matters they are so much delighted with gold, driver, ivory, marble, gems, and silks, that unless everything is overlaid with costly show, or rather insane luxury, they think God is not duly worshipped.

It was a Father who said, "He ate flesh freely on the day on which others abstained from it, because he was a Christian." They overleap the boundaries, therefore, when they doom to perdition every soul that, during Lent, shall have tasted flesh.

There were two Fathers, the one of whom said, "A monk not labouring with his own hands is no better than a violent man and a robber;" and the other, "Monks, however as- siduous they may be in study, meditation, and prayer, must not live by others." This boundary, too, they transgressed, when they placed lazy gormandising monks in dens and stews, to gorge themselves on other men's substance.

It was a Father who said, "It is a horrid abomination to see in Christian temples a painted image either of Christ or of any saint." Nor was this pronounced by the voice era single individual; but an Ecclesiastical Council also decreed, "Let nought that is worshipped be depicted on walls."Very far are they from keeping within these boundaries when they leave not a corner without images.

Another Father counselled, "That after performing the office of humanity to the dead in their burial, we should leave them at rest." These limits they burst through when they keep up a perpetual anxiety about the dead.

It is a Father who testifies, "That the substance of bread and wine in the Eucharist does not cease but remains, just as the nature and substance of man remains united to the Godhead in the Lord Jesus Christ." This boundary they pass in pretending that, as soon as the words of our Lord are pronounced, the substance of bread and wine ceases, and is transubstantiated into body and blood.

They were Fathers, who, as they exhibited only one Eucharist to the whole Church, and kept back from it the profane and flagitious; so they, in the severest terms, censured all those who, being present, did not communicate How far have they removed these land- marks, in filling not churches only, but also private houses, with their masses, admitting all and sundry to be present, each the more willingly the more largely he pays, however wicked and impure he may be,—not inviting any one to faith in Christ and faithful communion in the sacraments, but rather vending their own work for the grace and merits of Christ!

There were two Fathers, the one of whom decided that those were to be excluded altogether from partaking of Christ's sacred supper, who, contented with communion in one kind, abstained from the other; while the other Father strongly contends31 that the blood of the Lord ought not to be denied to the Christian people, who, in confessing him, are en- joined to shed their own blood. These landmarks, also, they removed, when, by an unalterable law, they ordered the very thing which the former Father punished with excommunication, and the latter condemned for a valid reason. It was a Father who pronounced it rashness, in an obscure question, to decide in either way without clear and evident authority from Scripture. They forgot this landmark when they enacted so many constitutions, so many canons, and so many dogmatical decisions, without sanction from the word of God.

It was a Father who reproved Montanus, among other heresies, for being the first who imposed laws of fasting. They have gone far beyond this landmark also in enjoining fasting under the strictest laws.

It was a Father who denied that the ministers of the Church should be interdicted from marrying, and pronounced married life to be a state of chastity; and there were other Fathers who assented to his decision. These boundaries they overstepped in rigidly binding their priests to celibacy.

It was a Father who thought that Christ only should be listened to, from its being said, "hear him;" and that regard is due not to what others before us have said or done, but only to what Christ, the head of all, has commanded. This landmark they neither observe them- selves nor allow to be observed by others, while they subject themselves and others to any master whatever, rather than Christ.

There is a Father who contends that the Church ought not to prefer herself to Christ, who always judges truly, whereas ecclesiastical judges, who are but men, are generally deceived. Having burst through this barrier also, they hesitate not to suspend the whole authority of Scripture on the judgment of the Church.

All the Fathers with one heart execrated, and with one mouth protested against, contaminating the word of God with the subtleties sophists, and involving it in the brawls of dialecticians. Do they keep within these limits when the sole occupation of their lives is to entwine and entangle the simplicity of Scripture with endless disputes, and worse than sophistical jargon? So much so, that were the Fathers to rise from their graves, and listen to the brawling art which bears the name of speculative theology, there is nothing they would suppose it less to be than a discussion of a religious nature.

But my discourse would far exceed its just limits were I to show, in detail, how petulantly those men shake off the yoke of the Fathers, while they wish to be thought their most obedient sons. Months, nay, years would fail me; and yet so deplorable and desperate is their effrontery, that they presume to chastise us for overstepping the ancient landmarks!

5. Then, again, it is to no purpose they call us to the bar of custom. To make everything yield to custom would be to do the greatest injustice. Were the judgments of mankind correct, custom would be regulated by the good. But it is often far otherwise in point of fact; for, whatever the many are seen to do, forthwith obtains the force of custom. But human affairs have scarcely ever been so happily constituted as that the better course pleased the greater number. Hence the private vices of the multitude have generally resulted in public error, or rather that common consent in vice which these worthy men would have to be law. Any one with eyes may perceive that it is not one flood of evils which has deluged us; that many fatal plagues have invaded the globe; that all things rush headlong; so that either the affairs of men must be altogether despaired of, or we must not only resist, but boldly attack prevailing evils. The cure is prevented by no other cause than the length of time during which we have been accustomed to the disease. But be it so that public error must have a place in human society, still, in the kingdom of God, we must look and listen only to his eternal truth, against which no series of years, no custom, no conspiracy, can plead prescription. Thus Isaiah formerly taught the people of God, "Say ye not, A confederacy, to all to whom this people shall say, A confederacy;" i.e. do not unite with the people in an impious consent; "neither fear ye their fear, nor be afraid. Sanctify the Lord of hosts himself; and let him be your fear, and let him be your dread" (Is. 8:12). Now, therefore, let them, if they will, object to us both past ages and present examples; if we sanctify the Lord of hosts, we shall not be greatly afraid. Though many ages should have consented to like ungodliness, He is strong who taketh vengeance to the third and fourth generation; or the whole world should league together in the same iniquity. He taught

experimentally what the end is of those who sin with the multitude, when He destroyed the whole human race with a flood, saving Noah with his little family, who, by putting his faith in Him alone, "condemned the world" (Heb. 11:7). In short, depraved custom is just a kind of general pestilence in which men perish not the less that they fall in a crowd. It were well, moreover, to ponder the observation of Cyprian, that those who sin in ignorance, though they cannot be entirely exculpated, seem, however, to be, in some sense, excusable; whereas those who obstinately reject the truth, when presented to them by the kindness of God, have no defence to offer.

6. Their dilemma does not push us so violently as to oblige us to confess, either that the Church was a considerable time without life, or that we have now a quarrel with the Church. The Church of Christ assuredly has lived, and will live, as long as Christ shall reign at the right hand of the Father. By his hand it is sustained, by his protection defended, by his mighty power preserved in safety. For what he once undertook he will undoubtedly perform, he will be with his people always, "even to the end of the world" (Mt. 28:20). With the Church we wage no war, since, with one consent, in common with the whole body of the faithful, we worship and adore one God, and Christ Jesus the Lord, as all the pious have always adored him. But they themselves err not a little from the truth in not recognising any church but that which they behold with the bodily eye, and in endeavouring to circumscribe it by limits, within which it cannot be confined.

The hinges on which the controversy turns are these: first, in their contending that the form of the Church is always visible and apparent; and, secondly, in their placing this form in the see of the Church of Rome and its hierarchy. We, on the contrary, maintain, both that the Church may exist without any apparent form, and, moreover, that the form is not ascertained by that external splendour which they foolishly admire, but by a very different mark, namely, by the pure preaching of the word of God, and the due administration of the sacraments. They make an outcry whenever the Church cannot be pointed to with the finger. But how oft was it the fate of the Church among the Jews to be so defaced that no comeliness appeared? What do we suppose to have been the splendid form when Elijah complained that he was left alone? (1 Kings 19:14). How long after the advent of Christ did it lie hid without form? How often since has it been so oppressed by wars, seditions, and heresies, that it was nowhere seen in splendour? Had they lived at that time, would they have believed there was any Church? But Elijah learned that there remained seven thousand men who had not bowed the knee to Baal; nor ought we to doubt that Christ has always reigned on earth ever since he ascended to heaven. Had the faithful at that time required some discernible form, must they not have forthwith given way to despondency? And, indeed, Hilary accounted it a very great fault in his day, that men were so possessed with a foolish admiration of Episcopal dignity as not to perceive the deadly hydra lurking under that mask. His words are (Cont. Auxentium), "One advice I give: Beware of Antichrist; for, unhappily, a love of walls has seized you; unhappily, the Church of God which you venerate exists in houses and buildings; unhappily, under these you find the name of peace. Is it doubtful that in these Antichrist will have his seat? Safer to me are mountains, and woods, and lakes, and dungeons, and whirlpools; since in these prophets, dwelling or immersed, did prophesy."

And what is it at the present day that the world venerates in its horned bishops, unless that it imagines those who are seen presiding over celebrated cities to be holy prelates of religion? Away, then, with this absurd mode of judging! Let us rather reverently admit, that as God alone knows who are his, so he may sometimes withdraw the external manifestation of his Church from the view of men. This, I allow, is a fearful punishment which God sends on the earth; but if the wickedness of men so deserves, why do we strive to oppose the just vengeance of God? It was thus that God, in past ages, punished the ingratitude of men; for after they had refused to obey his truth, and had extinguished his light, he allowed them, when blinded by sense, both to be deluded by lying vanities and plunged in thick darkness, so that no face of a true Church appeared. Meanwhile, however, though his own people were dispersed and concealed amidst errors and darkness, he saved them from destruction. No wonder; for he knew how to preserve them even in the confusion of Babylon and the flame of the fiery furnace.

But as to the wish that the form of the Church should be ascertained by some kind of vain pomp, how perilous it is I will briefly indicate, rather than explain, that I may not exceed all bounds. What they say is, that the Pontiff, who holds the apostolic see, and the priests who are anointed and consecrated by him, provided they have the insignia of fillets and mitres, represent the Church, and ought to be considered as in the place of the Church, and therefore cannot err. Why so? because they are pastors of the Church, and consecrated to the Lord. And were not Aaron and other prefects of Israel pastors? But Aaron and his sons, though already set apart to the priesthood, erred notwithstanding when they made the calf (Exod. 32:4). Why, according to this view, should not the four hundred prophets who lied to Ahab represent the Church? (1 Kings 22:11, &c.). The Church, however, stood on the side of Micaiah. He was alone, indeed, and despised, but from his mouth the truth proceeded. Did not the prophets also exhibit both the name and face of the Church, when, with one accord, they rose up against Jeremiah, and with menaces boasted of it as a thing impossible that the law should perish from the priest, or counsel from the wise, or the word from the prophet?

(Jer. 18:18). In opposition to the whole body of the prophets, Jeremiah is sent alone to declare from the Lord (Jer. 4:9), that a time would come when the law would perish from the priest, counsel from the wise, and the word from the prophet. Was not like splendour displayed in that council when the chief priests, scribes, and Pharisees assembled to consult how they might put Jesus to death? Let them go, then, and cling to the external mask, while they make Christ and all the prophets of God schismatics, and, on the other hand, make Satan's ministers the organs of the Holy Spirit!

But if they are sincere, let them answer me in good faith,—in what place, and among whom, do they think the Church resided, after the Council of Basle degraded and deposed Eugenius from the popedom, and substituted Amadeus in his place? Do their utmost, they cannot deny that that Council was legitimate as far as regards external forms, and was summoned not only by one Pontiff, but by two. Eugenius, with the whole herd of cardinals and bishops who had joined him in plotting the dissolution of the Council, was there con- demned of contumacy, rebellion, and schism. Afterwards, however, aided by the favour of princes, he got back his popedom safe. The election of Amadeus, duly made by the authority of a general holy synod, went to smoke; only he himself was appeased with a cardinal's cap, like a piece of offal thrown to a barking dog. Out of the lap of these rebellious and contumacious schismatics proceeded all future popes, cardinals, bishops, abbots, and presbyters. Here they are caught, and cannot escape. For, on which party will they bestow the name of Church? Will they deny it to have been a general Council, though it lacked nothing as regards external majesty, having been solemnly called by two bulls, consecrated by the legate of the Roman See as its president, constituted regularly in all respects, and continuing in possession of all its honours to the last? Will they admit that Eugenius, and his whole train, through whom they have all been consecrated, were schismatical? Let them, then, either define the form of the Church differently, or, however numerous they are, we will hold them all to be schismatics in having knowingly and willingly received ordination from heretics. But had it never been discovered before that the Church is not tied to external pomp, we are furnished with a lengthened proof in their own conduct, in proudly vending themselves to the world under the specious title of Church, notwithstanding that they are the deadly pests of the Church. I speak not of their manners and of those tragical atrocities with which their whole life teems, since it is said that they are Pharisees who should be heard, not imitated. By de- voting some portion of your leisure to our writings, you will see, not obscurely, that their doctrine—the very doctrine to which they say it is owing that they are the Church—is a deadly murderer of souls, the firebrand, ruin, and destruction of the Church.

7. Lastly, they are far from candid when they invidiously number up the disturbances, tumults, and disputes, which the preaching of our doctrine has brought in its train, and the fruits which, in many instances, it now produces; for the doctrine itself is undeservedly charged with evils which ought to be ascribed to the malice of Satan. It is one of the characteristics of the divine word, that whenever it appears, Satan ceases to slumber and sleep. This is the surest and most unerring test for distinguishing it from false doctrines which readily betray themselves, while they are received by all with willing ears, and welcomed by an applauding world. Accordingly, for several ages, during which all things were immersed in profound darkness, almost all mankind were mere jest and sport to the god of this world, who, like any Sardanapalus, idled and luxuriated undisturbed. For what else could he do but laugh and sport while in tranquil and undisputed possession of his kingdom? But when light beaming from

31

above somewhat dissipated the darkness—when the strong
man arose and aimed a blow at his kingdom—then, indeed,
he began to shake off his wonted torpor, and rush to arms.
And first he stirred up the hands of men, that by them he
might violently suppress the dawning truth; but when this
availed him not, he turned to snares, exciting dissensions
and disputes about doctrine by means of his Catabaptists,
and other portentous miscreants, that he might thus
obscure, and, at length, extinguish the truth. And now he
persists in assailing it with both engines, endeavouring to
pluck up the true seed by the violent hand of man, and
striving, as much as in him lies, to choke it with his tares,
that it may not grow and bear knit. But it will be in vain, if
we listen to the admonition of the Lord, who long ago
disclosed his wiles, that we might not be taken unawares,
and armed us with full protection against all his
machinations. But how malignant to throw upon the word
of God itself the blame either of the seditions which wicked
men and rebels, or of the sects which impostors stir up
against it! The example, however, is not new. Elijah was
inter- rogated whether it were not he that troubled Israel.
Christ was seditious, according to the Jews; and the
apostles were charged with the crime of popular
commotion. What else do those who, in the present day,
impute to us all the disturbances, tumults, and contentions
which break out against us? Elijah, however, has taught us
our answer (1 Kings 18:17, 18). It is not we who
disseminate errors or stir up tumults, but they who resist the
mighty power of God.

But while this single answer is sufficient to rebut the
rash charges of these men, it is necessary, on the other
hand, to consult for the weakness of those who take the
alarm at such scandals, and not unfrequently waver in
perplexity. But that they may not fall away in this
perplexity, and forfeit their good degree, let them know that
the apostles in their day experienced the very things which

now befall us. There were then unlearned and unstable men who, as Peter tells us (2 Pet. 3:16), wrested the inspired writings of Paul to their own destruction. There were despisers of God, who, when they heard that sin abounded in order that grace might more abound, immediately inferred, "We will continue in sin that grace may abound" (Rom. 6:1); when they heard that believers were not under the law, but under grace, forthwith sung out, "We will sin because we are not under the law, but under grace" (Rom. 6:15). There were some who charged the apostle with being the minister of sin. Many false prophets entered in privily to pull down the churches which he had reared. Some preached the gospel through envy and strife, not sincerely (Phil. 1:15)—maliciously even—thinking to add affliction to his bonds. Elsewhere the gospel made little progress. All sought their own, not the things which were Jesus Christ's. Others went back like the dog to his vomit, or the sow that was washed to her wallowing in the mire. Great numbers perverted their spiritual freedom to carnal licentiousness. False brethren crept in to the imminent danger of the faithful. Among the brethren themselves various quarrels arose. What, then, were the apostles to do? Were they either to dissemble for the time, or rather lay aside and abandon that gospel which they saw to be the seed—bed of so many strifes, the source of so many perils, the occasion of so many scandals? In straits of this kind, they remembered that "Christ was a stone of stumbling, and a rock of offence," "set up for the fall and rising again of many," and "for a sign to be spoken against" (Luke 2:34); and, armed with this assurance, they proceeded boldly through all perils from tumults and scandals. It becomes us to be supported by the same consideration, since Paul declares that it is a neverfailing characteristic of the gospel to be a "savour of death unto death in them that perish" (2 Cor. 2:16), although rather destined to us for the purpose of being a savour of life unto life, and the power of God for the salvation of believers. This we should certainly experience it to be, did we not by our ingratitude corrupt this unspeakable gift of God, and turn to our destruction what ought to be our only saving defence.

But to return, Sire. Be not moved by the absurd insinuations with which our adversaries are striving to frighten you into the belief that nothing else is wished and aimed at by this new gospel (for so they term it), than opportunity for sedition and impunity for all kinds of vice. Our God is not the author of division, but of peace; and the Son of God, who came to destroy the works of the devil, is not the minister of sin. We, too, are undeservedly charged with desires of a kind for which we have never given even the smallest suspicion. We, forsooth, meditate the subversion of kingdoms; we, whose voice was never heard in faction, and whose life, while passed under you, is known to have been always quiet and simple; even now, when exiled from our home, we nevertheless cease not to pray for all prosperity to your person and your kingdom. We, forsooth, are aiming after an unchecked indulgence in vice, in whose manners, though there is much to be blamed, there is nothing which deserves such an imputation; nor (thank God) have we profited so little in the gospel that our life may not be to these slanderers an example of chastity, kindness, pity, temperance, patience, moderation, or any other virtue. It is plain, indeed, that we fear God sincerely, and worship him in truth, since, whether by life or by death, we desire his name to be hallowed; and hatred herself has been forced to bear testimony to the innocence and civil integrity of some of our people on whom death was inflicted for the very thing which deserved the highest praise. But if any, under pretext of the gospel, excite tumults (none such have as yet been detected in your realm), if any use the liberty of the grace of God as a cloak for licentiousness (I know of numbers who do), there are laws and legal punishments by which they may be punished up to the measure of their deserts—only, in the mean time, let not the gospel of God be evil spoken of because of the iniquities of evil men.

Sire, That you may not lend too credulous an ear to the accusations of our enemies, their virulent injustice has been set before you at sufficient length; I fear even more than sufficient, since this preface has grown almost to the bulk of a full apology. My object, however, was not to frame a defence, but only with a view to the hearing of our cause, to mollify your mind, now indeed turned away and estranged from us—I add, even inflamed against us—but whose good will, we are confident, we should regain, would you but once, with calmness and composure, read this our Confession, which we desire your Majesty to accept instead of a defence. But if the whispers of the malevolent so possess your ear, that the accused are to have no opportunity of pleading their cause; if those vindictive furies, with your connivance, are always to rage with bonds, scourgings, tortures, maimings, and burnings, we, indeed, like sheep doomed to slaughter, shall be reduced to every extremity; yet so that, in our patience, we will possess our souls, and wait for the strong hand of the Lord, which, doubtless, will appear in its own time, and show itself armed, both to rescue the poor from affliction, and also take vengeance on the despisers, who are now exulting so securely.

Most illustrious King, may the Lord, the King of kings, establish your throne in righteousness, and your sceptre in equity.

Basle, 1st *August* 1536.

THE EPISTLE TO THE READER
[PREFIXED TO THE SECOND EDITION, PUBLISHED AT STRASBURG IN 1539.]

In the First Edition of this work, having no expectation of the success which God has, in his goodness, been pleased to give it, I had, for the greater part, performed my office perfunctorily, as is usual in trivial undertakings. But when I perceived that almost all the godly had received it with a favour which I had never dared to wish, far less to hope for, being sincerely conscious that I had received much more than I deserved, I thought I should be very ungrateful if I did not endeavour, at least according to my humble ability, to respond to the great kindness which had been expressed towards me, and which spontaneously urged me to diligence. I therefore ask no other favour from the studious for my new work than that which they have already bestowed upon me beyond my merits. I feel so much obliged, that I shall be satisfied if I am thought not to have made a bad return for the gratitude I owe. This return I would have made much earlier, had not the Lord, for almost two whole years, exercised me in an extraordinary manner. But it is soon enough if well enough. I shall think it has appeared in good season when I perceive that it produces some fruit to the Church of God. I may add, that my object in this work was to prepare and train students of theology for the study of the Sacred Volume, so that they might both have an easy introduction to it, and be able to proceed in it, with unfaltering step, seeing I have endeavoured to give such a summary of religion in all its parts, and have digested it into such an order as may make it not difficult for any one, who is rightly acquainted with it, to ascertain both what he ought principally to look for in Scripture, and also to what head he ought to refer whatever is contained in it. Having thus, as it were, paved the way, I shall not feel it necessary, in any Commentaries on Scripture which I may afterwards publish, to enter into long discussions of doctrines or dilate on common places, and will, therefore, always compress them. In this way the pious reader will be saved much trouble and weariness, provided he comes furnished with a knowledge of the present work as an essential prerequisite. As my Commentary on the Epistle to the Romans will give a specimen of this plan, I would much rather let it speak for itself than declare it in words. Farewell, dear reader, and if you derive any fruit from my labours, give me the benefit of your prayers to the Lord.

SUBJECT OF THE PRESENT WORK.
[PREFIXED TO THE FRENCH EDITION, PUBLISHED AT GENEVA IN 1545.]

In order that my Readers may be the better able to profit by the present work, I am desirous briefly to point out the advantage which they may derive from it. For by so doing I will show them the end at which they ought to aim, and to which they ought to give their attention in reading it.

Although the Holy Scriptures contain a perfect doctrine, to which nothing can be added—our Lord having been pleased therein to unfold the infinite treasures of his wisdom—still every person, not intimately acquainted with them, stands in need of some guidance and direction, as to what he ought to look for in them, that he may not wander up and down, but pursue a certain path, and so attain the end to which the Holy Spirit invites him.

Hence it is the duty of those who have received from God more light than others to assist the simple in this matter, and, as it were, lend them their hand to guide and assist them in finding the sum of what God has been pleased to teach us in his word. Now, this cannot be better done in writing than by treating in succession of the principal matters which are comprised in Christian philosophy. For he who understands these will be prepared to make more progress in the school of God in one day than any other person in three months, inasmuch as he, in a great measure, knows to what he should refer each sentence, and has a rule by which to test whatever is presented to him.

Seeing, then, how necessary it was in this manner to aid those who desire to be instructed in the doctrine of salvation, I have endeavoured, according to the ability which God has given me, to employ myself in so doing, and with this view have composed the present book. And first I wrote it in Latin, that it might be serviceable to all studious persons, of what nation soever they might be; afterwards, desiring to communicate any fruit which might be in it to my French countrymen, I translated it into our own tongue. I dare not bear too strong a testimony in its favour, and declare how profitable the reading of it will be, lest I should seem to prize my own work too highly. However I may promise this much, that it will be a kind of key opening up to all the children of God a right and ready access to the understand- ing of the sacred volume. Wherefore, should our Lord give me henceforth means and opportunity of composing some Commentaries, I will use the greatest possible brevity, as there will be no occasion to make long digressions, seeing that I have in a manner deduced at length all the articles which pertain to Christianity.

And since we are bound to acknowledge that all truth and sound doctrine proceed from God, I will venture boldly to declare what I think of this work, acknowledging it to be God's work rather than mine. To him, indeed, the praise due to it must be ascribed. My opinion of the work then is this: I exhort all, who reverence the word of the Lord, to read it, and diligently imprint it on their memory, if they would, in the first place, have a summary of Christian doctrine, and, in the second place, an introduction to the profitable reading both of the Old and New Testament. When they shall have done so, they will know by experience that I have not wished to impose upon them with words. Should any one be unable to comprehend all that is contained in it, he must not, however, give it up in despair; but continue always to read on, hoping that one passage will give him a more familiar exposition of another. Above all things, I would recommend that recourse be had to Scripture in considering the proofs which I adduce from it.

EPISTLE TO THE READER.
[PREFIXED TO THE LAST EDITION, REVISED BY THE AUTHOR.]

In the first edition of this work, having not the least expectation of the success which God, in his boundless goodness, has been pleased to give it, I had, for the greater part, performed my task in a perfunctory manner (as is usual in trivial undertakings); but when I understood that it had been received, by almost all the pious with a favour which I had never dared to ask, far less to hope for, the more I was sincerely conscious that the reception was beyond my deserts, the greater I thought my ingratitude would be, if, to the very kind wishes which had been expressed towards me, and which seemed of their own accord to invite me to diligence, I did not endeavour to respond, at least according to my humble ability. This I attempted not only in the Second Edition, but in every subsequent one the work has received some improvement. But though I do not regret the labour previously expended, I never felt satisfied until the work was arranged in the order in which it now appears. Now I trust it will approve itself to the Judgment of all my readers. As a clear proof of the diligence with which I have laboured to perform this service to the Church of God, I may be permitted to mention, that last winter, when I thought I was dying of quartan ague, the more the disorder increased, the less I spared myself, in order that I might leave this book behind me, and thus make some return to the pious for their kind urgency. I could have wished to give it sooner, but it is soon enough if good enough. I shall think it has appeared in good time when I see it more productive of benefit than formerly to the Church of God. This is my only wish.

And truly it would fare ill with me if, not contented with the approbation of God alone, I were unable to despise the foolish and perverse censures of ignorant as well as the malicious and unjust censures of ungodly men. For although, by the blessing of God, my most ardent desire has been to advance his kingdoms and promote the public good,—although I feel perfectly conscious, and take God and his angels to witness, that ever since I began to discharge the office of teacher in the Church, my only object has been to do good to the Church, by maintaining the pure doctrine of godliness, yet I believe there never was a man more assailed, stung, and torn by calumny [as well by the declared enemies of the truth of God, as by many worthless persons who have crept into his Church—as well by monks who have brought forth their frocks from their cloisters to spread infection wherever they come, as by other miscreants not better than they1]. After this letter to the reader was in the press, I had undoubted information that, at Augsburg, where the Imperial Diet was held, a rumour of my defection to the papacy was circulated, and entertained in the courts of the princes more readily than might have been expected. This, forsooth, is the return made me by those who certainly are not unaware of numerous proofs of my constancy—proofs which, while they rebut the foul charge, ought to have defended me against it, with all humane and impartial judges. But the devil, with all his crew, is mistaken if he imagines that, by assailing me with vile falsehoods, he can either cool my zeal, or diminish my exertions. I trust that God, in his infinite goodness, will enable me to persevere with unruffled patience in the course of his holy vocation. Of this I give the pious reader a new proof in the present edition.

I may further observe, that my object in this work has been, so to prepare and train candidates for the sacred office, for the study of the sacred volume, that they may both have an easy introduction to it, and be able to prosecute it with unfaltering step; for, if I mistake not, I have given a summary of religion in all its parts, and digested it in an order which will make it easy for any one, who rightly comprehends it, to ascertain both what he ought chiefly to look for in Scripture, and also to what head he ought to refer whatever is contained in it. Having thus, as it were, paved the way, as it will be unnecessary, in any Commentaries on Scripture which I may afterwards publish, to enter into long discussions of doctrinal points, and enlarge on commonplaces, I will compress them into narrow compass. In this way much trouble and fatigue will be spared to the pious reader, provided he comes prepared with a knowledge of the present work as an indispensable prerequisite. The system here followed being set forth as in a mirror in all my Commentaries, I think it better to let it speak for itself than to give any verbal explanation of it.

Farewell, kind reader: if you derive any benefit from my labours, aid me with your prayers to our heavenly Father.

Geneva, 1*st August* 1559.

The zeal of those whose cause I undertook,
    Has swelled a short defence into a book.

"I profess to be one of those who, by profiting, write,
and by writing profit."
—*Augustine*, Epist. 7.

METHOD AND ARRANGEMENT, OR SUBJECT OF THE WHOLE WORK.
[FROM AN EPITOME OF THE INSTITUTIONS, BY GASPAR OLEVIAN.]

The subject handled by the author of these Christian Institutes is twofold: the former, the knowledge of God, which leads to a blessed immortality; and the latter (which is subordinate to the former), the knowledge of ourselves. With this view the author simply adopts the arrangement of the Apostles' Creed, as that with which all Christians are most familiar. For as the Creed consists of four parts, the first relating to God the Father, the second to the Son, the third to the Holy Spirit, and the fourth to the Church, so the author, in fulfilment of his task, divides his Institutes into four parts, corresponding to those of the Creed. Each of these parts it will now be proper to explain separately.

I. The first article of the Apostles' Creed is concerning *God the Father*, the creation, preservation, and government of the universe, as implied in his omnipotence. Accordingly, the First Book of the Institutes treats of the knowledge of God, considered as the Creator, Preserver, and Governor of the world, and of every thing contained in it. It shows both wherein the true knowledge of the Creator consists, and what the end of this knowledge is, chap. 1 and 2; that it is not learned at school, but that every one is self-taught it from the womb, chap. 3. Such, however, is man's depravity, that he stifles and corrupts this knowledge, partly by ignorance, partly by wicked design; and hence does not by means of it either glorify God as he ought, or attain to happiness, chap. 4. This inward knowledge is aided from without, namely by the creatures in which, as in a mirror, the perfections of God may be contemplated. But man does

43

not properly avail himself of this assistance, and hence to those to whom God is pleased to make himself more intimately known for salvation, he communicates his written word. This leads to a consideration of the Holy Scriptures, in which God has revealed that not the Father only, but along with the Father, the Son, and Holy Spirit, is that Creator of heaven and earth, whom, in consequence of our innate depravity we were unable, either from innate natural knowledge, or the beautiful mirror of the world, to know so as to glorify. Here the author treats of the manifestation of God in Scripture; and in connection with it, of the one divine essence in three persons. But, lest man should lay the blame of his voluntary blindness on God, the author shows in what state man was created at first, introducing dissertations on the image of God, free will, and original righteousness. The subject of Creation being thus disposed of, the preservation and government of the world is considered in the three last chapters, which contain a very full discussion of the doctrine of Divine Providence.

II. As man, by sinning, forfeited the privileges conferred on him at his creation, recourse must be had to Christ. Accordingly, the next article in the Creed is, *And in Jesus Christ his only Son, &c.* In like manner, the Second Book of the Institutes treats of the knowledge of God considered as a Redeemer in Christ, And showing man his falls conducts him to Christ the Mediator. Here the subject of original sin is considered, and it is shown that man has no means within himself, by which he can escape from guilt, and the impending curse: that, on the contrary, until he is reconciled and renewed, every thing that proceeds from him is of the nature of sin. This subject is considered as far as the 6th chapter. Man being thus utterly undone in himself, and incapable of working out his own cure by thinking a good thought, or doing what is acceptable to God, must seek redemption without himself—viz. in Christ. The end for which the Law was given, was not to secure worshipers for itself, but to conduct them unto Christ. This leads to an exposition of the Moral Law. Christ was known to the Jews under the Law as the author of salvation, but is more fully revealed under the Gospel in which he was manifested to the world. Hence arises the doctrine concerning the similarity and difference of the two Testaments, the Old and the New, the Law and the Gospel. These topics occupy as far as the 12th chapter. It is next shown that, in order to secure a complete salvation, it was necessary that the eternal Son of God should become man, and assume a true human nature. It is also shown in what way these two natures constitute one person. In order to purchase a full salvation by his own merits, and effectually apply it, Christ was appointed to the offices of Prophet, Priest, and King. The mode in which Christ performs these offices is considered, and also whether in point of fact he did accomplish the work of redemption. Here an exposition is given of the articles relating to Christ's death, resurrection, and ascension into heaven. In conclusion, it is proved that Christ is rightly and properly said to have merited divine grace and salvation for us.

III. So long as Christ is separated from us we have no benefit from him. We must be ingrafted in him like branches in the vine. Hence the Creed, after treating of Christ, proceeds in its third article, *I believe in the Holy Spirit*,—the Holy Spirit being the bond of union between us and Christ. In like manner, the Third Book of the Institutes treats of the Holy Spirit which unites us to Christ, and, in connection with it, of faith, by which we embrace Christ with a double benefit—viz. that of gratuitous righteousness which he imputes to us, and regeneration, which he begins in us by giving us repentance. In order to show the worthlessness of a faith which is not accompanied with a desire of repentance, the author, before proceeding to a full discussion of justification, treats at length from chapter 3-10 of repentance, and the constant study of it—

repentance, which Christ, when apprehended by faith, begets in us by his Spirit. Chapter 11 treats of the primary and peculiar benefit of Christ when united to us by the Holy Spirit—viz. justification. This subject is continued to the 20th chapter, which treats of prayer, the hand, as it were, to receive the blessings which faith knows to be treasured up for it with God, according to the word of promise. But, as the Holy Spirit, who creates and preserves our faith, does not unite all men to Christ, who is the sole author of salvation, chapter 21 treats of the eternal election of God, to which it is owing that we, in whom he foresaw no good which he had not previously bestowed, are given to Christ, and united to him by the effectual calling of the Gospel. This subject is continued to the 25th chapter, which treats of complete regeneration and felicity, namely, the final resurrection to which we must raise our eyes, seeing that, in regard to fruition, the happiness of the godly is only begun in this world.

IV. Since the Holy Spirit does not ingraft all men into Christ, or endue them with faith, and those whom he does so endue he does not ordinarily endue without means, but uses for that purpose the preaching of the Gospel and the dispensation of the Sacraments, together with the administration of all kinds of discipline, the Creed contains the following article, *I believe in the Holy Catholic Church*, namely, that Church which, when lying in eternal death, the Father, by gratuitous election, freely reconciled to himself in Christ, and endued with the Holy Spirit, that, being ingrafted into Christ, it might have communion with him as its proper head; whence flow perpetual remission of sins, and full restoration to eternal life. Accordingly the Church is treated of in the first fourteen chapters of the Fourth Book, which thereafter treats of the means which the Holy Spirit employs in calling us effectually from spiritual death, and preserving the Church, in other words, Baptism and the Lord's Supper. These means are, as it were, the royal sceptre of Christ, by which, through the efficacy of his Spirit, he commences his spiritual reign in the Church, advances it from day to day, and after this life, without the use of means, finally perfects it. This subject is continued to the 20th chapter.

And because civil governments are, in this life, the hospitable entertainers (*hospitia*) of the Church (though civil government is distinct from the spiritual kingdom of Christ), the author shows how great blessings they are, blessings which the Church is bound gratefully to acknowledge, until we are called away from this tabernacle to the heavenly inheritance, where God will be all in all.

Such is the arrangement of the Institutes which may be thus summed up: Man being at first created upright, but afterwards being not partially but totally ruined, finds his entire salvation out of himself in Christ, to whom being united by the Holy Spirit freely given without any foresight of future works, he thereby obtains a double blessing — viz. full imputation of righteousness, which goes along with us even to the grave, and the commencement of sanctification, which daily advances till at length it is perfected in the day of regeneration or resurrection of the body, and this, in order that the great mercy of God may be celebrated in the heavenly mansions, throughout eternity.

BOOK I

ARGUMENT.

The First Book treats of the knowledge of God the Creator. But as it is in the creation of man that the divine perfections are best displayed, so man also is made the subject of discourse. Thus the whole book divides itself into two principal heads—the former relating to the knowledge of God, and the latter to the knowledge of man. In the first chapter, these are considered jointly; and in each of the following chapters, separately: occasionally, however, intermingled with other matters which refer to one or other of the heads; *e.g.*, the discussions concerning Scripture and images, falling under the former head, and the other three concerning the creation of the world, the holy angels and devils, falling under the latter. The last point discussed—viz. the method of the divine government, relates to both.

With regard to the former head—viz. the knowledge of God, it is shown, in the first place, what the kind of knowledge is which God requires, Chap. 2. And, in the second place (Chap. 3-9), where this knowledge must be sought, namely, not in man; because, although naturally implanted in the human mind, it is stifled, partly by ignorance, partly by evil intent, Chap. 3 and 4; not in the frame of the world: because, although it shines most clearly there, we are so stupid that these manifestations, however perspicuous, pass away without any beneficial result, Chap. 5; but in Scripture (Chap. 6), which is treated of, Chap. 7-9. In the third place, it is shown what the character of God is, Chap. 10. In the fourth place, how impious it is to give a visible form to God (here images, the worship of them, and its origin, are considered), Chap. 11. In the fifth place, it is shown that God is to be solely and wholly worshipped, Chap. 12. Lastly, Chap. 13 treats of the unity of the divine essence, and the distinction of three persons.

With regard to the latter head—viz. the knowledge of man, first, Chap. 14 treats of the creation of the world, and of good and bad angels (these all having reference to man). And then Chap. 15, taking up the subject of man himself, examines his nature and his powers.

The better to illustrate the nature both of God and man, the three remaining Chapters—viz. 16-18, proceed to treat of the general government of the world, and particularly of human actions, in opposition to fortune and fate, explaining both the doctrine and its use. In conclusion, it is shown, that though God employs the instrumentality of the wicked, he is pure from sin and from taint of every kind.

CHAPTER 1.

THE KNOWLEDGE OF GOD AND OF OURSELVES MUTUALLY CONNECTED. — NATURE OF THE CONNECTION.

Sections.

1. The sum of true wisdom—viz. the knowledge of God and of ourselves. Effects of the latter.

2. Effects of the knowledge of God, in humbling our pride, unveiling our hypocrisy, demonstrating the absolute perfections of God, and our own utter helplessness.

3. Effects of the knowledge of God illustrated by the examples, 1. of holy patriarchs; 2. of holy angels; 3. of the sun and moon.

1. Our wisdom, in so far as it ought to be deemed true and solid Wisdom, consists almost entirely of two parts: the knowledge of God and of ourselves. But as these are connected together by many ties, it is not easy to determine which of the two precedes and gives birth to the other. For, in the first place, no man can survey himself without forthwith turning his thoughts towards the God in whom he lives and moves; because it is perfectly obvious, that the endowments which we possess cannot possibly be from ourselves; nay, that our very being is nothing else than subsistence in God alone. In the second place, those blessings which unceasingly distil to us from heaven, are like streams conducting us to the fountain. Here, again, the infinitude of good which resides in God becomes more apparent from our poverty. In particular, the miserable ruin into which the revolt of the first man has plunged us, compels us to turn our eyes upwards; not only that while hungry and famishing we may thence ask what we want,

but being aroused by fear may learn humility. For as there exists in man something like a world of misery, and ever since we were stript of the divine attire our naked shame discloses an immense series of disgraceful properties every man, being stung by the consciousness of his own unhappiness, in this way necessarily obtains at least some knowledge of God. Thus, our feeling of ignorance, vanity, want, weakness, in short, depravity and corruption, reminds us (see Calvin on John 4:10), that in the Lord, and none but He, dwell the true light of wisdom, solid virtue, exuberant goodness. We are accordingly urged by our own evil things to consider the good things of God; and, indeed, we cannot aspire to Him in earnest until we have begun to be displeased with ourselves. For what man is not disposed to rest in himself? Who, in fact, does not thus rest, so long as he is unknown to himself; that is, so long as he is contented with his own endowments, and unconscious or unmindful of his misery? Every person, therefore, on coming to the knowledge of himself, is not only urged to seek God, but is also led as by the hand to find him.

2. On the other hand, it is evident that man never attains to a true self-knowledge until he has previously contemplated the face of God, and come down after such contemplation to look into himself. For (such is our innate pride) we always seem to ourselves just, and upright, and wise, and holy, until we are convinced, by clear evidence, of our injustice, vileness, folly, and impurity. Convinced, however, we are not, if we look to ourselves only, and not to the Lord also —He being the only standard by the application of which this conviction can be produced. For, since we are all naturally prone to hypocrisy, any empty semblance of righteousness is quite enough to satisfy us instead of righteousness itself. And since nothing appears within us or around us that is not tainted with very great impurity, so long as we keep our mind within the confines of human pollution, anything which is in some small degree ·

52

less defiled delights us as if it were most pure just as an eye, to which nothing but black had been previously presented, deems an object of a whitish, or even of a brownish hue, to be perfectly white. Nay, the bodily sense may furnish a still stronger il- lustration of the extent to which we are deluded in estimating the powers of the mind. If, at mid-day, we either look down to the ground, or on the surrounding objects which lie open to our view, we think ourselves endued with a very strong and piercing eyesight; but when we look up to the sun, and gaze at it unveiled, the sight which did excellently well for the earth is instantly so dazzled and confounded by the refulgence, as to oblige us to confess that our acuteness in discerning terrestrial objects is mere dimness when applied to the sun. Thus too, it happens in estimating our spiritual qualities. So long as we do not look beyond the earth, we are quite pleased with our own righteousness, wisdom, and virtue; we address ourselves in the most flattering terms, and seem only less than demigods. But should we once begin to raise our thoughts to God, and reflect what kind of Being he is, and how absolute the perfection of that righteousness, and wisdom, and virtue, to which, as a standard, we are bound to be conformed, what formerly delighted us by its false show of righteousness will become polluted with the greatest iniquity; what strangely imposed upon us under the name of wisdom will disgust by its extreme folly; and what presented the appearance of virtuous energy will be condemned as the most miserable impotence. So far are those qualities in us, which seem most perfect, from corresponding to the divine purity.

3. Hence that dread and amazement with which as Scripture uniformly relates, holy men were struck and overwhelmed whenever they beheld the presence of God. When we see those who previously stood firm and secure so quaking with terror, that the fear of death takes hold of them, nay, they are, in a manner, swallowed up and

annihilated, the inference to be drawn is that men are never duly touched and impressed with a conviction of their insignificance, until they have contrasted themselves with the majesty of God. Frequent examples of this consternation occur both in the Book of Judges and the Prophetical Writings; so much so, that it was a common expression among the people of God, "We shall die, for we have seen the Lord." Hence the Book of Job, also, in humbling men under a conviction of their folly, feebleness, and pollution, always derives its chief argument from descriptions of the Divine wisdom, virtue, and purity. Nor without cause: for we see Abraham the readier to acknowledge himself but dust and ashes the nearer he approaches to behold the glory of the Lord, and Elijah unable to wait with unveiled face for His approach; so dreadful is the sight. And what can man do, man who is but rottenness and a worm, when even the Cherubim themselves must veil their faces in very terror? To this, undoubtedly, the Prophet Isaiah refers, when he says (Isaiah 24:23), "The moon shall be confounded, and the sun ashamed, when the Lord of Hosts shall reign;" *i.e.*, when he shall exhibit his refulgence, and give a nearer view of it, the brightest objects will, in comparison, be covered with darkness.

But though the knowledge of God and the knowledge of ourselves are bound together by a mutual tie, due arrangement requires that we treat of the former in the first place, and then descend to the latter.

CHAPTER 2.

WHAT IT IS TO KNOW GOD,—TENDENCY OF THIS KNOWLEDGE.

Sections.

1. The knowledge of God the Creator defined. The substance of this knowledge, and the use to be made of it.

2. Further illustration of the use, together with a necessary reproof of vain curiosity, and refutation of the Epicureans. The character of God as it appears to the pious mind, contrasted with the absurd views of the Epicureans. Religion defined.

1. By the knowledge of God, I understand that by which we not only conceive that there is some God, but also apprehend what it is for our interest, and conducive to his glory, what, in short, it is befitting to know concerning him. For, properly speaking, we cannot say that God is known where there is no religion or piety. I am not now referring to that species of knowledge by which men, in themselves lost and under curse, apprehend God as a Redeemer in Christ the Mediator. I speak only of that simple and primitive knowledge, to which the mere course of nature would have conducted us, had Adam stood upright. For although no man will now, in the present ruin of the human race, perceive God to be either a father, or the author of salvation, or propitious in any respect, until Christ interpose to make our peace; still it is one thing to perceive that God our Maker supports us by his power, rules us by his providence, fosters us by his goodness, and visits us with all kinds of blessings, and another thing to embrace the grace of reconciliation offered to us in Christ. Since, then, the Lord first appears, as well in the creation of the world

as in the general doctrine of Scripture, simply as a Creator, and afterwards as a Redeemer in Christ,—a twofold knowledge of him hence arises: of these the former is now to be considered, the latter will afterwards follow in its order. But although our mind cannot conceive of God, without rendering some worship to him, it will not, however, be sufficient simply to hold that he is the only being whom all ought to worship and adore, unless we are also persuaded that he is the fountain of all goodness, and that we must seek everything in him, and in none but him. My meaning is: we must be persuaded not only that as he once formed the world, so he sustains it by his boundless power, governs it by his wisdom, preserves it by his goodness, in particular, rules the human race with justice and Judgment, bears with them in mercy, shields them by his protection; but also that not a particle of light, or wisdom, or justice, or power, or rectitude, or genuine truth, will anywhere be found, which does not flow from him, and of which he is not the cause; in this way we must learn to expect and ask all things from him, and thankfully ascribe to him whatever we receive. For this sense of the divine perfections is the proper master to teach us piety, out of which religion springs. By piety I mean that union of reverence and love to God which the knowledge of his benefits inspires. For, until men feel that they owe everything to God, that they are cherished by his paternal care, and that he is the author of all their blessings, so that nought is to be looked for away from him, they will never submit to him in voluntary obedience; nay, unless they place their entire happiness in him, they will never yield up their whole selves to him in truth and sincerity.

2. Those, therefore, who, in considering this question, propose to inquire what the essence of God is, only delude us with frigid speculations,—it being much more our interest to know what kind of being God is, and what things are agreeable to his nature. For, of what use is it to join

Epicures in acknowledging some God who has cast off the care of the world, and only delights himself in ease? What avails it, in short, to know a God with whom we have nothing to do? The effect of our knowledge rather ought to be, *first*, to teach us reverence and fear; and, *secondly*, to induce us, under its guidance and teaching, to ask every good thing from him, and, when it is received, ascribe it to him. For how can the idea of God enter your mind without instantly giving rise to the thought, that since you are his workmanship, you are bound, by the very law of creation, to submit to his authority?—that your life is due to him?—that whatever you do ought to have reference to him? If so, it undoubtedly follows that your life is sadly corrupted, if it is not framed in obedience to him, since his will ought to be the law of our lives. On the other hand, your idea of his nature is not clear unless you acknowledge him to be the origin and fountain of all goodness. Hence would arise both confidence in him, and a desire of cleaving to him, did not the depravity of the human mind lead it away from the proper course of investigation.

For, first of all, the pious mind does not devise for itself any kind of God, but looks alone to the one true God; nor does it feign for him any character it pleases, but is contented to have him in the character in which he manifests himself always guarding, with the utmost diligences against transgressing his will, and wandering, with daring presumptions from the right path. He by whom God is thus known perceiving how he governs all things, confides in him as his guardian and protector, and casts himself entirely upon his faithfulness,—perceiving him to be the source of every blessing, if he is in any strait or feels any want, he instantly recurs to his protection and trusts to his aid,—persuaded that he is good and merciful, he reclines upon him with sure confidence, and doubts not that, in the divine clemency, a remedy will be provided for his every time of need,—acknowledging him as his Father and his Lord he considers himself bound to have respect to his authority in all things, to reverence his majesty, aim at the advancement of his glory, and obey his commands,— regarding him as a just judge, armed with severity to punish crimes, he keeps the Judgment-seat always in his view. Standing in awe of it, he curbs himself, and fears to provoke his anger. Nevertheless, he is not so terrified by an apprehension of Judgment as to wish he could withdraw himself, even if the means of escape lay before him; nay, he embraces him not less as the avenger of wickedness than as the rewarder of the righteous; because he perceives that it equally appertains to his glory to store up punishment for the one, and eternal life for the other. Besides, it is not the mere fear of punishment that restrains him from sin. Loving and revering God as his father, honouring and obeying him as his master, although there were no hell, he would revolt at the very idea of offending him. Such is pure and genuine religion, namely, confidence in God coupled with serious fear—fear, which both includes in it willing reverence, and brings along with it such legitimate worship as is prescribed by the law. And it ought to be more carefully considered that all men promiscuously do homage to God, but very few truly reverence him. On all hands there is abundance of ostentatious ceremonies, but sincerity of heart is rare.

CHAPTER 3.

THE KNOWLEDGE OF GOD NATURALLY IMPLANTED IN THE HUMAN MIND.

Sections.

1. The knowledge of God being manifested to all makes the reprobate without excuse. Universal belief and acknowledge- ment of the existence of God.

2. Objection—that religion and the belief of a Deity are the inventions of crafty politicians. Refutation of the objection. This universal belief confirmed by the examples of wicked men and Atheists.

3. Confirmed also by the vain endeavours of the wicked to banish all fear of God from their minds. Conclusion, that the knowledge of God is naturally implanted in the human mind.

1. That there exists in the human minds and indeed by natural instinct, some sense of Deity, we hold to be beyond dispute, since God himself, to prevent any man from pretending ignorance, has endued all men with some idea of his Godhead, the memory of which he constantly renews and occasionally enlarges, that all to a man being aware that there is a God, and that he is their Maker, may be condemned by their own conscience when they neither worship him nor consecrate their lives to his service. Certainly, if there is any quarter where it may be supposed that God is unknown, the most likely for such an instance to exist is among the dullest tribes farthest removed from civilisation. But, as a heathen tells us, there is no nation so barbarous, no race so brutish, as not to be imbued with the conviction that there is a God. Even those who, in other respects, seem to differ least from the lower animals, constantly retain some sense of religion; so thoroughly has

this common conviction possessed the mind, so firmly is it stamped on the breasts of all men. Since, then, there never has been, from the very first, any quarter of the globe, any city, any household even, without religion, this amounts to a tacit confession, that a sense of Deity is inscribed on every heart. Nay, even idolatry is ample evidence of this fact. For we know how reluctant man is to lower himself, in order to set other creatures above him. Therefore, when he chooses to worship wood and stone rather than be thought to have no God, it is evident how very strong this impression of a Deity must be; since it is more difficult to obliterate it from the mind of man, than to break down the feelings of his nature,—these certainly being broken down, when, in opposition to his natural haughtiness, he spontaneously humbles himself before the meanest object as an act of reverence to God.

2. It is most absurd, therefore, to maintain, as some do, that religion was devised by the cunning and craft of a few individuals, as a means of keeping the body of the people in due subjection, while there was nothing which those very individuals, while teaching others to worship God, less believed than the existence of a God. I readily acknowledge, that designing men have introduced a vast number of fictions into religion, with the view of inspiring the populace with reverence or striking them with terror, and thereby rendering them more obsequious; but they never could have succeeded in this, had the minds of men not been previously imbued with that uniform belief in God, from which, as from its seed, the religious propensity springs. And it is altogether incredible that those who, in the matter of religion, cunningly imposed on their ruder neighbours, were altogether devoid of a knowledge of God. For though in old times there were some, and in the present day not a few are found who deny the being of a God, yet, whether they will or not, they occasionally feel the truth which they are desirous not to know. We do not read of any

man who broke out into more unbridled and audacious contempt of the Deity than C. Caligula, and yet none showed greater dread when any indication of divine wrath was manifested. Thus, however unwilling, he shook with terror before the God whom he professedly studied to condemn. You may every day see the same thing happening to his modern imitators. The most audacious despiser of God is most easily disturbed, trembling at the sound of a falling leaf. How so, unless in vindication of the divine majesty, which smites their consciences the more strongly the more they endeavour to flee from it. They all, indeed, look out for hiding-places where they may conceal themselves from the presence of the Lord, and again efface it from their mind; but after all their efforts they remain caught within the net. Though the conviction may occasionally seem to vanish for a moment, it immediately returns, and rushes in with new impetuosity, so that any interval of relief from the gnawing of conscience is not unlike the slumber of the intoxicated or the insane, who have no quiet rest in sleep, but are continually haunted with dire horrific dreams. Even the wicked themselves, therefore, are an example of the fact that some idea of God always exists in every human mind.

3. All men of sound Judgment will therefore hold, that a sense of Deity is indelibly en- graven on the human heart. And that this belief is naturally engendered in all, and thoroughly fixed as it were in our very bones, is strikingly attested by the contumacy of the wicked, who, though they struggle furiously, are unable to extricate themselves from the fear of God. Though Diagoras, and others of like stamps make themselves merry with whatever has been believed in all ages concerning religion, and Dionysus scoffs at the Judgment of heaven, it is but a Sardonian grin; for the worm of conscience, keener than burning steel, is gnawing them within. I do not say with Cicero, that errors wear out by age, and that religion increases and grows

better day by day. For the world (as will be shortly seen) labours as much as it can to shake off all knowledge of God, and corrupts his worship in innumerable ways. I only say, that, when the stupid hardness of heart, which the wicked eagerly court as a means of despising God, becomes enfeebled, the sense of Deity, which of all things they wished most to be extinguished, is still in vigour, and now and then breaks forth. Whence we infer, that this is not a doctrine which is first learned at school, but one as to which every man is, from the womb, his own master; one which nature herself allows no individual to forget, though many, with all their might, strive to do so. Moreover, if all are born and live for the express purpose of learning to know God, and if the knowledge of God, in so far as it fails to produce this effect, is fleeting and vain, it is clear that all those who do not direct the whole thoughts and actions of their lives to this end fail to fulfil the law of their being. This did not escape the observation even of philosophers. For it is the very thing which Plato meant (in *Phœd. et Theact.*) when he taught, as he often does, that the chief good of the soul consists in re- semblance to God; *i.e.,* when, by means of knowing him, she is wholly transformed into him. Thus Gryllus, also, in Plutarch (*lib. guod bruta anim. ratione utantur*), reasons most skilfully, when he affirms that, if once religion is banished from the lives of men, they not only in no respect excel, but are, in many respects, much more wretched than the brutes, since, being exposed to so many forms of evil, they continually drag on a troubled and restless existence: that the only thing, therefore, which makes them superior is the worship of God, through which alone they aspire to immortality.

CHAPTER 4.

THE KNOWLEDGE OF GOD STIFLED OR CORRUPTED, IGNORANTLY OR MALICIOUSLY.

Sections.

1. The knowledge of God suppressed by ignorance, many falling away into superstition. Such persons, however, inexcusable, because their error is accompanied with pride and stubbornness.

2. Stubbornness the companion of impiety.

3. No pretext can justify superstition. This proved, first, from reason; and, secondly, from Scripture.

4. The wicked never willingly come into the presence of God. Hence their hypocrisy. Hence, too, their sense of Deity leads to no good result.

1. But though experience testifies that a seed of religion is divinely sown in all, scarcely one in a hundred is found who cherishes it in his heart, and not one in whom it grows to maturity so far is it from yielding fruit in its season. Moreover, while some lose themselves in superstitious observances, and others, of set purpose, wickedly revolt from God, the result is that, in regard to the true knowledge of him, all are so degenerate, that in no part of the world can genuine godliness be found. In saying that some fall away into superstition, I mean not to insinuate that their excessive absurdity frees them from guilt; for the blindness under which they labour is almost invariably accompanied with vain pride and stubbornness. Mingled vanity and pride appear in this, that when miserable men do seek after God, instead of ascending higher than themselves as they ought to do, they measure him by their own carnal stupidity, and, neglecting solid inquiry, fly off to indulge their curiosity in

vain speculation. Hence, they do not conceive of him in the character in which he is manifested, but imagine him to be whatever their own rashness has devised. This abyss standing open, they cannot move one footstep without rushing headlong to destruction. With such an idea of God, nothing which they may attempt to offer in the way of worship or obedience can have any value in his sight, because it is not him they worship, but, instead of him, the dream and figment of their own heart. This corrupt procedure is admirably described by Paul, when he says, that "thinking to be wise, they became fools" (Rom. 1:22). He had previously said that "they became vain in their imaginations," but lest any should suppose them blameless, he afterwards adds that they were deservedly blinded, because, not contented with sober inquiry, because, arrogating to themselves more than they have any title to do, they of their own accord court darkness, nay, bewitch themselves with perverse, empty show. Hence it is that their folly, the result not only of vain curiosity, but of licentious desire and overweening confidence in the pursuit of forbidden knowledge, cannot be excused.

2. The expression of David (Psalm 14:1, 53:1), "The fool hath said in his heart, There is no God," is primarily applied to those who, as will shortly farther appear, stifle the light of nature, and intentionally stupefy themselves. We see many, after they have become hardened in a daring course of sin, madly banishing all remembrance of God, though spontaneously suggested to them from within, by natural sense. To show how detestable this madness is, the Psalmist introduces them as distinctly denying that there is a God, because although they do not disown his essence, they rob him of his justice and providence, and represent him as sitting idly in heaven. Nothing being less accordant with the nature of God than to cast off the government of the world, leaving it to chance, and so to wink at the crimes of men that they may wanton with impunity in evil courses;

it follows, that every man who indulges in security, after extinguishing all fear of divine Judgment, virtually denies that there is a God. As a just punishment of the wicked, after they have closed their own eyes, God makes their hearts dull and heavy, and hence, seeing, they see not. David, indeed, is the best interpreter of his own meaning, when he says elsewhere, the wicked has "no fear of God before his eyes," (Psalm 36:1); and, again, "He has said in his heart, God has forgotten; he hideth his face; he will never see it." Thus although they are forced to acknowledge that there is some God, they, however, rob him of his glory by denying his power. For, as Paul declares, "If we believe not, he abideth faithful, he cannot deny himself," (2 Tim. 2:13); so those who feign to themselves a dead and dumb idol, are truly said to deny God. It is, moreover, to be observed, that though they struggle with their own convictions, and would fain not only banish God from their minds, but from heaven also, their stupefaction is never so complete as to secure them from being occasionally dragged before the divine tribunal. Still, as no fear restrains them from rushing violently in the face of God, so long as they are hurried on by that blind impulse, it cannot be denied that their prevailing state of mind in regard to him is brutish oblivion.

3. In this way, the vain pretext which many employ to clothe their superstition is overthrown. They deem it enough that they have some kind of zeal for religion, how preposterous soever it may be, not observing that true religion must be conformable to the will of God as its unerring standard; that he can never deny himself, and is no spectra or phantom, to be metamorphosed at each individual's caprice. It is easy to see how superstition, with its false glosses, mocks God, while it tries to please him. Usually fastening merely on things on which he has declared he sets no value, it either contemptuously overlooks, or even undisguisedly rejects, the things which

he expressly enjoins, or in which we are assured that he takes pleasure. Those, therefore, who set up a fictitious worship, merely worship and adore their own delirious fancies; indeed, they would never dare so to trifle with God, had they not previously fashioned him after their own childish conceits. Hence that vague and wandering opinion of Deity is declared by an apostle to be ignorance of God: "Howbeit, then, when ye knew not God, ye did service unto them which by nature are no gods." And he elsewhere declares, that the Ephesians were "without God" (Eph. 2:12) at the time when they wandered without any correct knowledge of him. It makes little difference, at least in this respect, whether you hold the existence of one God, or a plurality of gods, since, in both cases alike, by departing from the true God, you have nothing left but an execrable idol. It remains, therefore, to conclude with Lactantius (*Instit. Div.* lib 1:2, 6), "No religion is genuine that is not in accordance with truth."

4. To this fault they add a second—viz. that when they do think of God it is against their will; never approaching him without being dragged into his presence, and when there, instead of the voluntary fear flowing from reverence of the divine majesty, feeling only that forced and servile fear which divine Judgment extorts Judgment which, from the impossibility of escape, they are compelled to dread, but which, while they dread, they at the same time also hate. To impiety, and to it alone, the saying of Statius properly applies: "Fear first brought gods into the world," (*Theb.* lib. 1). Those whose inclinations are at variance with the justice of God, knowing that his tribunal has been erected for the punishment of transgression, earnestly wish that that tribunal were overthrown. Under the influence of this feeling they are actually warring against God, justice being one of his essential attributes. Perceiving that they are always within reach of his power, that resistance and evasion are alike impossible, they fear

and tremble. Accordingly, to avoid the appearance of condemning a majesty by which all are overawed, they have recourse to some species of religious observance, never ceasing meanwhile to defile themselves with every kind of vice, and add crime to crime, until they have broken the holy law of the Lord in every one of its requirements, and set his whole righteousness at nought; at all events, they are not so restrained by their semblance of fear as not to luxuriate and take pleasure in iniquity, choosing rather to indulge their carnal propensities than to curb them with the bridle of the Holy Spirit. But since this shadow of religion (it scarcely even deserves to be called a shadow) is false and vain, it is easy to infer how much this confused knowledge of God differs from that piety which is instilled into the breasts of believers, and from which alone true religion springs. And yet hypocrites would fain, by means of tortuous windings, make a show of being near to God at the very time they are fleeing from him. For while the whole life ought to be one perpetual course of obedience, they rebel without fear in almost all their actions, and seek to appease him with a few paltry sacrifices; while they ought to serve him with integrity of heart and holiness of life, they endeavour to procure his favour by means of frivolous devices and punctilios of no value. Nay, they take greater license in their grovelling indulgences, because they imagine that they can fulfil their duty to him by preposterous expiations; in short, while their confidence ought to have been fixed upon him, they put him aside, and rest in them- selves or the creatures. At length they bewilder themselves in such a maze of error, that the darkness of ignorance obscures, and ultimately extinguishes, those sparks which were de- signed to show them the glory of God. Still, however, the conviction that there is some Deity continues to exist, like a plant which can never be completely eradicated, though so corrupt, that it is only capable of producing the worst of fruit. Nay, we have still stronger evidence of the proposition for which I now contend—viz. that a sense of Deity is naturally engraven on the human heart, in the fact, that the very reprobate are forced to acknowledge it. When at their ease, they can jest about God, and talk pertly and loquaciously in disparagement of his power; but should despair, from any cause, overtake them, it will stimulate them to seek

CHAPTER 5.

THE KNOWLEDGE OF GOD CONSPICUOUS IN THE CREATION, AND CONTINUAL GOVERNMENT OF THE WORLD.

This chapter consists of two parts: 1. The former, which occupies the first ten sections, divides all the works of God into two great classes, and elucidates the knowledge of God as displayed in each class. The one class is treated of in the first six, and the other in the four following sections: 2. The latter part of the chapter shows, that, in consequence of the extreme stupidity of men, those manifestations of God, however perspicuous, lead to no useful result. This latter part, which commences at the eleventh section, is continued to the end of the chapter.

Sections.

1. The invisible and incomprehensible essence of God, to a certain extent, made visible in his works.

2. This declared by the first class of works — viz. the admirable motions of the heavens and the earth, the symmetry of the human body, and the connection of its parts; in short, the various objects which are presented to every eye.

3. This more especially manifested in the structure of the human body.

4. The shameful ingratitude of disregarding God, who, in such a variety of ways, is manifested within us. The still more shameful ingratitude of contemplating the endowments of the soul, without ascending to Him who gave them. No objection can be founded on any supposed organism in the soul.

5. The powers and actions of the soul, a proof of its separate existence from the body. Proofs of the soul's

immortality. Objection that the whole world is quickened by one soul. Reply to the objection. Its impiety.

6. Conclusion from what has been said—viz. that the omnipotence, eternity, and goodness of God, may be learned from the first class of works, *i.e.*, those which are in accordance with the ordinary course of nature.

7. The second class of works—viz. those above the ordinary course of nature, afford clear evidence of the perfections of God, especially his goodness, justice, and mercy.

8. Also his providence, power, and wisdom.

9. Proofs and illustrations of the divine Majesty. The use of them—viz. the acquisition of divine knowledge in combination with true piety.

10. The tendency of the knowledge of God to inspire the righteous with the hope of future life, and remind the wicked of the punishments reserved for them. Its tendency, moreover, to keep alive in the hearts of the righteous a sense of the divine goodness.

11. The second part of the chapter, which describes the stupidity both of learned and unlearned, in ascribing the whole order of things, and the admirable arrangements of divine Providence, to fortune.

12. Hence Polytheism, with all its abominations, and the endless and irreconcilable opinions of the philosophers concerning God.

13. All guilty of revolt from God, corrupting pure religion, either by following general custom, or the impious consent of antiquity.

14. Though irradiated by the wondrous glories of creation, we cease not to follow our own ways.

15. Our conduct altogether inexcusable, the dullness of perception being attributable to ourselves, while we are fully reminded of the true path, both by the structure and the government of the world.

1. Since the perfection of blessedness consists in the knowledge of God, he has been pleased, in order that none might be excluded from the means of obtaining felicity, not only to deposit in our minds that seed of religion of which we have already spoken, but so to manifest his perfections in the whole structure of the universe, and daily place himself in our view, that we cannot open our eyes without being compelled to behold him. His essence, indeed, is incomprehensible, utterly transcending all human thought; but on each of his works his glory is engraven in characters so bright, so distinct, and so illustrious, that none, however dull and illiterate, can plead ignorance as their excuse. Hence, with perfect truth, the Psalmist exclaims, "He covereth himself with light as with a garment," (Psalm 104:2); as if he had said, that God for the first time was arrayed in visible attire when, in the creation of the world, he displayed those glorious banners, on which, to whatever side we turn, we behold his perfections visibly portrayed. In the same place, the Psalmist aptly compares the expanded heavens to his royal tent, and says, "He layeth the beams of his chambers in the waters, maketh the clouds his chariot, and walketh upon the wings of the wind," sending forth the winds and lightnings as his swift messengers. And because the glory of his power and wisdom is more refulgent in the firmament, it is frequently designated as his palace. And, first, wherever you turn your eyes, there is no portion of the world, however minute, that does not exhibit at least some sparks of beauty; while it is impossible to contemplate the vast and beautiful fabric as it extends around, without being overwhelmed by the immense weight of glory. Hence, the author of the Epistle to the Hebrews elegantly describes the visible worlds as images of the invisible (Heb. 11:3), the elegant structure of the world serving us as a kind of mirror, in which we may behold God, though otherwise invisible. For the same reason, the Psalmist attributes language to celestial objects,

a language which all nations understand (Psalm 19:1), the manifestation of the Godhead being too clear to escape the notice of any people, however obtuse. The apostle Paul, stating this still more clearly, says, "That which may be known of God is manifest in them, for God has showed it unto them. For the invisible things of him from the creation of the world are clearly seen, being under- stood by the things that are made, even his eternal power and Godhead," (Rom. 1:20).

2. In attestation of his wondrous wisdom, both the heavens and the earth present us with innumerable proofs not only those more recondite proofs which astronomy, medicine, and all the natural sciences, are designed to illustrate, but proofs which force themselves on the notice of the most illiterate peasant, who cannot open his eyes without beholding them. It is true, indeed, that those who are more or less intimately acquainted with those liberal studies are thereby assisted and enabled to obtain a deeper insight into the secret workings of divine wisdom. No man, however, though he be ignorant of these, is incapacitated for discerning such proofs of creative wisdom as may well cause him to break forth in admiration of the Creator. To investigate the motions of the heavenly bodies, to determine their positions, measure their distances, and ascertain their properties, demands skill, and a more careful examination; and where these are so employed, as the Providence of God is thereby more fully unfolded, so it is reasonable to suppose that the mind takes a loftier flight, and obtains brighter views of his glory. Still, none who have the use of their eyes can be ignorant of the divine skill manifested so conspicuously in the endless variety, yet distinct and well ordered array, of the heavenly host; and, therefore, it is plain that the Lord has furnished every man with abundant proofs of his wisdom. The same is true in regard to the structure of the human frame. To determine the connection of its parts, its symmetry and beauty, with

the skill of a Galen (Lib. De Usu Partium), requires singular acuteness; and yet all men acknowledge that the human body bears on its face such proofs of ingenious contrivance as are sufficient to proclaim the admirable wisdom of its Maker.

3. Hence certain of the philosophers have not improperly called man a *microcosm* (*miniature world*), as being a rare specimen of divine power, wisdom, and goodness, and containing within himself wonders sufficient to occupy our minds, if we are willing so to employ them. Paul, accordingly, after reminding the Athenians that they "might feel after God and find him," immediately adds, that "he is not far from every one of us," (Acts 17:27); every man having within himself undoubted evidence of the heavenly grace by which he lives, and moves, and has his being. But if, in order to apprehend God, it is unnecessary to go farther than ourselves, what excuse can there be for the sloth of any man who will not take the trouble of descending into himself that he may find Him? For the same reason, too, David, after briefly celebrating the wonderful name and glory of God, as everywhere displayed, immediately exclaims, "What is man, that thou art mindful of him?" and again, "Out of the mouths of babes and sucklings thou hast ordained strength," (Psalm 8:2, 4). Thus he declares not only that the human race are a bright mirror of the Creator's works, but that infants hanging on their mothers' breasts have tongues eloquent enough to proclaim his glory without the aid of other orators. Accordingly, he hesitates not to bring them forward as fully instructed to refute the madness of those who, from devilish pride, would fain extinguish the name of God. Hence, too, the passage which Paul quotes from Aratus, "We are his offspring," (Acts 17:28), the excellent gifts with which he has endued us attesting that he is our Father. In the same way also, from natural instinct, and, as it were, at the dictation of experience, heathen poets call him the

father of men. No one, indeed, will voluntarily and willingly devote himself to the service of God unless he has previously tasted his paternal love, and been thereby allured to love and reverence Him.

4. But herein appears the shameful ingratitude of men. Though they have in their own persons a factory where innumerable operations of God are carried on, and a magazine stored with treasures of inestimable value — instead of bursting forth in his praise, as they are bound to do, they, on the contrary, are the more inflated and swelled with pride. They feel how wonderfully God is working in them, and their own experience tells them of the vast variety of gifts which they owe to his liberality. Whether they will or not, they cannot but know that these are proofs of his Godhead, and yet they inwardly suppress them. They have no occasion to go farther than themselves, provided they do not, by appropriating as their own that which has been given them from heaven, put out the light intended to exhibit God clearly to their minds. At this day, however, the earth sustains on her bosom many monster minds — minds which are not afraid to employ the seed of Deity deposited in human nature as a means of suppressing the name of God. Can any thing be more detestable than this madness in man, who, finding God a hundred times both in his body and his soul, makes his excellence in this respect a pretext for denying that there is a God? He will not say that chance has made him differ from the brutes that perish; but, substituting nature as the architect of the universe, he suppresses the name of God. The swift motions of the soul, its noble faculties and rare endowments, bespeak the agency of God in a manner which would make the suppression of it impossible, did not the Epicureans, like so many Cyclops, use it as a vantage-ground, from which to wage more audacious war with God. Are so many treasures of heavenly wisdom employed in the guidance of such a worm as man, and shall the whole universe be denied the

same privilege? To hold that there are organs in the soul corresponding to each of its faculties, is so far from obscuring the glory of God, that it rather illustrates it. Let Epicurus tell what concourse of atoms, cooking meat and drink, can form one portion into refuse and another portion into blood, and make all the members separately perform their office as carefully as if they were so many souls acting with common consent in the superintendence of one body.

5. But my business at present is not with that stye: I wish rather to deal with those who, led away by absurd subtleties, are inclined, by giving an indirect turn to the frigid doctrine of Aristotle, to employ it for the purpose both of disproving the immortality of the soul, and robbing God of his rights. Under the pretext that the faculties of the soul are organised, they chain it to the body as if it were incapable of a separate existence, while they endeavour as much as in them lies, by pronouncing eulogiums on nature, to suppress the name of God. But there is no ground for maintaining that the powers of the soul are confined to the performance of bodily functions. What has the body to do with your measuring the heavens, counting the number of the stars, ascertaining their magnitudes, their relative distances, the rate at which they move, and the orbits which they describe? I deny not that Astronomy has its use; all I mean to show is, that these lofty investigations are not conducted by organised symmetry, but by the faculties of the soul itself apart altogether from the body. The single example I have given will suggest many others to the reader. The swift and versatile movements of the soul in glancing from heaven to earth, connecting the future with the past, retaining the remembrance of former years, nay, forming creations of its own—its skill, moreover, in making astonishing discoveries, and inventing so many wonderful arts, are sure indications of the agency of God in man. What shall we say of its activity when the body is asleep, its many revolving thoughts, its many useful

suggestions, its many solid arguments, nay, its presentiment of things yet to come? What shall we say but that man bears about with him a stamp of immortality which can never be effaced? But how is it possible for man to be divine, and yet not acknowledge his Creator? Shall we, by means of a power of judging implanted in our breast, distinguish between justice and injustice, and yet there be no judge in heaven? Shall some remains of intelligence continue with us in sleep, and yet no God keep watch in heaven? Shall we be deemed the inventors of so many arts and useful properties that God may be defrauded of his praise, though experience tells us plainly enough, that whatever we possess is dispensed to us in unequal measures by another hand? The talk of certain persons concerning a secret inspiration quickening the whole world, is not only silly, but altogether profane. Such persons are delighted with the following celebrated passage of Virgil: —

"Know, first, that heaven, and earth's compacted frame,
And flowing waters, and the starry flame,
And both the radiant lights, one common soul
Inspires and feeds—and animates the whole.

This active mind, infused through all the space, Unites and mingles with the mighty mass: Hence, men and beasts the breath of life obtain, And birds of air, and monsters of the main.

Th' ethereal vigour is in all the same,
And every soul is filled with equal flame."

The meaning of all this is, that the world, which was made to display the glory of God, is its own creator. For the same poet has, in another place, adopted a view common to both Greeks and Latins: —

"Hence to the bee some sages have assigned
A portion of the God, and heavenly mind;
For God goes forth, and spreads throughout the whole,
Heaven, earth, and sea, the universal soul;

Each, at its birth, from him all beings share,
Both man and brute, the breath of vital air;
To him return, and, loosed from earthly chain,
Fly whence they sprung, and rest in God again;
Spurn at the grave, and, fearless of decay,
Dwell in high heaven, art star th' ethereal way."

Here we see how far that jejune speculation, of a universal mind animating and invigorating the world, is fitted to beget and foster piety in our minds. We have a still clearer proof of this in the profane verses which the licentious Lucretius has written as a deduction from the same principle. The plain object is to form an unsubstantial deity, and thereby banish the true God whom we ought to fear and worship. I admit, indeed that the expressions "Nature is God," may be piously used, if dictated by a pious mind; but as it is inaccurate and harsh (Nature being more properly the order which has been established by God), in matters which are so very important, and in regard to which special reverence is due, it does harm to confound the Deity with the inferior operations of his hands.

6. Let each of us, therefore, in contemplating his own nature, remember that there is one God who governs all natures, and, in governing, wishes us to have respect to himself, to make him the object of our faith, worship, and adoration. Nothing, indeed, can be more preposterous than to enjoy those noble endowments which bespeak the divine presence within us, and to neglect him who, of his own good pleasure, bestows them upon us. In regard to his power, how glorious the manifestations by which he urges us to the contemplation of himself; unless, indeed, we pretend not to know whose energy it is that by a word sustains the boundless fabric of the universe — at one time making heaven reverberate with thunder, sending forth the scorching lightning, and setting the whole atmosphere in a blaze; at another, causing the raging tempests to blow, and forthwith, in one moment, when it so pleases him, making a

perfect calm; keeping the sea, which seems constantly threatening the earth with devastation, suspended as it were in air; at one time, lashing it into fury by the impetuosity of the winds; at another, appeasing its rage, and stilling all its waves. Here we might refer to those glowing descriptions of divine power, as illustrated by natural events, which occur throughout Scripture; but more especially in the book of Job, and the prophecies of Isaiah. These, however, I purposely omit, because a better opportunity of introducing them will be found when I come to treat of the Scriptural account of the creation. (*Infra*, chap. 14 s. 1, 2, 20, *sq*). I only wish to observe here, that this method of investigating the divine perfections, by tracing the lineaments of his countenance as shadowed forth in the firmament and on the earth, is common both to those within and to those without the pale of the Church. From the power of God we are naturally led to consider his eternity since that from which all other things derive their origin must necessarily be selfexistent and eternal. Moreover, if it be asked what cause induced him to create all things at first, and now inclines him to preserve them, we shall find that there could be no other cause than his own goodness. But if this is the only cause, nothing more should be required to draw forth our love towards him; every creature, as the Psalmist reminds us, participating in his mercy. "His tender mercies are over all his works," (Ps. 145:9).

7. In the second class of God's works, namely those which are above the ordinary course of nature, the evidence of his perfections are in every respect equally clear. For in conducting the affairs of men, he so arranges the course of his providence, as daily to declare, by the clearest manifestations, that though all are in innumerable ways the partakers of his bounty, the righteous are the special objects of his favour, the wicked and profane the special objects of his severity. It is impossible to doubt his punishment of crimes; while at the same time he, in no unequivocal

manner, declares that he is the protector, and even the avenger of innocence, by shedding blessings on the good, helping their necessities, soothing and solacing their griefs, relieving their sufferings, and in all ways providing for their safety. And though he often permits the guilty to exult for a time with impunity, and the innocent to be driven to and fro in adversity, nay, even to be wickedly and iniquitously oppressed, this ought not to produce any uncertainty as to the uniform justice of all his procedure. Nay, an opposite inference should be drawn. When any one crime calls forth visible manifestations of his anger, it must be because he hates all crimes; and, on the other hand, his leaving many crimes unpunished, only proves that there is a Judgment in reserve, when the punishment now delayed shall be inflicted. In like manner, how richly does he supply us with the means of contemplating his mercy when, as frequently happens, he continues to visit miserable sinners with unwearied kindness, until he subdues their depravity, and woos them back with more than a parent's fondness?

8. To this purpose the Psalmist (Ps. 107) mentioning how God, in a wondrous manner, often brings sudden and unexpected succour to the miserable when almost on the brink of despair, whether in protecting them when they stray in deserts, and at length leading them back into the right path, or supplying them with food when famishing for want, or delivering them when captive from iron fetters and foul dungeons, or conducting them safe into harbour after shipwreck, or bringing them back from the gates of death by curing their diseases, or, after burning up the fields with heat and drought, fertilising them with the river of his grace, or exalting the meanest of the people, and casting down the mighty from their lofty seats:—the Psalmist, after bringing forward examples of this description, infers that those things which men call fortuitous events, are so many proofs of divine providence, and more especially of paternal clemency, furnishing ground of joy to the

righteous, and at the same time stopping the mouths of the ungodly. But as the greater part of mankind, enslaved by error, walk blindfold in this glorious theatre, he exclaims that it is a rare and singular wisdom to meditate carefully on these works of God, which many, who seem most sharp-sighted in other respects, behold without profit. It is indeed true, that the brightest manifestation of divine glory finds not one genuine spectator among a hundred. Still, neither his power nor his wisdom is shrouded in darkness. His power is strikingly displayed when the rage of the wicked, to all appearance irresistible, is crushed in a single moment; their arrogance subdued, their strongest bulwarks overthrown, their armour dashed to pieces, their strength broken, their schemes defeated without an effort, and audacity which set itself above the heavens is precipitated to the lowest depths of the earth. On the other hand, the poor are raised up out of the dust, and the needy lifted out of the dung hill (Ps. 113:7), the oppressed and afflicted are rescued in extremity, the despairing animated with hope, the unarmed defeat the armed, the few the many, the weak the strong. The excellence of the divine wisdom is manifested in distributing everything in due season, confounding the wisdom of the world, and taking the wise in their own craftiness (1 Cor. 3:19); in short, conducting all things in perfect accordance with reason.

9. We see there is no need of a long and laborious train of argument in order to obtain proofs which illustrate and assert the Divine Majesty. The few which we have merely touched, show them to be so immediately within our reach in every quarter, that we can trace them with the eye, or point to them with the finger. And here we must observe again (see chap. 2 s. 2), that the knowledge of God which we are invited to cultivate is not that which, resting satisfied with empty speculation, only flutters in the brain, but a knowledge which will prove substantial and fruitful wherever it is duly perceived, and rooted in the heart. The

Lord is manifested by his perfections. When we feel their power within us, and are conscious of their benefits, the knowledge must impress us much more vividly than if we merely imagined a God whose presence we never felt. Hence it is obvious, that in seeking God, the most direct path and the fittest method is, not to attempt with presumptuous curiosity to pry into his essence, which is rather to be adored than minutely discussed, but to contemplate him in his works, by which he draws near, becomes familiar, and in a manner communicates himself to us. To this the Apostle referred when he said, that we need not go far in search of him (Acts 17:27), because, by the continual working of his power, he dwells in every one of us. Accordingly, David (Psalm 145), after acknowledging that his greatness is unsearchable, proceeds to enumerate his works, declaring that his greatness will thereby be unfolded. It therefore becomes us also diligently to prosecute that investigation of God which so enraptures the soul with admiration as, at the same time, to make an efficacious impression on it. And, as Augustine expresses it (in Psalm 144), since we are unable to comprehend Him, and are, as it were, overpowered by his greatness, our proper course is to contemplate his works, and so refresh ourselves with his goodness.

10. By the knowledge thus acquired, we ought not only to be stimulated to worship God, but also aroused and elevated to the hope of future life. For, observing that the manifestations which the Lord gives both of his mercy and severity are only begun and incomplete, we ought to infer that these are doubtless only a prelude to higher manifestations, of which the full display is reserved for another state. Conversely, when we see the righteous brought into affliction by the ungodly, assailed with injuries, overwhelmed with calumnies, and lacerated by insult and contumely, while, on the contrary, the wicked flourish, prosper, acquire ease and honour, and all these

with impunity, we ought forthwith to infer, that there will be a future life in which iniquity shall receive its punishment, and righteousness its reward. Moreover, when we observe that the Lord often lays his chastening rod on the righteous, we may the more surely conclude, that far less will the unrighteous ultimately escape the scourges of his anger. There is a well-known passage in Augustine (De Civitat. Dei, lib. 1 c. 8), "Were all sin now visited with open punishment, it might be thought that nothing was reserved for the final Judgment; and, on the other hand, were no sin now openly punished, it might be supposed there was no divine providence." It must be acknowledged, therefore, that in each of the works of God, and more especially in the whole of them taken together, the divine perfections are delineated as in a picture, and the whole human race thereby invited and allured to acquire the knowledge of God, and, in consequence of this knowledge, true and complete felicity. Moreover, while his perfections are thus most vividly displayed, the only means of ascertaining their practical operation and tendency is to descend into ourselves, and consider how it is that the Lord there manifests his wisdom, power, and energy,—how he there displays his justice, goodness, and mercy. For although David (Psalm 92:6) justly complains of the extreme infatuation of the ungodly in not pondering the deep counsels of God, as exhibited in the government of the human race, what he elsewhere says (Psalm 40) is most true, that the wonders of the divine wisdom in this respect are more in number than the hairs of our head. But I leave this topic at present, as it will be more fully considered afterwards in its own place (Book I. c. 16, see. 6-9).

11. Bright, however, as is the manifestation which God gives both of himself and his immortal kingdom in the mirror of his works, so great is our stupidity, so dull are we in regard to these bright manifestations, that we derive no benefit from them. For in regard to the fabric and admirable

arrangement of the universe, how few of us are there who, in lifting our eyes to the heavens, or looking abroad on the various regions of the earth, ever think of the Creator? Do we not rather overlook Him, and sluggishly content ourselves with a view of his works? And then in regard to supernatural events, though these are occurring every day, how few are there who ascribe them to the ruling providence of God—how many who imagine that they are casual results produced by the blind evolutions of the wheel of chance? Even when under the guidance and direction of these events, we are in a manner forced to the contemplation of God (a circumstance which all must occasionally experience), and are thus led to form some impressions of Deity, we immediately fly off to carnal dreams and depraved fictions, and so by our vanity corrupt heavenly truth. This far, indeed, we differ from each other, in that every one appropriates to himself some peculiar error; but we are all alike in this, that we substitute monstrous fictions for the one living and true God—a disease not confined to obtuse and vulgar minds, but affecting the noblest, and those who, in other respects, are singularly acute. How lavishly in this respect have the whole body of philosophers betrayed their stupidity and want of sense? To say nothing of the others whose absurdities are of a still grosser description, how completely does Plato, the soberest and most religious of them all, lose himself in his round globe? What must be the case with the rest, when the leaders, who ought to have set them an example, commit such blunders, and labour under such hallucinations? In like manner, while the government of the world places the doctrine of providence beyond dispute, the practical result is the same as if it were believed that all things were carried hither and thither at the caprice of chance; so prone are we to vanity and error. I am still referring to the most distinguished of the philosophers, and not to the common herd, whose madness in profaning the truth of God exceeds all bounds.

12. Hence that immense flood of error with which the whole world is overflowed. Every individual mind being a kind of labyrinth, it is not wonderful, not only that each nation has adopted a variety of fictions, but that almost every man has had his own god. To the darkness of ignorance have been added presumption and wantonness, and hence there is scarcely an individual to be found without some idol or phantom as a substitute for Deity. Like water gushing forth from a large and copious spring, immense crowds of gods have issued from the human mind, every man giving himself full license, and devising some peculiar form of divinity, to meet his own views. It is unnecessary here to attempt a catalogue of the superstitions with which the world was overspread. The thing were endless; and the corruptions themselves, though not a word should be said, furnish abundant evidence of the blindness of the human mind. I say nothing of the rude and illiterate vulgar; but among the philosophers who attempted, by reason and learning, to pierce the heavens, what shameful disagreement! The higher any one was endued with genius, and the more he was polished by science and art, the more specious was the colouring which he gave to his opinions. All these, however, if examined more closely, will be found to be vain show. The Stoics plumed themselves on their acuteness, when they said that the various names of God might be extracted from all the parts of nature, and yet that his unity was not thereby divided: as if we were not already too prone to vanity, and had no need of being presented with an endless multiplicity of gods, to lead us further and more grossly into error. The mystic theology of the Egyptians shows how sedulously they laboured to be thought rational on this subject. And, perhaps, at the first glance, some show of probability might deceive the simple and unwary; but never did any mortal devise a scheme by

which religion was not foully corrupted. This endless variety and confusion emboldened the Epicureans, and other gross despisers of piety, to cut off all sense of God. For when they saw that the wisest contradicted each others they hesitated not to infer from their dissensions, and from the frivolous and absurd doctrines of each, that men foolishly, and to no purpose, brought torment upon themselves by searching for a God, there being none: and they thought this inference safe, because it was better at once to deny God altogether, than to feign uncertain gods, and thereafter engage in quarrels without end. They, indeed, argue absurdly, or rather weave a cloak for their impiety out of human ignorance; though ignorance surely cannot derogate from the prerogatives of God. But since all confess that there is no topic on which such difference exists, both among learned and unlearned, the proper inference is, that the human mind, which thus errs in inquiring after God, is dull and blind in heavenly mysteries. Some praise the answer of Simonides, who being asked by King Hero what God was, asked a day to consider. When the king next day repeated the question, he asked two days; and after repeatedly doubling the number of days, at length replied, "The longer I consider, the darker the subject appears." He, no doubt, wisely suspended his opinion, when he did not see clearly: still his answer shows, that if men are only naturally taught, instead of having any distinct, solid, or certain knowledge, they fasten only on contradictory principles, and, in consequence, worship an unknown God.

13. Hence we must hold, that whosoever adulterates pure religion (and this must be the case with all who cling to their own views), make a departure from the one God. No doubt, they will allege that they have a different intention; but it is of little consequence what they intend or persuade themselves to believe, since the Holy Spirit pronounces all to be apostates, who, in the blindness of

their minds, substitute demons in the place of God. For this reason Paul declares that the Ephesians were "without God," (Eph. 2:12), until they had learned from the Gospel what it is to worship the true God. Nor must this be restricted to one people only, since, in another place, he declares in general, that all men "became vain in their imaginations," after the majesty of the Creator was manifested to them in the structure of the world. Accordingly, in order to make way for the only true God, he condemns all the gods celebrated among the Gentiles as lying and false, leaving no Deity anywhere but in Mount Zion where the special knowledge of God was professed (Hab. 2:18, 20). Among the Gentiles in the time of Christ, the Samaritans undoubtedly made the nearest approach to true piety; yet we hear from his own mouth that they worshipped they knew not what (John 4:22); whence it follows that they were deluded by vain errors. In short, though all did not give way to gross vice, or rush headlong into open idolatry, there was no pure and authentic religion founded merely on common belief. A few individuals may not have gone all insane lengths with the vulgar; still Paul's declaration remains true, that the wisdom of God was not apprehended by the princes of this world (1 Cor. 2:8). But if the most distinguished wandered in darkness, what shall we say of the refuse? No wonder, therefore, that all worship of man's device is repudiated by the Holy Spirit as degenerate. Any opinion which man can form in heavenly mysteries, though it may not beget a long train of errors, is still the parent of error. And though nothing worse should happen, even this is no light sin—to worship an unknown God at random. Of this sin, however, we hear from our Saviour's own mouth (John 4:22), that all are guilty who have not been taught out of the law who the God is whom they ought to worship. Nay, even Socrates in Xenophon (lib. 1 Memorabilia), lauds the response of Apollo enjoining every man to worship the gods according to the rites of his country, and the particular practice of his own city. But what right have mortals thus to decide of their own authority in a matter which is far above the world; or who can so acquiesce in the will of his forefathers, or the decrees of the people, as unhesitatingly to receive a god at their hands? Every one will adhere to his own Judgment, sooner than submit to the dictation of others. Since, therefore, in regulating the worship of God, the custom of a city, or the consent of antiquity, is a too feeble and fragile bond of piety; it remains that God himself must bear witness to himself from heaven.

14. In vain for us, therefore, does Creation exhibit so many bright lamps lighted up to show forth the glory of its Author. Though they beam upon us from every quarter, they are altogether insufficient of themselves to lead us into the right path. Some sparks, undoubtedly, they do throw out; but these are quenched before they can give forth a brighter effulgence. Wherefore, the apostle, in the very place where he says that the worlds are images of invisible things, adds that it is *by faith* we understand that they were framed by the word of God (Heb. 11:3); thereby intimating that the invisible Godhead is indeed represented by such displays, but that we have no eyes to perceive it until they are enlightened through faith by internal revelation from God. When Paul says that that which may be known of God is manifested by the creation of the world, he does not mean such a manifestation as may be comprehended by the wit of man (Rom. 1:19); on the contrary, he shows that it has no further effect than to render us inexcusable (Acts 17:27). And though he says, elsewhere, that we have not far to seek for God, inasmuch as he dwells within us, he shows, in another passage, to what extent this nearness to God is availing. God, says he, "in times past, suffered all nations to walk in their own ways. Nevertheless, he left not himself without witness, in that he did good, and gave us rain from heaven, and fruitful seasons, filling our hearts

with food and gladness," (Acts 14:16, 17). But though God is not left without a witness, while, with numberless varied acts of kindness, he woos men to the knowledge of himself, yet they cease not to follow their own ways, in other words, deadly errors.

15. But though we are deficient in natural powers which might enable us to rise to a pure and clear knowledge of God, still, as the dullness which prevents us is within, there is no room for excuse. We cannot plead ignorance, without being at the same time convicted by our own consciences both of sloth and ingratitude. It were, indeed, a strange defence for man to pretend that he has no ears to hear the truth, while dumb creatures have voices loud enough to declare it; to allege that he is unable to see that which creatures without eyes demonstrate, to excuse himself on the ground of weakness of mind, while all creatures without reason are able to teach. Wherefore, when we wander and go astray, we are justly shut out from every species of excuse, because all things point to the right path. But while man must bear the guilt of corrupting the seed of divine knowledge so wondrously deposited in his mind, and preventing it from bearing good and genuine fruit, it is still most true that we are not sufficiently instructed by that bare and simple, but magnificent testimony which the creatures bear to the glory of their Creator. For no sooner do we, from a survey of the world, obtain some slight knowledge of Deity, than we pass by the true God, and set up in his stead the dream and phantom of our own brain, drawing away the praise of justice, wisdom, and goodness, from the fountain-head, and transferring it to some other quarter. Moreover, by the erroneous estimate we form, we either so obscure or pervert his daily works, as at once to rob them of their glory and the author of them of his just praise.

CHAPTER 6.

THE NEED OF SCRIPTURE, AS A GUIDE AND TEACHER, IN COMING TO GOD AS A CREATOR.

Sections.

1. God gives his elect a better help to the knowledge of himself—viz. the Holy Scriptures. This he did from the very first.

2. First, By oracles and visions, and the ministry of the Patriarchs. Secondly, By the promulgation of the Law, and the preaching of the Prophets. Why the doctrines of religion are committed to writing.

3. This view confirmed, 1. By the depravity of our nature making it necessary in every one who would know God to have recourse to the word; 2. From those passages of the Psalms in which God is introduced as reigning.

4. Another confirmation from certain direct statements in the Psalms. Lastly, From the words of our Saviour.

1. Therefore, though the effulgence which is presented to every eye, both in the heavens and on the earth, leaves the ingratitude of man without excuse, since God, in order to bring the whole human race under the same condemnation, holds forth to all, without exception, a mirror of his Deity in his works, another and better help must be given to guide us properly to God as a Creator. Not in vain, therefore, has he added the light of his Word in order that he might make himself known unto salvation, and bestowed the privilege on those whom he was pleased to bring into nearer and more familiar relation to himself. For, seeing how the minds of men were carried to and fro, and found no certain resting-place, he chose the Jews for a

peculiar people, and then hedged them in that they might not, like others, go astray. And not in vain does he, by the same means, retain us in his knowledge, since but for this, even those who, in comparison of others, seem to stand strong, would quickly fall away. For as the aged, or those whose sight is defective, when any books however fair, is set before them, though they perceive that there is something written are scarcely able to make out two consecutive words, but, when aided by glasses, begin to read distinctly, so Scripture, gathering together the impressions of Deity, which, till then, lay confused in our minds, dissipates the darkness, and shows us the true God clearly. God therefore bestows a gift of singular value, when, for the instruction of the Church, he employs not dumb teachers merely, but opens his own sacred mouth; when he not only proclaims that some God must be worshipped, but at the same time declares that He is the God to whom worship is due; when he not only teaches his elect to have respect to God, but manifests himself as the God to whom this respect should be paid.

The course which God followed towards his Church from the very first, was to supplement these common proofs by the addition of his Word, as a surer and more direct means of discovering himself. And there can be no doubt that it was by this help, Adam, Noah, Abraham, and the other patriarchs, attained to that familiar knowledge which, in a manner, distinguished them from unbelievers. I am not now speaking of the peculiar doctrines of faith by which they were elevated to the hope of eternal blessedness. It was necessary, in passing from death unto life, that they should know God, not only as a Creator, but as a Redeemer also; and both kinds of knowledge they certainly did obtain from the Word. In point of order, however, the knowledge first given was that which made them acquainted with the God by whom the world was made and is governed. To this first knowledge was afterwards added the more intimate knowledge which alone quickens dead souls, and by which God is known not only as the Creator of the worlds and the sole author and disposer of all events, but also as a Redeemer, in the person of the Mediator. But as the fall and the corruption of nature have not yet been considered, I now postpone the consideration of the remedy (for which, see Book 2 c. 6 &c). Let the reader then remember, that I am not now treating of the covenant by which God adopted the children of Abraham, or of that branch of doctrine by which, as founded in Christ, believers have, properly speaking, been in all ages separated from the profane heathen. I am only showing that it is necessary to apply to Scripture, in order to learn the sure marks which distinguish God, as the Creator of the world, from the whole herd of fictitious gods. We shall afterward, in due course, consider the work of Redemption. In the meantime, though we shall adduce many passages from the New Testament, and some also from the Law and the Prophets, in which express mention is made of Christ, the only object will be to show that God, the Maker of the world, is manifested to us in Scripture, and his true character expounded, so as to save us from wandering up and down, as in a labyrinth, in search of some doubtful deity.

2. Whether God revealed himself to the fathers by oracles and visions, or, by the instrumentality and ministry of men, suggested what they were to hand down to posterity, there cannot be a doubt that the certainty of what he taught them was firmly engraven on their hearts, so that they felt assured and knew that the things which they learnt came forth from God, who invariably accompanied his word with a sure testimony, infinitely superior to mere opinion. At length, in order that, while doctrine was continually enlarged, its truth might subsist in the world during all ages, it was his pleasure that the same oracles which he had deposited with the fathers should be

consigned, as it were, to public records. With this view the law was promulgated, and prophets were afterwards added to be its interpreters. For though the uses of the law were manifold (Book 2 c. 7 and 8), and the special office assigned to Moses and all the prophets was to teach the method of reconciliation between God and man (whence Paul calls Christ "the end of the law," Rom. 10:4); still I repeat that, in addition to the proper doctrine of faith and repentance in which Christ is set forth as a Mediator, the Scriptures employ certain marks and tokens to distinguish the only wise and true God, considered as the Creator and Governor of the world, and thereby guard against his being confounded with the herd of false deities. Therefore, while it becomes man seriously to employ his eyes in considering the works of God, since a place has been assigned him in this most glorious theatre that he may be a spectator of them, his special duty is to give ear to the Word, that he may the better profit. Hence it is not strange that those who are born in darkness become more and more hardened in their stupidity; because the vast majority instead of confining themselves within due bounds by listening with docility to the Word, exult in their own vanity. If true religion is to beam upon us, our principle must be, that it is necessary to begin with heavenly teaching, and that it is impossible for any man to obtain even the minutest portion of right and sound doctrine without being a disciple of Scripture. Hence, the first step in true knowledge is taken, when we reverently embrace the testimony which God has been pleased therein to give of himself. For not only does faith, full and perfect faith, but all correct knowledge of God, originate in obedience. And surely in this respect God has with singular Providence provided for mankind in all ages.

3. For if we reflect how prone the human mind is to lapse into forgetfulness of God, how readily inclined to every kind of error, how bent every now and then on

devising new and fictitious religions, it will be easy to understand how necessary it was to make such a depository of doctrine as would secure it from either perishing by the neglect, vanishing away amid the errors, or being corrupted by the presumptuous audacity of men. It being thus manifest that God, foreseeing the inefficiency of his image imprinted on the fair form of the universe, has given the assistance of his Word to all whom he has ever been pleased to instruct effectually, we, too, must pursue this straight path, if we aspire in earnest to a genuine contemplation of God;—we must go, I say, to the Word, where the character of God, drawn from his works is described accurately and to the life; these works being estimated, not by our depraved Judgment, but by the standard of eternal truth. If, as I lately said, we turn aside from it, how great soever the speed with which we move, we shall never reach the goal, because we are off the course. We should consider that the brightness of the Divine countenance, which even an apostle declares to be inaccessible (1 Tim. 6:16), is a kind of labyrinth,—a labyrinth to us inextricable, if the Word do not serve us as a thread to guide our path; and that it is better to limp in the way, than run with the greatest swiftness out of it. Hence the Psalmist, after repeatedly declaring (Psalm 93, 96, 97, 99, &c). that superstition should be banished from the world in order that pure religion may flourish, introduces God as *reigning*; meaning by the term, not the power which he possesses and which he exerts in the government of universal nature, but the doctrine by which he maintains his due suprem- acy: because error never can be eradicated from the heart of man until the true knowledge of God has been implanted in it.

4. Accordingly, the same prophet, after mentioning that the heavens declare the glory of God, that the firmament sheweth forth the works of his hands, that the regular succession of day and night proclaim his Majesty, proceeds

to make mention of the Word:—"The law of the Lord," says he, "is perfect, converting the soul; the testimony of the Lord is sure, making wise the simple. The statutes of the Lord are right, rejoicing the heart; the commandment of the Lord is pure, enlightening the eyes," (Psalm 19:1-9). For though the law has other uses besides (as to which, see Book 2 c. 7, sec. 6, 10, 12), the general meaning is, that it is the proper school for training the children of God; the invitation given to all nations, to behold him in the heavens and earth, proving of no avail. The same view is taken in the 29th Psalm, where the Psalmist, after discoursing on the dreadful voice of God, which, in thunder, wind, rain, whirlwind, and tempest, shakes the earth, makes the mountains tremble, and breaks the cedars, concludes by saying, "that in his temple does every one speak of his glory," unbelievers being deaf to all God's words when they echo in the air. In like manner another Psalm, after describing the raging billows of the sea, thus concludes, "Thy testimonies are very sure; holiness becometh thine house for ever," (Psalm 93:5). To the same effect are the words of our Saviour to the Samaritan woman, when he told her that her nation and all other nations worshipped they knew not what; and that the Jews alone gave worship to the true God (John 4:22). Since the human mind, through its weakness, was altogether unable to come to God if not aided and upheld by his sacred word, it necessarily followed that all mankind, the Jews excepted, inasmuch as they sought God without the Word, were labouring under vanity and error.

CHAPTER 7.

THE TESTIMONY OF THE SPIRIT NECESSARY TO GIVE FULL AUTHORITY TO SCRIPTURE. THE IMPIETY OF PRETENDING THAT THE CREDIBILITY OF SCRIP- TURE DEPENDS ON THE JUDGMENT OF THE CHURCH.

Section.

1. The authority of Scripture derived not from men, but from the Spirit of God. Objection, That Scripture depends on the decision of the Church. Refutation, I. The truth of God would thus be subjected to the will of man. II. It is insulting to the Holy Spirit. III. It establishes a tyranny in the Church. IV. It forms a mass of errors. V. It subverts conscience. VI. It exposes our faith to the scoffs of the profane.

2. Another reply to the objection drawn from the words of the Apostle Paul. Solution of the difficulties started by opponents. A second objection refuted.

3. A third objection founded on a sentiment of Augustine considered.

4. Conclusion, That the authority of Scripture is founded on its being spoken by God. This confirmed by the conscience of the godly, and the consent of all men of the least candour. A fourth objection common in the mouths of the profane. Refutation.

5. Last and necessary conclusion, That the authority of Scripture is sealed on the hearts of believers by the testimony of the Holy Spirit. The certainty of this testimony. Confirmation of it from a passage of Isaiah, and the experience of believers. Also, from another passage of Isaiah.

1. Before proceeding farther, it seems proper to make some observations on the authority of Scripture, in order that our minds may not only be prepared to receive it with reverence, but be divested of all doubt.

When that which professes to be the Word of God is acknowledged to be so, no person, unless devoid of common sense and the feelings of a man, will have the desperate hardihood to refuse credit to the speaker. But since no daily responses are given from heaven, and the Scriptures are the only records in which God has been pleased to consign his truth to perpetual remembrance, the full authority which they ought to possess with the faithful is not recognised, unless they are believed to have come from heaven, as directly as if God had been heard giving utterance to them. This subject well deserves to be treated more at large, and pondered more accurately. But my readers will pardon me for having more regard to what my plan admits than to what the extent of this topic requires.

A most pernicious error has very generally prevailed — viz. that Scripture is of importance only in so far as conceded to it by the suffrage of the Church; as if the eternal and inviolable truth of God could depend on the will of men. With great insult to the Holy Spirit, it is asked, who can assure us that the Scriptures proceeded from God; who guarantee that they have come down safe and unimpaired to our times; who persuade us that *this* book is to be received with reverence, and *that one* expunged from the list, did not the Church regulate all these things with certainty? On the determination of the Church, therefore, it is said, depend both the reverence which is due to Scripture, and the books which are to be admitted into the canon. Thus profane men, seeking, under the pretext of the Church, to introduce unbridled tyranny, care not in what absurdities they entangle themselves and others, provided they extort from the simple this one acknowledgement — viz. that there is nothing which the Church cannot do. But what is to become of miserable consciences in quest of some solid assurance of eternal life, if all the promises with regard to it have no better support than man's Judgment? On being told so, will they cease to doubt and tremble? On the other hand, to what jeers of the wicked is our faith subjected—into how great suspicion is it brought with all, if believed to have only a precarious authority lent to it by the good will of men?

2. These ravings are admirably refuted by a single expression of an apostle. Paul testifies that the Church is "built on the foundation of the apostles and prophets," (Eph. 2:20). If the doctrine of the apostles and prophets is the foundation of the Church, the former must have had its certainty before the latter began to exist. Nor is there any room for the cavil, that though the Church derives her first beginning from thence, it still remains doubtful what writings are to be attributed to the apostles and prophets, until her Judgment is interposed. For if the Christian Church was founded at first on the writings of the prophets, and the preaching of the apostles, that doctrine, wheresoever it may be found, was certainly ascertained and sanctioned antecedently to the Church, since, but for this, the Church herself never could have existed. Nothings therefore can be more absurd than the fiction, that the power of judging Scripture is in the Church, and that on her nod its certainty depends. When the Church receives it, and gives it the stamp of her authority, she does not make that authentic which was otherwise doubtful or controverted but, acknowledging it as the truth of God, she, as in duty bounds shows her reverence by an unhesitating assent. As to the question, How shall we be persuaded that it came from God without recurring to a decree of the Church? it is just the same as if it were asked, How shall we learn to distinguish light from darkness, white from black, sweet from bitter? Scripture bears upon the face of it as clear

evidence of its truth, as white and black do of their colour, sweet and bitter of their taste.

3. I am aware it is usual to quote a sentence of Augustine in which he says that he would not believe the gospel, were he not moved by the authority of the Church (Aug. Cont. Epist. Fundament. c. 5). But it is easy to discover from the context, how inaccurate and unfair it is to give it such a meaning. He was reasoning against the Manichees, who insisted on being implicitly believed, alleging that they had the truth, though they did not show they had. But as they pretended to appeal to the gospel in support of Manes, he asks what they would do if they fell in with a man who did not even believe the gospel—what kind of argument they would use to bring him over to their opinion. He afterwards adds, "But I would not believe the gospel," &c.; meaning, that were he a stranger to the faith, the only thing which could induce him to embrace the gospel would be the authority of the Church. And is it any thing wonderful, that one who does not know Christ should pay respect to men?

Augustine, therefore, does not here say that the faith of the godly is founded on the authority of the Church; nor does he mean that the certainty of the gospel depends upon it; he merely says that unbelievers would have no certainty of the gospel, so as thereby to win Christ, were they not influenced by the consent of the Church. And he clearly shows this to be his meaning, by thus expressing himself a little before: "When I have praised my own creed, and ridiculed yours, who do you suppose is to judge between us; or what more is to be done than to quit those who, inviting us to certainty, afterwards command us to believe uncertainty, and follow those who invite us, in the first instance, to believe what we are not yet able to comprehend, that waxing stronger through faith itself, we may become able to understand what we believe—no longer men, but God himself internally strengthening and

98

illuminating our minds? These unquestionably are the words of Augustine (August. Cont. Epist. Fundament. cap. 4); and the obvious inference from them is, that this holy man had no intention to suspend our faith in Scripture on the nod or decision of the Church, but only to intimate (what we too admit to be true) that those who are not yet enlightened by the Spirit of God, become teachable by reverence for the Church, and thus submit to learn the faith of Christ from the gospel. In this way, though the authority of the Church leads us on, and prepares us to believe in the gospel, it is plain that Augustine would have the certainty of the godly to rest on a very different foundation.

At the same time, I deny not that he often presses the Manichees with the consent of the whole Church, while arguing in support of the Scriptures, which they rejected. Hence he upbraids Faustus (lib. 32) for not submitting to evangelical truth—truth so well founded, so firmly established, so gloriously renowned, and handed down by sure succession from the days of the apostles. But he nowhere insinuates that the authority which we give to the Scriptures depends on the definitions or devices of men. He only brings forward the universal Judgment of the Church, as a point most pertinent to the cause, and one, moreover, in which he had the advantage of his opponents. Any one who desires to see this more fully proved may read his short treatises, *De Utilitate Credendi* (The Advantages of Believing), where it will be found that the only facility of believing which he recommends is that which affords an introduction, and forms a fit commencement to inquiry; while he declares that we ought not to be satisfied with opinion, but to strive after substantial truth.

4. It is necessary to attend to what I lately said, that our faith in doctrine is not established until we have a perfect conviction that God is its author. Hence, the highest proof of Scripture is uniformly taken from the character of him whose Word it is. The prophets and apostles boast not their

99

own acuteness or any qualities which win credit to speakers, nor do they dwell on reasons; but they appeal to the sacred name of God, in order that the whole world may be compelled to submission. The next thing to be considered is, how it appears not probable merely, but certain, that the name of God is neither rashly nor cunningly pretended. If, then, we would consult most effectually for our consciences, and save them from being driven about in a whirl of uncertainty, from wavering, and even stumbling at the smallest obstacle, our conviction of the truth of Scripture must be derived from a higher source than human conjectures, Judgments, or reasons; namely, the secret testimony of the Spirit. It is true, indeed, that if we choose to proceed in the way of arguments it is easy to establish, by evidence of various kinds, that if there is a God in heaven, the Law, the Prophecies, and the Gospel, proceeded from him. Nay, although learned men, and men of the greatest talent, should take the opposite side, summoning and ostentatiously displaying all the powers of their genius in the discussion; if they are not possessed of shameless effrontery, they will be compelled to confess that the Scripture exhibits clear evidence of its being spoken by God, and, consequently, of its containing his heavenly doctrine. We shall see a little farther on, that the volume of sacred Scripture very far surpasses all other writings. Nay, if we look at it with clear eyes, and unblessed Judgment, it will forthwith present itself with a divine majesty which will subdue our presumptuous opposition, and force us to do it homage.

Still, however, it is preposterous to attempt, by discussion, to rear up a full faith in Scripture. True, were I called to contend with the craftiest despisers of God, I trust, though I am not possessed of the highest ability or eloquence, I should not find it difficult to stop their obstreperous mouths; I could, without much ado, put down the boastings which they mutter in corners, were anything to be gained by refuting their cavils. But although we may maintain the sacred Word of God against gainsayers, it does not follow that we shall forthwith implant the certainty which faith requires in their hearts. Profane men think that religion rests only on opinion, and, therefore, that they may not believe foolishly, or on slight grounds, desire and insist to have it proved by reason that Moses and the prophets were divinely in- spired. But I answer, that the testimony of the Spirit is superior to reason. For as God alone can properly bear witness to his own words, so these words will not obtain full credit in the hearts of men, until they are sealed by the inward testimony of the Spirit. The same Spirit, therefore, who spoke by the mouth of the prophets, must penetrate our hearts, in order to convince us that they faithfully delivered the message with which they were divinely entrusted. This connection is most aptly expressed by Isaiah in these words, "My Spirit that is upon thee, and my words which I have put in thy mouth, shall not depart out of thy mouth, nor out of the mouth of thy seed, nor out of the mouth of thy seed's seed, saith the Lord, from henceforth and for ever," (Isa. 59:21). Some worthy persons feel disconcerted, because, while the wicked murmur with impunity at the Word of God, they have not a clear proof at hand to silence them, forgetting that the Spirit is called an earnest and seal to confirm the faith of the godly, for this very reason, that, until he enlightens their minds, they are tossed to and fro in a sea of doubts.

5. Let it therefore be held as fixed, that those who are inwardly taught by the Holy Spirit acquiesce implicitly in Scripture; that Scripture, carrying its own evidence along with it, deigns not to submit to proofs and arguments, but owes the full conviction with which we ought to receive it to the testimony of the Spirit. Enlightened by him, we no longer believe, either on our own Judgment or that of others, that the Scriptures are from God; but, in a way superior to human Judgment, feel perfectly assured—as

much so as if we beheld the divine image visibly impressed on it—that it came to us, by the instrumentality of men, from the very mouth of God. We ask not for proofs or probabilities on which to rest our Judgment, but we subject our intellect and Judgment to it as too transcendent for us to estimate. This, however, we do, not in the manner in which some are wont to fasten on an unknown object, which, as soon as known, displeases, but because we have a thorough conviction that, in holding it, we hold unassailable truth; not like miserable men, whose minds are enslaved by superstition, but because we feel a divine energy living and breathing in it—an energy by which we are drawn and animated to obey it, willingly indeed, and knowingly, but more vividly and effectually than could be done by human will or knowledge. Hence, God most justly exclaims by the mouth of Isaiah, "Ye are my witnesses, saith the Lord, and my servant whom I have chosen, that ye may know and believe me, and understand that I am he," (Isa. 43:10).

Such, then, is a conviction which asks not for reasons; such, a knowledge which accords with the highest reason, namely knowledge in which the mind rests more firmly and securely than in any reasons; such in fine, the conviction which revelation from heaven alone can produce. I say nothing more than every believer experiences in himself, though my words fall far short of the reality. I do not dwell on this subject at present, because we will return to it again: only let us now understand that the only true faith is that which the Spirit of God seals on our hearts. Nay, the modest and teachable reader will find a sufficient reason in the promise contained in Isaiah, that all the children of the renovated Church "shall be taught of the Lord," (Isaiah 54:13). This singular privilege God bestows on his elect only, whom he separates from the rest of mankind. For what is the beginning of true doctrine but prompt alacrity to hear the Word of God? And God, by the mouth of Moses, thus demands to be heard: "It is not in heavens that thou shouldest say, Who shall go up for us to heaven, and bring it unto us, that we may hear and do it? But the word is very nigh unto thee, in thy mouth and in thy heart," (Deut. 30:12, 14). God having been pleased to reserve the treasure of intelligence for his children, no wonder that so much ignorance and stupidity is seen in the *generality* of mankind. In the generality, I include even those specially chosen, until they are ingrafted into the body of the Church. Isaiah, moreover, while reminding us that the prophetical doctrine would prove incredible not only to strangers, but also to the Jews, who were desirous to be thought of the household of God, subjoins the reason, when he asks, "To whom has the arm of the Lord been revealed?" (Isaiah 53:1). If at any time, then we are troubled at the small number of those who believe, let us, on the other hand, call to mind, that none comprehend the mysteries of God save those to whom it is given.

CHAPTER 8.

THE CREDIBILITY OF SCRIPTURE SUFFICIENTLY PROVED IN SO FAR AS NATURAL REASON ADMITS.

This chapter consists of four parts. The first contains certain general proofs which may be easily gathered out of the writings both of the Old and New Testament—viz. the arrangement of the sacred volume, its dignity, truth, simplicity, efficacy, and majesty, sec. 1, 2. The second part contains special proofs taken from the Old Testament—viz. the antiquity of the books of Moses, their authority, his miracles and prophecies, sec. 3-7; also, the predictions of the other prophets and their wondrous harmony, sec. 8. There is subjoined a refutation of two objections to the books of Moses and the Prophets, sec. 9, 10. The third part exhibits proofs gathered out of the New Testament, *e.g.*, the harmony of the Evangelists in their account of heavenly mysteries, the majesty of the writings of John, Peter, and Paul, the remarkable calling of the Apostles and conversion of Paul, sec. 11. The last part exhibits the proofs drawn from ecclesiastical history, the perpetual consent of the Church in receiving and preserving divine truth, the invincible force of the truth in defending itself, the agreement of the godly (though otherwise differing so much from one another), the pious profession of the same doctrine by many illustrious men; in fine, the more than human constancy of the martyrs, sec. 12, 13. This is followed by a conclusion of the particular topic discussed.

Sections.

1. Secondary helps to establish the credibility of Scripture. I. The arrangement of the sacred volume. II. Its dignity. III. Its truth. IV. Its simplicity. V. Its efficacy.

2. The majesty conspicuous in the writings of the Prophets.

3. Special proofs from the Old Testament. I. The antiquity of the Books of Moses.

4. This antiquity contrasted with the dreams of the Egyptians. II. The majesty of the Books of Moses.

5. The miracles and prophecies of Moses. A profane objection refuted.

6. Another profane objection refuted.

7. The prophecies of Moses as to the sceptre not departing from Judah, and the calling of the Gentiles.

8. The predictions of other prophets. The destruction of Jerusalem; and the return from the Babylonish captivity. Harmony of the Prophets. The celebrated prophecy of Daniel.

9. Objection against Moses and the Prophets. Answer to it.

10. Another objection and answer. Of the wondrous Providence of God in the preservation of the sacred books. The Greek Translation. The carefulness of the Jews.

11. Special proofs from the New Testament. I. The harmony of the Evangelists, and the sublime simplicity of their writings. II. The majesty of John, Paul, and Peter. III. The calling of the Apostles. IV. The conversion of Paul.

12. Proofs from Church history. I. Perpetual consent of the Church in receiving and preserving the truth. II. The invincible power of the truth itself. III. Agreement among the godly, not withstanding of their many differences in other respects. 13. The constancy of the martyrs. Conclusion. Proofs of this description only of use after the certainty of Scripture has been established in the heart by the Holy Spirit.

1. In vain were the authority of Scripture fortified by argument, or supported by the consent of the Church, or confirmed by any other helps, if unaccompanied by an assurance higher and stronger than human Judgment can give. Till this better foundation has been laid, the authority of Scripture remains in suspense. On the other hand, when recognising its exemption from the common rule, we receive it reverently, and according to its dignity, those proofs which were not so strong as to produce and rivet a full conviction in our minds, become most appropriate helps. For it is wonderful how much we are confirmed in our belief, when we more attentively consider how admirably the system of divine wisdom contained in it is arranged—how perfectly free the doctrine is from every thing that savours of earth—how beautifully it harmonises in all its parts—and how rich it is in all the other qualities which give an air of majesty to composition. Our hearts are still more firmly assured when we reflect that our admiration is elicited more by the dignity of the matter than by the graces of style. For it was not without an admirable arrangement of Providence, that the sublime mysteries of the kingdom of heaven have for the greater part been delivered with a contemptible meanness of words. Had they been adorned with a more splendid eloquence, the wicked might have cavilled, and alleged that this constituted all their force. But now, when an unpolished simplicity, almost bordering on rudeness, makes a deeper impression than the loftiest flights of oratory, what does it indicate if not that the Holy Scriptures are too mighty in the power of truth to need the rhetorician's art?

Hence there was good ground for the Apostle's declaration, that the faith of the Cor- inthians was founded not on "the wisdom of men," but on "the power of God," (1 Cor. 2:5), this speech and preaching among them having been "not with enticing words of man's wisdom, but in demonstration of the Spirit and of power," (1 Cor. 2:5). For the truth is vindicated in opposition to every doubt, when, unsupported by foreign aid, it has its sole sufficiency in itself. How peculiarly this property belongs to Scripture appears from this, that no human writings, however skilfully composed, are at all capable of affecting us in a similar way. Read Demosthenes or Cicero, read Plato, Aristotle, or any other of that class: you will, I admit, feel wonderfully allured, pleased, moved, enchanted; but turn from them to the reading of the Sacred Volume, and whether you will or not, it will so affect you, so pierce your heart, so work its way into your very marrow, that, in comparison of the impression so produced, that of orators and philosophers will almost disappear; making it manifest that in the Sacred Volume there is a truth divine, a something which makes it immeasurably superior to all the gifts and graces attainable by man.

2. I confess, however, that in elegance and beauty, nay, splendour, the style of some of the prophets is not surpassed by the eloquence of heathen writers. By examples of this description, the Holy Spirit was pleased to show that it was not from want of eloquence he in other instances used a rude and homely style. But whether you read David, Isaiah, and others of the same class, whose discourse flows sweet and pleasant; or Amos the herdsman, Jeremiah, and Zechariah, whose rougher idiom savours of rusticity; that majesty of the Spirit to which I adverted appears conspicuous in all. I am not unaware, that as Satan often apes God, that he may by a fallacious resemblance the better insinuate himself into the minds of the simple, so he craftily disseminated the impious errors with which he deceived miserable men in an uncouth and semi-barbarous style, and frequently employed obsolete forms of expression in order to cloak his impostures. None possessed of any moderate share of sense need be told how vain and vile such affectation is. But in regard to the Holy Scriptures, however petulant men may attempt to carp at

them, they are replete with sentiments which it is clear that man never could have conceived. Let each of the prophets be examined, and not one will be found who does not rise far higher than human reach. Those who feel their works insipid must be absolutely devoid of taste.

3. As this subject has been treated at large by others, it will be sufficient here merely to touch on its leading points. In addition to the qualities already mentioned, great weight is due to the antiquity of Scripture (Euseb. Prepar. Evang. lib. 2 c. 1). Whatever fables Greek writers may retail concerning the Egyptian Theology, no monument of any religion exists which is not long posterior to the age of Moses. But Moses does not introduce a new Deity. He only sets forth that doctrine concerning the eternal God which the Israelites had received by tradition from their fathers, by whom it had been transmitted, as it were, from hand to hand, during a long series of ages. For what else does he do than lead them back to the covenant which had been made with Abraham? Had he referred to matters of which they had never heard, he never could have succeeded; but their deliverance from the bondage in which they were held must have been a fact of familiar and universal notoriety, the very mention of which must have immediately aroused the attention of all. It is, moreover, probable, that they were intimately acquainted with the whole period of four hundred years. Now, if Moses (who is so much earlier than all other writers) traces the tradition of his doctrine from so remote a period, it is obvious how far the Holy Scriptures must in point of antiquity surpass all other writings.

4. Some perhaps may choose to credit the Egyptians in carrying back their antiquity to a period of six thousand years before the world was created. But their garrulity, which even some profane authors have held up to derision, it cannot be necessary for me to refute. Josephus, however, in his work against Appion, produces important passages from very ancient writers, implying that the doctrine

delivered in the law was celebrated among all nations from the remotest ages, though it was neither read nor accurately known. And then, in order that the malignant might have no ground for suspicion, and the ungodly no handle for cavil, God has provided, in the most effectual manner, against both dangers. When Moses relates the words which Jacob, under Divine inspiration, uttered concerning his posterity almost three hundred years before, how does he ennoble his own tribe? He stigmatises it with eternal infamy in the person of Levi. "Simon and Levi," says he, "are brethren; instruments of cruelty are in their habitations. O my soul, come not thou into their secret; unto their assembly mine honour be not thou united," (Gen. 49:5, 6). This stigma he certainly might have passed in silence, not only that he might spare his own ancestor, but also save both himself and his whole family from a portion of the disgrace. How can any suspicion attach to him, who, by voluntarily proclaiming that the first founder of his family was declared detestable by a Divine oracle, neither consults for his own private interest, nor declines to incur obloquy among his tribe, who must have been offended by his statement of the fact? Again, when he relates the wicked murmuring of his brother Aaron, and his sister Miriam (Numb. 12:1), shall we say that he spoke his own natural feelings, or that he obeyed the command of the Holy Spirit? Moreover, when invested with supreme authority, why does he not bestow the office of High Priest on his sons, instead of consigning them to the lowest place? I only touch on a few points out of many; but the Law itself contains throughout numerous proofs, which fully vindicate the credibility of Moses, and place it beyond dispute, that he was in truth a messenger sent forth from God.

5. The many striking miracles which Moses relates are so many sanctions of the law delivered, and the doctrine propounded, by him. His being carried up into the mount in a cloud; his remaining there forty days separated from

human society; his countenance glistening during the promulgation of the law, as with meridian effulgence; the lightnings which flashed on every side; the voices and thunderings which echoed in the air; the clang of the trumpet blown by no human mouth; his entrance into the tabernacle, while a cloud hid him from the view of the people; the miraculous vindication of his authority, by the fearful destruction of Korah, Nathan, and Abiram, and all their impious faction; the stream instantly gushing forth from the rock when struck with his rod; the manna which rained from heaven at his prayer;—did not God by all these proclaim aloud that he was an un- doubted prophet? If any one object that I am taking debatable points for granted, the cavil is easily answered. Moses published all these things in the assembly of the people. How, then, could he possibly impose on the very eye-witnesses of what was done? Is it conceivable that he would have come forward, and, while accusing the people of unbelief, obstinacy, ingratitude, and other crimes, have boasted that his doctrine had been confirmed in their own presence by miracles which they never saw?

6. For it is also worthy of remark, that the miracles which he relates are combined with disagreeable circumstances, which must have provoked opposition from the whole body of the people, if there had been the smallest ground for it. Hence it is obvious that they were induced to assent, merely because they had been previously convinced by their own experience. But because the fact was too ascribed them to magic (Exod. 9:11). But with what probability is a charge of magic brought against him, who held it in such abhorrence, that he ordered every one who should consult soothsayers and magicians to be stoned? (Lev. 20:27). Assuredly, no impostor deals in tricks, without studying to raise his reputation by amazing the common people. But what does Moses do? By crying out, that he and Aaron his brother are nothing (Exod. 16:7), that

they merely execute what God has commanded, he clears himself from every approach to suspicion. Again, if the facts are considered in themselves, what kind of incantation could cause manna to rain from heaven every day, and in sufficient quantity to maintain a people, while any one, who gathered more than the appointed measure, saw his incredulity divinely punished by its turning to worms? To this we may add, that God then suffered his servant to be subjected to so many serious trials, that the ungodly cannot now gain anything by their glamour. When (as often happened) the people proudly and petulantly rose up against him, when individuals conspired, and attempted to overthrow him, how could any impostures have enabled clear to leave it free for heathen writers to deny that Moses did perform miracles, the father of lies suggested a calumny, and him to elude their rage? The event plainly shows that by these means his doctrine was attested to all succeeding ages.

7. Moreover, it is impossible to deny that he was guided by a prophetic spirit in assigning the first place to the tribe of Judah in the person of Jacob, especially if we take into view the fact itself, as explained by the event. Suppose that Moses was the inventor of the prophecy, still, after he committed it to writing, four hundred years pass away, during which no mention is made of a sceptre in the tribe of Judah. After Saul is anointed, the kingly office seems fixed in the tribe of Benjamin (1 Sam. 11:15; 16:13). When David is anointed by Samuel, what apparent ground is there for the transference? Who could have looked for a king out of the plebeian family of a herdsman? And out of seven brothers, who could have thought that the honour was destined for the youngest? And then by what means did he afterwards come within reach of the throne? Who dare say that his anointing was regulated by human art, or skill, or prudence, and was not rather the fulfilment of a divine prophecy? In like manner, do not the predictions, though

obscure, of the admission of the Gentiles into the divine covenant, seeing they were not fulfilled till almost two thousand years after, make it palpable that Moses spoke under divine inspiration? I omit other predictions which so plainly betoken divine revelation, that all men of sound mind must see they were spoken by God. In short, his Song itself (Deut. 32) is a bright mirror in which God is manifestly seen.

8. In the case of the other prophets the evidence is even clearer. I will only select a few examples, for it were too tedious to enumerate the whole. Isaiah, in his own day, when the kingdom of Judah was at peace, and had even some ground to confide in the protection of the Chaldeans, spoke of the destruction of the city and the captivity of the people (Isaiah 55:1). Supposing it not to be sufficient evidence of divine inspiration to foretell, many years before, events which, at the time, seemed fabulous, but which ultimately turned out to be true, whence shall it be said that the prophecies which he uttered concerning their return proceeded, if it was not from God? He names Cyrus, by whom the Chaldeans were to be subdued and the people restored to freedom. After the prophet thus spoke, more than a hundred years elapsed before Cyrus was born, that being nearly the period which elapsed between the death of the one and the birth of the other. It was impossible at that time to guess that some Cyrus would arise to make war on the Babylonians, and after subduing their powerful monarchy, put an end to the captivity of the children of Israel. Does not this simple, unadorned narrative plainly demonstrate that what Isaiah spoke was not the conjecture of man, but the undoubted oracle of God? Again, when Jeremiah, a considerable time before the people were led away, assigned seventy years as the period of captivity, and fixed their liberation and return, must not his tongue have been guided by the Spirit of God? What effrontery were it to deny that, by these evidences, the authority of the

prophets is established, the very thing being fulfilled to which they appeal in support of their credibility! "Behold, the former things are come to pass, and new things do I declare; before they spring forth I tell you of them," (Isaiah 42:9). I say nothing of the agreement between Jeremiah and Ezekiel, who, living so far apart, and yet prophesying at the same time, harmonise as completely in all they say as if they had mutually dictated the words to one another. What shall I say of Daniel? Did not he deliver prophecies embracing a future period of almost six hundred years, as if he had been writing of past events generally known? (Dan. 9, &c). If the pious will duly meditate on these things, they will be sufficiently instructed to silence the cavils of the ungodly. The demonstration is too clear to be gainsaid.

9. I am aware of what is muttered in corners by certain miscreants, when they would display their acuteness in assailing divine truth. They ask, how do we know that Moses and the prophets wrote the books which now bear their names? Nay, they even dare to question whether there ever was a Moses. Were any one to question whether there ever was a Plato, or an Aristotle, or a Cicero, would not the rod or the whip be deemed the fit chastisement of such folly? The law of Moses has been wonderfully preserved, more by divine providence than by human care; and though, owing to the negligence of the priests, it lay for a short time buried,—from the time when it was found by good King Josiah (2 Kings 22:8; 2 Chron. 34:15),—it has continued in the hands of men, and been transmitted in unbroken succession from generation to generation. Nor, indeed, when Josiah brought it forth, was it as a book unknown or new, but one which had always been matter of notoriety, and was then in full remembrance. The original writing had been deposited in the temple, and a copy taken from it had been deposited in the royal archives (Deut. 17:18, 19); the only thing which had occurred was, that the priests had ceased to publish the law itself in due form, and

the people also had neglected the wonted reading of it. I may add, that scarcely an age passed during which its authority was not confirmed and renewed. Were the books of Moses unknown to those who had the Psalms of David in their hands? To sum up the whole in one word, it is certain beyond dispute, that these writings passed down, if I may so express it, from hand to hand, being transmitted in an unbroken series from the fathers, who either with their own ears heard them spoken, or learned them from those who had, while the remembrance of them was fresh.

10. An objection taken from the history of the Maccabees (1 Macc. 1:57, 58) to impugn the credibility of Scripture, is, on the contrary, fitted the best possible to confirm it. First, however, let us clear away the gloss which is put upon it: having done so, we shall turn the engine which they erect against us upon themselves. As Antiochus ordered all the books of Scripture to be burnt, it is asked, where did the copies we now have come from? I, in my turn, ask, In what workshop could they have been so quickly fabricated? It is certain that they were in existence the moment the persecution ceased, and that they were acknowledged without dispute by all the pious who had been educated in their doctrine, and were familiarly acquainted with them. Nay, while all the wicked so wantonly insulted the Jews as if they had leagued together for the purpose, not one ever dared to charge them with having introduced spurious books. Whatever, in their opinion, the Jewish religion might be, they acknowledged that Moses was the founder of it. What, then, do those babblers, but betray their snarling petulance in falsely alleging the spuriousness of books whose sacred antiquity is proved by the consent of all history? But not to spend labour in vain in refuting these vile calumnies, let us rather attend to the care which the Lord took to preserve his Word, when against all hope he rescued it from the truculence of a most cruel tyrant as from the midst of the

flames—inspiring pious priests and others with such constancy that they hesitated not, though it should have been purchased at the expense of their lives, to transmit this treasure to posterity, and defeating the keenest search of prefects and their satellites.

Who does not recognise it as a signal and miraculous work of God, that those sacred monuments which the ungodly persuaded themselves had utterly perished, immediately returned to resume their former rights, and, indeed, in greater honour? For the Greek translation appeared to disseminate them over the whole world. Nor does it seem so wonderful that God rescued the tables of his covenant from the sanguinary edicts of Antiochus, as that they remained safe and entire amid the manifold disasters by which the Jewish nation was occasionally crushed, devastated, and almost exterminated. The Hebrew language was in no estimation, and almost unknown; and assuredly, had not God provided for religion, it must have utterly perished. For it is obvious from the prophetical writings of that age, how much the Jews, after their return from the captivity, had lost the genuine use of their native tongue. It is of importance to attend to this, because the comparison more clearly establishes the antiquity of the Law and the Prophets. And whom did God employ to preserve the doctrine of salvation contained in the Law and the Prophets, that Christ might manifest it in its own time? The Jews, the bitterest enemies of Christ; and hence Augustine justly calls them the librarians of the Christian Church, because they supplied us with books of which they themselves had not the use.

11. When we proceed to the New Testament, how solid are the pillars by which its truth is supported! Three evangelists give a narrative in a mean and humble style. The proud often eye this simplicity with disdain, because they attend not to the principal heads of doctrine; for from these they might easily infer that these evangelists treat of

heavenly mysteries beyond the capacity of man. Those who have the least particle of candour must be ashamed of their fastidiousness when they read the first chapter of Luke. Even our Saviour's discourses, of which a summary is given by these three evangelists, ought to prevent every one from treating their writings with contempt. John, again, fulminating in majesty, strikes down more powerfully than any thunderbolt the petulance of those who refuse to submit to the obedience of faith. Let all those acute censors, whose highest pleasure it is to banish a reverential regard of Scripture from their own and other men's hearts, come forward; let them read the Gospel of John, and, willing or unwilling, they will find a thousand sentences which will at least arouse them from their sloth; nay, which will burn into their consciences as with a hot iron, and check their derision. The same thing may be said of Peter and Paul, whose writings, though the greater part read them blindfold, exhibit a heavenly majesty, which in a manner binds and rivets every reader. But one circumstance, sufficient of itself to exalt their doctrine above the world, is, that Matthew, who was formerly fixed down to his money table, Peter and John, who were employed with their little boats, being all rude and illiterate, had never learned in any human school that which they delivered to others. Paul, more over, who had not only been an avowed but a cruel and bloody foe, being changed into a new man, shows, by the sudden and unhoped-for change, that a heavenly power had compelled him to preach the doctrine which once he destroyed. Let those dogs deny that the Holy Spirit descended upon the apostles, or, if not, let them refuse credit to the history, still the very circumstances proclaim that the Holy Spirit must have been the teacher of those who, formerly contemptible among the people, all of a sudden began to discourse so magnificently of heavenly mysteries.

12. Add, moreover, that, for the best of reasons, the consent of the Church is not without its weight. For it is not to be accounted of no consequence, that, from the first publication of Scripture, so many ages have uniformly concurred in yielding obedience to it, and that, notwithstanding of the many extraordinary attempts which Satan and the whole world have made to oppress and overthrow it, or completely efface it from the memory of men, it has flourished like the palm tree and continued invincible. Though in old times there was scarcely a sophist or orator of any note who did not exert his powers against it, their efforts proved unavailing. The powers of the earth armed themselves for its destruction, but all their at-tempts vanished into smoke. When thus powerfully assailed on every side, how could it have resisted if it had trusted only to human aid? Nay, its divine origin is more completely established by the fact, that when all human wishes were against it, it advanced by its own energy. Add that it was not a single city or a single nation that concurred in receiving and embracing it. Its authority was recognised as far and as wide as the world extends—various nations who had nothing else in common entering for this purpose into a holy league. Moreover, while we ought to attach the greatest weight to the agreement of minds so diversified, and in all other things so much at variance with each other —an agreement which a Divine Providence alone could have produced—it adds no small weight to the whole when we attend to the piety of those who thus agree; not of all of them indeed, but of those in whom as lights God was pleased that his Church should shine.

13. Again, with what confidence does it become us to subscribe to a doctrine attested and confirmed by the blood of so many saints? They, when once they had embraced it, hesitated not boldly and intrepidly, and even with great alacrity, to meet death in its defence. Being transmitted to us with such an earnest, who of us shall not receive it with

firm and unshaken conviction? It is therefore no small proof of the authority of Scripture, that it was sealed with the blood of so many witnesses, especially when it is considered that in bearing testimony to the faith, they met death not with fanatical enthusiasm (as erring spirits are sometimes wont to do), but with a firm and constant, yet sober godly zeal. There are other reasons, neither few nor feeble, by which the dignity and majesty of the Scriptures may be not only proved to the pious, but also completely vindicated against the cavils of slanderers. These, however, cannot of themselves produce a firm faith in Scripture until our heavenly Father manifest his presence in it, and thereby secure implicit reverence for it. Then only, therefore, does Scripture suffice to give a saving knowledge of God when its certainty is founded on the inward persuasion of the Holy Spirit. Still the human testimonies which go to confirm it will not be without effect, if they are used in subordination to that chief and highest proof, as secondary helps to our weakness. But it is foolish to attempt to prove to infidels that the Scripture is the Word of God. This it cannot be known to be, except by faith. Justly, therefore, does Augustine remind us, that every man who would have any understanding in such high matters must previously possess piety and mental peace.

CHAPTER 9.

ALL THE PRINCIPLES OF PIETY SUBVERTED BY FANATICS, WHO SUBSTITUTE REVELATIONS FOR SCRIPTURE.

Sections.

1. The temper and error of the Libertines, who take to themselves the name of spiritual, briefly described. Their refutation. 1. The Apostles and all true Christians have embraced the written Word. This confirmed by a passage in Isaiah; also by the example and words of Paul. 2. The Spirit of Christ seals the doctrine of the written Word on the minds of the godly.

2. Refutation continued. 3. The impositions of Satan cannot be detected without the aid of the written Word. First Ob- jection. The Answer to it.

3. Second Objection from the words of Paul as to the *letter and spirit*. The Answer, with an explanation of Paul's meaning. How the Spirit and the written Word are indissolubly connected.

1. Those who, rejecting Scripture, imagine that they have some peculiar way of penetrating to God, are to be deemed not so much under the influence of error as madness. For certain giddy men have lately appeared, who, while they make a great display of the superiority of the Spirit, reject all reading of the Scriptures themselves, and deride the simplicity of those who only delight in what they call the dead and deadly letter. But I wish they would tell me what spirit it is whose inspiration raises them to such a sublime height that they dare despise the doctrine of Scripture as mean and childish. If they answer that it is the Spirit of Christ, their confidence is exceedingly ridiculous;

since they will, I presume, admit that the apostles and other believers in the primitive Church were not illuminated by any other Spirit. None of these thereby learned to despise the word of God, but every one was imbued with greater reverence for it, as their writings most clearly testify. And, indeed, it had been so foretold by the mouth of Isaiah. For when he says, "My Spirit that is upon thee, and my words which I have put in thy mouth, shall not depart out of thy mouth, nor out of the mouth of thy seed, nor out of the mouth of thy seed's seed, saith the Lord, from henceforth and for ever," he does not tie down the ancient Church to external doctrine, as he were a mere teacher of elements;24 he rather shows that, under the reign of Christ, the true and full felicity of the new Church will consist in their being ruled not less by the Word than by the Spirit of God. Hence we infer that these miscreants are guilty of fearful sacrilege in tearing asunder what the prophet joins in indissoluble union. Add to this, that Paul, though carried up even to the third heaven, ceased not to profit by the doctrine of the law and the prophets, while, in like manner, he exhorts Timothy, a teacher of singular excellence, to give attention to reading (1 Tim. 4:13). And the eulogium which he pronounces on Scripture well deserves to be remembered — viz. that "it is profitable for doctrine, for reproof, for correction, and for instruction in righteousness, that the man of God may be perfect," (2 Tim. 3:16). What an infatuation of the devil, therefore, to fancy that Scripture, which conducts the sons of God to the final goal, is of transient and temporary use? Again, I should like those people to tell me whether they have imbibed any other Spirit than that which Christ promised to his disciples. Though their madness is extreme, it will scarcely carry them the length of making this their boast. But what kind of Spirit did our Saviour promise to send? One who should not speak of himself (John 16:13), but suggest and instil the truths which he himself had delivered through the word.

Hence the office of the Spirit promised to us, is not to form new and unheard-of revelations, or to coin a new form of doctrine, by which we may be led away from the received doctrine of the gospel, but to seal on our minds the very doctrine which the gospel recommends.

2. Hence it is easy to understand that we must give diligent heed both to the reading and hearing of Scripture, if we would obtain any benefit from the Spirit of God (just as Peter praises those who attentively study the doctrine of the prophets (2 Pet. 1:19), though it might have been thought to be superseded after the gospel light arose), and, on the contrary, that any spirit which passes by the wisdom of God's Word, and suggests any other doctrine, is deservedly suspected of vanity and falsehood. Since Satan transforms himself into an angel of light, what authority can the Spirit have with us if he be not ascertained by an infallible mark? And assuredly he is pointed out to us by the Lord with sufficient clearness; but these miserable men err as if bent on their own destruction, while they seek the Spirit from themselves rather than from Him. But they say that it is insulting to subject the Spirit, to whom all things are to be subject, to the Scripture: as if it were disgraceful to the Holy Spirit to maintain a perfect resemblance throughout, and be in all respects without variation consistent with himself. True, if he were subjected to a human, an angelical, or to any foreign standard, it might be thought that he was rendered subordinate, or, if you will, brought into bondage, but so long as he is compared with himself, and considered in himself, how can it be said that he is thereby injured? I admit that he is brought to a test, but the very test by which it has pleased him that his majesty should be confirmed. It ought to be enough for us when once we hear his voice; but lest Satan should insinuate himself under his name, he wishes us to recognise him by the image which he has stamped on the Scriptures. The author of the Scriptures cannot vary, and change his

likeness. Such as he there appeared at first, such he will perpetually remain. There is nothing contumelious to him in this, unless we are to think it would be honourable for him to degenerate, and revolt against himself.

3. Their cavil about our cleaving to the dead letter carries with it the punishment which they deserve for despising Scripture. It is clear that Paul is there arguing against false apostles (2 Cor. 3:6), who, by recommending the law without Christ, deprived the people of the benefit of the New Covenant, by which the Lord engages that he will write his law on the hearts of believers, and engrave it on their inward parts. The letter therefore is dead, and the law of the Lord kills its readers when it is dissevered from the grace of Christ, and only sounds in the ear without touching the heart. But if it is effectually impressed on the heart by the Spirit; if it exhibits Christ, it is the word of life converting the soul, and making wise the simple. Nay, in the very same passage, the apostle calls his own preaching the ministration of the Spirit (2 Cor. 3:8), intimating that the Holy Spirit so cleaves to his own truth, as he has expressed it in Scripture, that he then only exerts and puts forth his strength when the word is received with due honour and respect.

There is nothing repugnant here to what was lately said (chap. 7) that we have no great certainty of the word itself, until it be confirmed by the testimony of the Spirit. For the Lord has so knit together the certainty of his word and his Spirit, that our minds are duly imbued with reverence for the word when the Spirit shining upon it enables us there to behold the face of God; and, on the other hand, we embrace the Spirit with no danger of delusion when we recognise him in his image, that is, in his word. Thus, indeed, it is. God did not produce his word before men for the sake of sudden display, intending to abolish it the moment the Spirit should arrive; but he employed the same Spirit, by whose agency he had administered the word, to complete his work by the efficacious confirmation of the word. In this way Christ explained to the two disciples (Luke 24:27), not that they were to reject the Scriptures and trust to their own wisdom, but that they were to understand the Scriptures. In like manner, when Paul says to the Thessalonians, "Quench not the Spirit," he does not carry them aloft to empty speculation apart from the word; he immediately adds, "Despise not prophesying," (1 Thess. 5:19, 20). By this, doubtless, he intimates that the light of the Spirit is quenched the moment prophesying fall into contempt. How is this answered by those swelling enthusiasts, in whose idea the only true illumination consists, in carelessly laying aside, and bidding adieu to the Word of God, while, with no less confidence than folly, they fasten upon any dreaming notion which may have casually sprung up in their minds? Surely a very different sobriety becomes the children of God. As they feel that without the Spirit of God they are utterly devoid of the light of truth, so they are not ignorant that the word is the instrument by which the illumination of the Spirit is dispensed. They know of no other Spirit than the one who dwelt and spake in the apostles — the Spirit by whose oracles they are daily invited to the hearing of the word.

CHAPTER 10.

IN SCRIPTURE, THE TRUE GOD OPPOSED, EXCLUSIVELY, TO ALL THE GODS OF THE HEATHEN.

Sections.

1. Explanation of the knowledge of God resumed. God as manifested in Scripture, the same as delineated in his works.

2. The attributes of God as described by Moses, David, and Jeremiah. Explanation of the attributes. Summary. Uses of this knowledge.

3. Scripture, in directing us to the true God, excludes the gods of the heathen, who, however, in some sense, held the unity of God.

1. We formerly observed that the knowledge of God, which, in other respects, is not obscurely exhibited in the frame of the world, and in all the creatures, is more clearly and familiarly explained by the word. It may now be proper to show, that in Scripture the Lord represents himself in the same character in which we have already seen that he is delineated in his works. A full discussion of this subject would occupy a large space. But it will here be sufficient to furnish a kind of index, by attending to which the pious reader may be enabled to understand what knowledge of God he ought chiefly to search for in Scripture, and be directed as to the mode of conducting the search. I am not now adverting to the peculiar covenant by which God distinguished the race of Abraham from the rest of the nations. For when by gratuitous adoption he admitted those who were enemies to the rank of sons, he even then acted in the character of a Redeemer. At present, however, we are employed in considering that knowledge which stops short at the creation of the world, without ascending to Christ the

Mediator. But though it will soon be necessary to quote certain passages from the New Testament (proofs being there given both of the power of God the Creator, and of his providence in the preservation of what he originally created), I wish the reader to remember what my present purpose is, that he may not wander from the proper subject. Briefly, then, it will be sufficient for him at present to understand how God, the Creator of heaven and earth, governs the world which was made by him. In every part of Scripture we meet with descriptions of his paternal kindness and readiness to do good, and we also meet with examples of severity which show that he is the just punisher of the wicked, especially when they continue obstinate notwithstanding of all his forbearance.

2. There are certain passages which contain more vivid descriptions of the divine character, setting it before us as if his genuine countenance were visibly portrayed. Moses, indeed, seems to have intended briefly to comprehend whatever may be known of God by man, when he said, "The Lord, The Lord God, merciful and gracious, long-suffering, and abundant in goodness and truth, keeping mercy for thousands, forgiving iniquity and transgression and sin, and that will by no means clear the guilty; visiting the iniquity of the fathers upon the children, and upon the children's children, unto the third and to the fourth generation," (Ex. 34:6, 7). Here we may observe, *first*, that his eternity and selfexistence are declared by his magnificent name twice repeated; and, *secondly*, that in the enumeration of his perfections, he is described not as he is in himself, but in relation to us, in order that our acknowledgement of him may be more a vivid actual impression than empty visionary speculation. Moreover, the perfections thus enumerated are just those which we saw shining in the heavens, and on the earth—compassion, goodness, mercy, justice, Judgment, and truth. For power and energy are comprehended under the name Jehovah.

Similar epithets are employed by the prophets when they would fully declare his sacred name. Not to collect a great number of passages, it may suffice at present to refer to one Psalm (145) in which a summary of the divine perfections is so carefully given that not one seems to have been omitted. Still, however, every perfection there set down may be contemplated in creation; and, hence, such as we feel him to be when experience is our guide, such he declares himself to be by his word. In Jeremiah, where God proclaims the character in which he would have us to acknowledge him, though the description is not so full, it is substantially the same. "Let him that glorieth," says he, "glory in this, that he understandeth and knoweth me, that I am the Lord which exercise loving-kindness, Judgment, and righteousness, in the earth," (Jer. 9:24). Assuredly, the attributes which it is most necessary for us to know are these three: Loving-kindness, on which alone our entire safety depends: Judgment, which is daily exercised on the wicked, and awaits them in a severer form, even for eternal destruction: Righteousness, by which the faithful are preserved, and most benignly cherished. The prophet declares, that when you understand these, you are amply furnished with the means of glorying in God. Nor is there here any omission of his truth, or power, or holiness, or goodness. For how could this knowledge of his loving-kindness, Judgment, and righteousness, exist, if it were not founded on his inviolable truth? How, again, could it be believed that he governs the earth with Judgment and righteousness, without presupposing his mighty power? Whence, too, his loving-kindness, but from his goodness? In fine, if all his ways are loving- kindness, Judgment, and righteousness, his holiness also is thereby conspicuous. Moreover, the knowledge of God, which is set before us in the Scriptures, is designed for the same purpose as that which shines in creation—viz. that we may thereby learn to worship him with perfect integrity of heart and unfeigned obedience, and also to depend entirely on his goodness.

3. Here it may be proper to give a summary of the general doctrine. First, then, let the reader observe that the Scripture, in order to direct us to the true God, distinctly excludes and rejects all the gods of the heathen, because religion was universally adulterated in almost every age. It is true, indeed, that the name of one God was everywhere known and celebrated. For those who worshipped a multitude of gods, whenever they spoke the genuine language of nature, simply used the name god, as if they had thought one god sufficient. And this is shrewdly noticed by Justin Martyr, who, to the same effect, wrote a treatise, entitled, On the Monarchy of God, in which he shows, by a great variety of evidence, that the unity of God is engraven on the hearts of all. Tertullian also proves the same thing from the common forms of speech. But as all, without exception, have in the vanity of their minds rushed or been dragged into lying fictions, these impressions, as to the unity of God, whatever they may have naturally been, have had no further effect than to render men inexcusable. The wisest plainly discover the vague wanderings of their minds when they express a wish for any kind of Deity, and thus offer up their prayers to unknown gods. And then, in imagining a manifold nature in God, though their ideas concerning Jupiter, Mercury, Venus, Minerva, and others, were not so absurd as those of the rude vulgar, they were by no means free from the delusions of the devil. We have elsewhere observed, that however subtle the evasions devised by philosophers, they cannot do away with the charge of rebellion, in that all of them have corrupted the truth of God. For this reason, Habakkuk (2:20), after condemning all idols, orders men to seek God in his temple, that the faithful may acknowledge none but Him, who has manifested himself in his word.

CHAPTER 11.

IMPIETY OF ATTRIBUTING A VISIBLE FORM TO GOD.—THE SETTING UP OF IDOLS A DEFECTION FROM THE TRUE GOD.

There are three leading divisions in this chapter. The first contains a refutation of those who ascribe a visible form to God (s. 1 and 2), with an answer to the objection of those who, because it is said that God manifested his presence by certain symbols, use it as a defence of their error (s. 3 and 4). Various arguments are afterwards adduced, disposing of the trite objection from Gregory's expression, that images are the books of the unlearned (s. 5-7). The second division of the chapter relates to the origin of idols or images, and the adoration of them, as approved by the Papists (s. 8-10). Their evasion refuted (s. 11). The third division treats of the use and abuse of images (s. 12). Whether it is expedient to have them in Christian Churches (s. 13). The concluding part contains a refutation of the second Council of Nice, which very absurdly contends for images in opposition to divine truth, and even to the disparagement of the Christian name.

Sections.

1. God is opposed to idols, that all may know he is the only fit witness to himself. He expressly forbids any attempt to represent him by a bodily shape.

2. Reasons for this prohibition from Moses, Isaiah, and Paul. The complaint of a heathen. It should put the worshipers of idols to shame.

3. Consideration of an objection taken from various passages in Moses. The Cherubim and Seraphim show that images are not fit to represent divine mysteries. The Cherubim belonged to the tutelage of the Law.

4. The materials of which idols are made, abundantly refute the fiction of idolaters. Confirmation from Isaiah and others. Absurd precaution of the Greeks.

5. Objection,—That images are the books of the unlearned. Objection answered, 1. Scripture declares images to be teachers of vanity and lies.

6. Answer continued, 2. Ancient Theologians condemn the formation and worship of idols.

7. Answer continued,—3. The use of images condemned by the luxury and meretricious ornaments given to them in Popish Churches. 4. The Church must be trained in true piety by another method.

8. The second division of the chapter. Origin of idols or images. Its rise shortly after the flood. Its continual progress.

9. Of the worship of images. Its nature. A pretext of idolaters refuted. Pretexts of the heathen. Genius of idolaters.

10. Evasion of the Papists. Their agreement with ancient idolaters.

11. Refutation of another evasion or sophism—viz. the distinction of δλα and λτι.

12. Third division of the chapter—viz. the use and abuse of images.

13. Whether it is expedient to have images in Christian temples.

14. Absurd defence of the worship of images by the second so-called Council of Nice. Sophisms or perversions of Scripture in defence of images in churches.

15. Passages adduced in support of the worship of images.

16. The blasphemous expressions of some ancient idolaters approved by not a few of the more modern, both in word and deed.

1. As Scripture, in accommodation to the rude and gross intellect of man, usually speaks in popular terms, so whenever its object is to discriminate between the true God and false deities, it opposes him in particular to idols; not that it approves of what is taught more elegantly and subtilely by philosophers, but that it may the better expose the folly, nay, madness of the world in its inquiries after God, so long as every one clings to his own speculations. This exclusive definition, which we uniformly meet with in Scripture, annihilates every deity which men frame for themselves of their own accord—God himself being the only fit witness to himself. Meanwhile, seeing that this brutish stupidity has overspread the globe, men longing after visible forms of God, and so forming deities of wood and stone, silver and gold, or of any other dead and corruptible matter, we must hold it as a first principle, that as often as any form is assigned to God, his glory is corrupted by an impious lie. In the Law, accordingly, after God had claimed the glory of divinity for himself alone, when he comes to show what kind of worship he approves and rejects, he immediately adds, "Thou shalt not make unto thee any graven image, or any likeness of any thing that is in heaven above, or in the earth beneath, or in the water under the earth," (Exod. 20:4). By these words he curbs any licentious attempt we might make to represent him by a visible shape, and briefly enumerates all the forms by which superstition had begun, even long before, to turn his truth into a lie. For we know that the Sun was worshipped by the Persian. As many stars as the foolish nations saw in the sky, so many gods they imagined them to be. Then to the Egyptians, every animal was a figure of God. The Greeks, again, plumed themselves on their superior wisdom in worshipping God under the human form (Maximum Tyrius Platonic. Serm. 38). But God makes no comparison between images, as if one were more, and another less befitting; he rejects, without

130

exception, all shapes and pictures, and other symbols by which the superstitious imagine they can bring him near to them.

2. This may easily be inferred from the reasons which he annexes to his prohibition. First, it is said in the books of Moses (Deut. 4:15), "Take ye therefore good heed unto yourselves; for ye saw no manner of similitude in the day that the Lord spake unto you in Horeb, out of the midst of the fire, lest ye corrupt yourselves, and make you a graven image, the similitude of any figure," &c. We see how plainly God declares against all figures, to make us aware that all longing after such visible shapes is rebellion against him. Of the prophets, it will be sufficient to mention Isaiah, who is the most copious on this subjects (Isaiah 40:18; 41:7, 29; 45:9; 46:5), in order to show how the majesty of God is defiled by an absurd and indecorous fiction, when he who is incorporeal is assimilated to corporeal matter; he who is invisible to a visible image; he who is a spirit to an inanimate object; and he who fills all space to a bit of paltry wood, or stone, or gold. Paul, too, reasons in the same way, "Forasmuch, then, as we are the offspring of God, we ought not to think that the Godhead is like unto gold, or silver, or stone, graven by art and man's device," (Acts 17:29). Hence it is manifest, that whatever statues are set up or pictures painted to represent God, are utterly displeasing to him, as a kind of insults to his majesty. And is it strange that the Holy Spirit thunders such responses from heaven, when he compels even blind and miserable idolaters to make a similar confession on the earth? Seneca's complaint, as given by Augustine De Civit. Dei, c. 10, is well known. He says "The sacred immortal, and invisible gods they exhibit in the meanest and most ignoble materials, and dress them in the clothing of men and beasts; some confound the sexes, and form a compound out of different bodies, giving the name of deities to objects, which, if they were met alive, would be deemed monsters."

Hence, again, it is obvious, that the defenders of images resort to a paltry quibbling evasion, when they pretend that the Jews were forbidden to use them on account of their proneness to superstition; as if a prohibition which the Lord founds on his own eternal essences and the uniform course of nature, could be restricted to a single nation. Besides, when Paul refuted the error of giving a bodily shape to God, he was addressing not Jews, but Athenians.

3. It is true that the Lord occasionally manifested his presence by certain signs, so that he was said to be seen face to face; but all the signs he ever employed were in apt accordance with the scheme of doctrine, and, at the same time, gave plain intimation of his incomprehensible essence. For the cloud, and smoke, and flame, though they were symbols of heavenly glory (Deut. 4:11), curbed men's minds as with a bridle, that they might not attempt to penetrate farther. Therefore, even Moses (to whom, of all men, God manifested himself most familiarly) was not permitted though he prayed for it, to behold that face, but received for answer, that the refulgence was too great for man (Exod. 33:20). The Holy Spirit appeared under the form of a dove, but as it instantly vanished, who does not see that in this symbol of a moment, the faithful were admonished to regard the Spirit as invisible, to be contented with his power and grace, and not call for any external figure? God sometimes appeared in the form of a man, but this was in anticipation of the future revelation in Christ, and, therefore, did not give the Jews the least pretext for setting up a symbol of Deity under the human form. The mercy-seat, also (Exod. 25:17, 18, 21), where, under the Law, God exhibited the presence of his power, was so framed, as to intimate that God is best seen when the mind rises in admiration above itself: the Cherubim with outstretched wings shaded, and the veil covered it, while the remoteness of the place was in itself a sufficient concealment. It is therefore mere infatuation to attempt to

defend images of God and the saints by the example of the Cherubim. For what, pray, did these figures mean, if not that images are unfit to represent the mysteries of God, since they were so formed as to cover the mercy-seat with their wings, thereby concealing the view of God, not only from the eye, but from every human sense, and curbing presumption? To this we may add, that the prophets depict the Seraphim, who are exhibited to us in vision, as having their faces veiled; thus intimating, that the refulgence of the divine glory is so great, that even the angels cannot gaze upon it directly, while the minute beams which sparkle in the face of angels are shrouded from our view. Moreover, all men of sound Judgment acknowledge that the Cherubim in question belonged to the old tutelage of the law. It is absurd, therefore, to bring them forward as an example for our age. For that period of puerility, if I may so express it, to which such rudiments were adapted, has passed away. And surely it is disgraceful, that heathen writers should be more skilful interpreters of Scripture than the Papists. Juvenal (Sat. 14) holds up the Jews to derision for worshipping the thin clouds and firmament. This he does perversely and impiously; still, in denying that any visible shape of Deity existed among them, he speaks more accurately than the Papists, who prate about there having been some visible image. In the fact that the people every now and then rushed forth with boiling haste in pursuit of idols, just like water gushing forth with violence from a copious spring, let us learn how prone our nature is to idolatry, that we may not, by throwing the whole blame of a common vice upon the Jews, be led away by vain and sinful enticements to sleep the sleep of death.

4. To the same effect are the words of the Psalmist (Psalms 115:4, 135:15), "Their idols are silver and gold, the works of men's hands." From the materials of which they are made, he infers that they are not gods, taking it for granted that every human device concerning God is a dull

fiction. He mentions silver and gold rather than clay or stone, that neither splendour nor cost may procure reverence to idols. He then draws a general conclusion, that nothing is more unlikely than that gods should be formed of any kind of inanimate matter. Man is forced to confess that he is but the creature of a day (see Book 3 c. 9 s. 2), and yet would have the metal which he has deified to be regarded as God. Whence had idols their origin, but from the will of man? There was ground, therefore, for the sarcasm of the heathen poet (Hor. Sat. I. 8), "I was once the trunk of a fig-tree, a useless log, when the tradesman, uncertain whether he should make me a stool, &c., chose rather that I should be a god." In other words, an earth-born creature, who breathes out his life almost every moment, is able by his own device to confer the name and honour of deity on a lifeless trunk. But as that Epicurean poet, in indulging his wit, had no regard for religion, without attending to his jeers or those of his fellows, let the rebuke of the prophet sting, nay, cut us to the heart, when he speaks of the extreme infatuation of those who take a piece of wood to kindle a fire to warm themselves, bake bread, roast or boil flesh, and out of the residue make a god, before which they prostrate themselves as suppliants (Isaiah 44:16). Hence, the same prophet, in another place, not only charges idolaters as guilty in the eye of the law, but up- braids them for not learning from the foundations of the earth, nothing being more incongruous than to reduce the immense and incomprehensible Deity to the stature of a few feet. And yet experience shows that this monstrous proceeding, though palpably repugnant to the order of nature, is natural to man. It is, moreover, to be observed, that by the mode of expression which is employed, every form of superstition is denounced. Being works of men, they have no authority from God (Isa. 2:8, 31:7; Hos. 14:3; Mic. 5:13); and, therefore, it must be regarded as a fixed principle, that all modes of worship devised by man are detest- able. The infatuation is placed in a still stronger light by the Psalmist (Psalm 115:8), when he shows how aid is implored from dead and senseless objects, by beings who have been endued with intelligence for the very purpose of enabling them to know that the whole universe is governed by Divine energy alone. But as the corruption of nature hurries away all mankind collectively and individually into this madness, the Spirit at length thunders forth a dreadful imprecation, "They that make them are like unto them, so is every one that trusteth in them." And it is to be observed, that the thing forbidden is *likeness*, whether sculptured or otherwise. This disposes of the frivolous precaution taken by the Greek Church. They think they do admirably, because they have no sculptured shape of Deity, while none go greater lengths in the licentious use of pictures. The Lord, however, not only forbids any image of himself to be erected by a statuary, but to be formed by any artist whatever, because every such image is sinful and insulting to his majesty.

5. I am not ignorant, indeed, of the assertion, which is now more than threadbare, "that images are the books of the unlearned." So said Gregory: but the Holy Spirit goes a very different decision; and had Gregory got his lesson in this matter in the Spirit's school, he never would have spoken as he did. For when Jeremiah declares that "the stock is a doctrine of vanities," (Jer. 10:8), and Habakkuk, "that the molten image" is "a teacher of lies," the general doctrine to be inferred certainly is, that every thing respecting God which is learned from images is futile and false. If it is objected that the censure of the prophets is directed against those who perverted images to purposes of impious superstition, I admit it to be so; but I add (what must be obvious to all), that the prophets utterly condemn what the Papists hold to be an undoubted axiom—viz. that images are substitutes for books. For they contrast images with the true God, as if the two were of an opposite nature,

and never could be made to agree. In the passages which I lately quoted, the conclusion drawn is, that seeing there is one true God whom the Jews worshipped, visible shapes made for the purpose of representing him are false and wicked fictions; and all, therefore, who have recourse to them for knowledge are miserably deceived. In short, were it not true that all such knowledge is fallacious and spurious, the prophets would not condemn it in such general terms. This at least I maintain, that when we teach that all human attempts to give a visible shape to God are vanity and lies, we do nothing more than state *verbatim* what the prophets taught.

6. Moreover, let Lactantius and Eusebius be read on this subject. These writers assume it as an indisputable fact, that all the beings whose images were erected were originally men. In like manner, Augustine distinctly declares, that it is unlawful not only to worship images, but to dedicate them. And in this he says no more than had been long before decreed by the Libertine Council, the thirty-sixth Canon of which is, "There must be no pictures used in churches: Let nothing which is adored or worshipped be painted on walls." But the most memorable passage of all is that which Augustine quotes in another place from Varro, and in which he expressly concurs: — "Those who first introduced images of the gods both took away fear and brought in error." Were this merely the saying of Varro, it might perhaps be of little weight, though it might well make us ashamed, that a heathen, groping as it were in darkness, should have attained to such a degree of light, as to see that corporeal images are unworthy of the majesty of God, and that, because they diminish reverential fear and encourage error. The sentiment itself bears witness that it was uttered with no less truth than shrewdness. But Augustine, while he borrows it from Varro, adduces it as conveying his own opinion. At the outset, indeed, he declares that the first errors into which men fell concerning God did not originate

with images, but increased with them, as if new fuel had been added. Afterwards, he explains how the fear of God was thereby extinguished or impaired, his presence being brought into contempt by foolish, and childish, and absurd representations. The truth of this latter remark I wish we did not so thoroughly experience. Whosoever, therefore, is desirous of being instructed in the true knowledge of God must apply to some other teacher than images.

7. Let Papists, then, if they have any sense of shame, henceforth desist from the futile plea, that images are the books of the unlearned—a plea so plainly refuted by innumerable passages of Scripture. And yet were I to admit the plea, it would not be a valid defence of their peculiar idols. It is well known what kind of monsters they obtrude upon us as divine. For what are the pictures or statues to which they append the names of saints, but exhibitions of the most shameless luxury or obscenity? Were any one to dress himself after their model, he would deserve the pillory. Indeed, brothels exhibit their inmates more chastely and modestly dressed than churches do images intended to represent virgins. The dress of the martyrs is in no respect more becoming. Let Papists then have some little regard to decency in decking their idols, if they would give the least plausibility to the false allegation, that they are books of some kind of sanctity. But even then we shall answer, that this is not the method in which the Christian people should be taught in sacred places. Very different from these follies is the doctrine in which God would have them to be there instructed. His injunction is, that the doctrine common to all should there be set forth by the preaching of the Word, and the administration of the sacraments,—a doctrine to which little heed can be given by those whose eyes are carried too and fro gazing at idols. And who are the unlearned, whose rudeness admits of being taught by images only? Just those whom the Lord acknowledges for his disciples; those whom he honours with a revelation of

his celestial philosophy, and desires to be trained in the saving mysteries of his kingdom. I confess, indeed, as matters now are, there are not a few in the present day who cannot want such books. But, I ask, whence this stupidity, but just because they are defrauded of the only doctrine which was fit to instruct them? The simple reason why those who had the charge of churches resigned the office of teaching to idols was, because they themselves were dumb. Paul declares, that by the true preaching of the gospel Christ is portrayed and in a manner crucified before our eyes (Gal. 3:1). Of what use, then, were the erection in churches of so many crosses of wood and stone, silver and gold, if this doctrine were faithfully and honestly preached —viz. Christ died that he might bear our curse upon the tree, that he might expiate our sins by the sacrifice of his body, wash them in his blood, and, in short, reconcile us to God the Father? From this one doctrine the people would learn more than from a thousand crosses of wood and stone. As for crosses of gold and silver, it may be true that the avaricious give their eyes and minds to them more eagerly than to any heavenly instructor.

8. In regard to the origin of idols, the statement contained in the Book of Wisdom has been received with almost universal consent—viz. that they originated with those who be- stowed this honour on the dead, from a superstitious regard to their memory. I admit that this perverse practice is of very high antiquity, and I deny not that it was a kind of torch by which the infatuated proneness of mankind to idolatry was kindled into a greater blaze. I do not, however, admit that it was the first origin of the practice. That idols were in use before the prevalence of that ambitious consecration of the images of the dead, frequently adverted to by profane writers, is evident from the words of Moses (Gen. 31:19). When he relates that Rachel stole her father's images, he speaks of the use of idols as a common vice. Hence we may infer, that the

human mind is, so to speak, a perpetual forge of idols. There was a kind of renewal of the world at the deluge, but before many years elapse, men are forging gods at will. There is reason to believe, that in the holy Patriarch's lifetime his grandchildren were given to idolatry: so that he must with his own eyes, not without the deepest grief, have seen the earth polluted with idols—that earth whose iniquities God had lately purged with so fearful a Judgment. For Joshua testifies (Josh. 24:2), that Torah and Nachor, even before the birth of Abraham, were the worshipers of false gods. The progeny of Shem having so speedily revolted, what are we to think of the posterity of Ham, who had been cursed long before in their father? Thus, indeed, it is. The human mind, stuffed as it is with presumptuous rashness, dares to imagine a god suited to its own capacity; as it labours under dullness, nay, is sunk in the grossest ignorance, it substitutes vanity and an empty phantom in the place of God. To these evils another is added. The god whom man has thus conceived inwardly he attempts to embody outwardly. The mind, in this way, conceives the idol, and the hand gives it birth. That idolatry has its origin in the idea which men have, that God is not present with them unless his presence is carnally exhibited, appears from the example of the Israelites: "Up," said they, "make us gods, which shall go before us; for as for this Moses, the man that brought us up out of the land of Egypt, we wet not what is become of him," (Exod. 22:1). They knew, indeed, that there was a God whose mighty power they had experienced in so many miracles, but they had no confidence of his being near to them, if they did not with their eyes behold a corporeal symbol of his presence, as an attestation to his actual government. They desired, therefore, to be assured by the image which went before them, that they were journeying under Divine guidance. And daily experience shows, that the flesh is always restless until it has obtained some figment like itself, with which it may vainly solace itself as a representation of God. In consequence of this blind passion men have, almost in all ages since the world began, set up signs on which they imagined that God was visibly depicted to their eyes.

9. After such a figment is formed, adoration forthwith ensues: for when once men imagined that they beheld God in images, they also worshipped him as being there. At length their eyes and minds becoming wholly engrossed by them, they began to grow more and more brutish, gazing and wondering as if some divinity were actually before them. It hence appears that men do not fall away to the worship of images until they have imbibed some idea of a grosser description: not that they actually believe them to be gods, but that the power of divinity somehow or other resides in them. Therefore, whether it be God or a creature that is imaged, the moment you fall prostrate before it in veneration, you are so far fascinated by superstition. For this reason, the Lord not only forbade the erection of statues to himself, but also the consecration of titles and stones which might be set up for adoration. For the same reason, also, the second commandment has an additional part concerning adoration. For as soon as a visible form is given to God, his power also is supposed to be annexed to it. So stupid are men, that wherever they figure God, there they fix him, and by necessary consequence proceed to adore him. It makes no difference whether they worship the idol simply, or God in the idol; it is always idolatry when divine honours are paid to an idol, be the colour what it may. And because God wills not to be worshipped superstitiously whatever is bestowed upon idols is so much robbed from him.

Let those attend to this who set about hunting for miserable pretexts in defence of the execrable idolatry in which for many past ages true religion has been buried and sunk. It is said that the images are not accounted gods. Nor were the Jews so utterly thoughtless as not to remember that there was a God whose hand led them out of Egypt before they made the calf. Indeed, Aaron saying, that these were the gods which had brought them out of Egypt, they intimated, in no ambiguous terms, that they wished to retain God, their deliverer, provided they saw him going before them in the calf. Nor are the heathen to be deemed to have been so stupid as not to understand that God was something else than wood and stone. For they changed the images at pleasure, but always retained the same gods in their minds; besides, they daily consecrated new images without thinking they were making new gods. Read the excuses which Augustine tells us were employed by the idolaters of his time (*August. in Ps.* 113). The vulgar, when accused, replied that they did not worship the visible object, but the Deity which dwelt in it invisibly. Those, again, who had what he calls a more refined religion, said, that they neither worshipped the image, nor any inhabiting Deity, but by means of the corporeal image beheld a symbol of that which it was their duty to worship. What then? All idolaters whether Jewish or Gentile, were actuated in the very way which has been described. Not contented with spiritual understanding, they thought that images would give them a surer and nearer impression. When once this preposterous representation of God was adopted, there was no limit until, deluded every now and then by new impostures, they came to think that God exerted his power in images. Still the Jews were persuaded, that under such images they worshipped the eternal God, the one true Lord of heaven and earth; and the Gentiles, also, in worshipping their own false gods, supposed them to dwell in heaven.

10. It is an impudent falsehood to deny that the thing which was thus anciently done is also done in our day. For why do men prostrate themselves before images? Why, when in the act of praying, do they turn towards them as to the ears of God? It is indeed true, as Augustine says (in Ps.

113), that no person thus prays or worships, looking at an image, without being impressed with the idea that he is heard by it, or without hoping that what he wishes will be performed by it. Why are such distinctions made between different images of the same God, that while one is passed by, or receives only common honour, another is worshipped with the highest solemnities? Why do they fatigue themselves with votive pilgrimages to images while they have many similar ones at home? Why at the present time do they fight for them to blood and slaughter, as for their altars and hearths, showing more willingness to part with the one God than with their idols? And yet I am not now detailing the gross errors of the vulgar—errors almost infinite in number, and in possession of almost all hearts. I am only referring to what those profess who are most desirous to clear themselves of idolatry. They say, we do not call them our gods. Nor did either the Jews or Gentiles of old so call them; and yet the prophets never ceased to charge them with their adulteries with wood and stone for the very acts which are daily done by those who would be deemed Christians, namely, for worshipping God carnally in wood and stone.

11. I am not ignorant, however, and I have no wish to disguise the fact, that they endeavour to evade the charge by means of a more subtle distinction, which shall afterwards be fully considered (see *infra*, s. 16, and chap. 12 s. 2). The worship which they pay to their images they cloak with the name of ειδωλοδυλεια (ιδολοδυλια), and deny to be ειδωλολατρεια (ιδολατρια). So they speaks holding that the worship which they call δυλια may, without insult to God, be paid to statues and pictures. Hence, they think themselves blameless if they are only the *servants*, and not the *worshippers*, of idols; as if it were not a lighter matter to *worship* than *to serve*. And yet, while they take refuge in a Greek term, they very childishly contradict themselves. For the Greek word λατρευειν

having no other meaning than *to worship*, what they say is just the same as if they were to confess that they worship their images without worshipping them. They cannot object that I am quibbling upon words. The fact is, that they only betray their ignorance while they attempt to throw dust in the eyes of the simple. But how eloquent soever they may be, they will never prove by their eloquence that one and the same thing makes two. Let them show how the things differ if they would be thought different from ancient idolaters. For as a murderer or an adulterer will not escape conviction by giving some adventitious name to his crime, so it is absurd for them to expect that the subtle device of a name will exculpate them, if they, in fact, differ in nothing from idolaters whom they themselves are forced to condemn. But so far are they from proving that their case is different, that the source of the whole evil consists in a preposterous rivalship with them, while they with their minds devise, and with their hands execute, symbolical shapes of God.

12. I am not, however, so superstitious as to think that all visible representations of every kind are unlawful. But as sculpture and painting are gifts of God, what I insist for is, that both shall be used purely and lawfully,—that gifts which the Lord has bestowed upon us, for his glory and our good, shall not be preposterously abused, nay, shall not be perverted to our destruction. We think it unlawful to give a visible shape to God, because God himself has forbidden it, and because it cannot be done without, in some degree, tarnishing his glory. And lest any should think that we are singular in this opinion, those acquainted with the productions of sound divines will find that they have always disapproved of it. If it be unlawful to make any corporeal representation of God, still more unlawful must it be to worship such a representation instead of God, or to worship God in it. The only things, therefore, which ought to be painted or sculptured, are things which can be

presented to the eye; the majesty of God, which is far beyond the reach of any eye, must not be dishonored by unbecoming representations. Visible representations are of two classes—viz. historical, which give a representation of events, and pictorial, which merely exhibit bodily shapes and figures. The former are of some use for instruction or admonition. The latter, so far as I can see, are only fitted for amusement. And yet it is certain, that the latter are almost the only kind which have hitherto been exhibited in churches. Hence we may infer, that the exhibition was not the result of judicious selection, but of a foolish and inconsiderate longing. I say nothing as to the improper and unbecoming form in which they are presented, or the wanton license in which sculptors and painters have here indulged (a point to which I alluded a little ago, *supra*, s. 7). I only say, that though they were otherwise faultless, they could not be of any utility in teaching.

13. But, without reference to the above distinction, let us here consider, whether it is expedient that churches should contain representations of any kind, whether of events or human forms. First, then, if we attach any weight to the authority of the ancient Church, let us remember, that for five hundred years, during which religion was in a more prosperous condition, and a purer doctrine flourished, Christian churches were completely free from visible representations (see Preface, and Book 4, c. 9 s. 9). Hence their first admission as an ornament to churches took place after the purity of the ministry had somewhat degenerated. I will not dispute as to the rationality of the grounds on which the first introduction of them proceeded, but if you compare the two periods, you will find that the latter had greatly declined from the purity of the times when images were unknown. What then? Are we to suppose that those holy fathers, if they had judged the thing to be useful and salutary, would have allowed the Church to be so long without it? Undoubtedly, because they saw very little or no

advantage, and the greatest danger in it, they rather rejected it intentionally and on rational grounds, than omitted it through ignorance or carelessness. This is clearly attested by Augustine in these words (Ep. 49. See also De Civit. Dei, lib 4 c. 31) "When images are thus placed aloft in seats of honour, to be beheld by those who are praying or sacrificing, though they have neither sense nor life, yet from appearing as if they had both, they affect weak minds just as if they lived and breathed," &c. And again, in another passage (in Ps. 112) he says, "The effect produced, and in a manner extorted, by the bodily shape, is, that the mind, being itself in a body, imagines that a body which is so like its oven must be similarly affected," &c. A little farther on he says, "Images are more capable of giving a wrong bent to an unhappy soul, from having mouth, eyes, ears, and feet, than of correcting it, as they neither speak, nor see, nor hear, nor walk." This undoubtedly is the reason why John (1 John 5:21) enjoins us to beware, not only of the worship of idols, but also of idols them- selves. And from the fearful infatuation under which the world has hitherto laboured, almost to the entire destruction of piety, we know too well from experience that the moment images appear in churches, idolatry has as it were raised its banner; because the folly of manhood cannot moderate itself, but forthwith falls away to superstitious worship. Even were the danger less imminent, still, when I consider the proper end for which churches are erected, it appears to me more unbecoming their sacredness than I well can tell, to admit any other images than those living symbols which the Lord has consecrated by his own word: I mean Baptism and the Lord's Supper, with the other ceremonies. By these our eyes ought to be more steadily fixed, and more vividly impressed, than to require the aid of any images which the wit of man may devise. Such, then, is the incomparable blessing of images—a blessing, the want of which, if we believe the Papists, cannot possibly be compensated!35

14. Enough, I believe, would have been said on this subject, were I not in a manner arrested by the Council of Nice; not the celebrated Council which Constantine the Great assembled, but one which was held eight hundred years ago by the orders and under the auspices of the Empress Irene. This Council decreed not only that images were to be used in churches, but also that they were to be worshipped. Every thing, therefore, that I have said, is in danger of suffering great prejudice from the authority of this Synod. To confess the truth, however, I am not so much moved by this consideration, as by a wish to make my readers aware of the lengths to which the infatuation has been carried by those who had a greater fondness for images than became Christians. But let us first dispose of this matter. Those who defend the use of images appeal to that Synod for support. But there is a refutation extant which bears the name of Charlemagne, and which is proved by its style to be a production of that period. It gives the opinions delivered by the bishops who were present, and the arguments by which they supported them. John, deputy of the Eastern Churches, said, "God created man in his own image," and thence inferred that images ought to be used. He also thought there was a recommendation of images in the following passage, "Show me thy face, for it is beautiful." Another, in order to prove that images ought to be placed on altars, quoted the passage, "No man, when he has lighted a candle, putteth it under a bushel." Another, to show the utility of looking at images, quoted a verse of the Psalms "The light of thy countenance, O Lord, has shone upon us." Another laid hold of this similitude: As the Patriarchs used the sacrifices of the Gentiles, so ought Christians to use the images of saints instead of the idols of the Gentiles. They also twisted to the same effect the words, "Lord, I have loved the beauty of thy house." But the most ingenious interpretation was the following, "As we have heard, so also have we seen;" therefore, God is

known not merely by the hearing of the word, but also by the seeing of images. Bishop Theodore was equally acute: "God," says he, "is to be admired in his saints;" and it is elsewhere said, "To the saints who are on earth;" therefore this must refer to images. In short, their absurdities are so extreme that it is painful even to quote them.

15. When they treat of adoration, great stress is laid on the worship of Pharaoh, the staff of Joseph, and the inscription which Jacob set up. In this last case they not only pervert the meaning of Scripture, but quote what is nowhere to be found. Then the passages, "Worship at his footstool"—"Worship in his holy mountain"—"The rulers of the people will worship before thy face," seem to them very solid and apposite proofs. Were one, with the view of turning the defenders of images into ridicule, to put words into their mouths, could they be made to utter greater and grosser absurdities? But to put an end to all doubt on the subject of images, Theodosius Bishop of Mira confirms the propriety of worshipping them by the dreams of his archdeacon, which he adduces with as much gravity as if he were in possession of a response from heaven. Let the patrons of images now go and urge us with the decree of this Synod, as if the venerable Fathers did not bring themselves into utter discredit by handling Scripture so childishly, or wresting it so shamefully and profanely.

16. I come now to monstrous impieties, which it is strange they ventured to utter, and twice strange that all men did not protest against with the utmost detestation. It is right to expose this frantic and flagitious extravagance, and thereby deprive the worship of images of that gloss of antiquity in which Papists seek to deck it. Theodosius Bishop of Amora fires oft an anathema at all who object to the worship of images. Another attributes all the calamities of Greece and the East to the crime of not having worshipped them. Of what punishment then are the Prophets, Apostles, and Martyrs worthy, in whose day no

images existed? They afterwards add, that if the statue of the Emperor is met with odours and incense, much more are the images of saints entitled to the honour. Constantius, Bishop of Constantia in Cyprus, professes to embrace images with reverence, and declares that he will pay them the respect which is due to the ever blessed Trinity: every person refusing to do the same thing he anathematises and classes with Marcionites and Manichees. Lest you should think this the private opinion of an individual, they all assent. Nay, John the Eastern legate, carried still farther by his zeal, declares it would be better to allow a city to be filled with brothels than be denied the worship of images. At last it is resolved with one consent that the Samaritans are the worst of all heretics, and that the enemies of images are worse than the Samaritans. But that the play may not pass off without the accustomed *Plaudite*, the whole thus concludes, "Rejoice and exult, ye who, having the image of Christ, offer sacrifice to it." Where is now the distinction of λατρια and δυλια with which they would throw dust in all eyes, human and divine? The Council unreservedly relies as much on images as on the living God.

CHAPTER 12.

GOD DISTINGUISHED FROM IDOLS, THAT HE MAY BE THE EXCLUSIVE OBJECT OF WORSHIP.

Sections.

1. Scripture, in teaching that there is but one God, does not make a dispute about words, but attributes all honour and religious worship to him alone. This proved, 1st, By the etymology of the term. 2d, By the testimony of God himself, when he declares that he is a jealous God, and will not allow himself to be confounded with any fictitious Deity.

2. The Papists in opposing this pure doctrine, gain nothing by their distinction of δυλια and λατρια.

3. Passages of Scripture subversive of the Papistical distinction, and proving that religious worship is due to God alone. Perversions of Divine worship.

1. We said at the commencement of our work (chap. 2), that the knowledge of God consists not in frigid speculation, but carries worship along with it; and we touched by the way (chap. 5 s. 6, 9, 10) on what will be more copiously treated in other places (Book 2, chap. 8)— viz. how God is duly worshipped. Now I only briefly repeat, that whenever Scripture asserts the unity of God, it does not contend for a mere name, but also enjoins that nothing which belongs to Divinity be applied to any other; thus making it obvious in what respect pure religion differs from superstition. The Greek word ευσεβεια means "right worship;" for the Greeks, though groping in darkness, were always aware that a certain rule was to be observed, in order that God might not be worshipped absurdly. Cicero truly and shrewdly derives the name *religion* from *relego*,

and yet the reason which he assigns is forced and farfetched — viz. that honest worshipers *read* and *read again*, and ponder what is true. I rather think the name is used in opposition to *vagrant license* — the greater part of mankind rashly taking up whatever first comes in their way, whereas piety, that it may stand with a firm step, confines itself within due bounds. In the same way superstition seems to take its name from its not being contented with the measure which reason prescribes, but accumulating a superfluous mass of vanities. But to say nothing more of words, it has been universally admitted in all ages, that religion is vitiated and perverted whenever false opinions are introduced into it, and hence it is inferred, that whatever is allowed to be done from inconsiderate zeal, cannot be defended by any pretext with which the superstitious may choose to cloak it. But although this confession is in every man's mouth, a shameful stupidity is forthwith manifested, inasmuch as men neither cleave to the one God, nor use any selection in their worship, as we have already observed.

But God, in vindicating his own right, first proclaims that he is a jealous God, and will be a stern avenger if he is confounded with any false god; and thereafter defines what due worship is, in order that the human race may be kept in obedience. Both of these he embraces in his Law when he first binds the faithful in allegiance to him as their only Lawgiver, and then prescribes a rule for worshipping him in accordance with his will. The Law, with its manifold uses and objects, I will consider in its own place; at present I only advert to this one, that it is designed as a bridle to curb men, and prevent them from turning aside to spurious worship. But it is necessary to attend to the observation with which I set out — viz. that unless everything peculiar to divinity is confined to God alone, he is robbed of his honour, and his worship is violated.

It may be proper here more particularly to attend to the subtleties which superstition employs. In revolting to strange gods, it avoids the appearance of abandoning the Supreme God, or reducing him to the same rank with others. It gives him the highest place, but at the same time surrounds him with a tribe of minor deities, among whom it portions out his peculiar offices. In this way, though in a dissembling and crafty manner, the glory of the Godhead is dissected, and not allowed to remain entire. In the same way the people of old, both Jews and Gentiles, placed an immense crowd in subordination to the father and ruler of the gods, and gave them, according to their rank, to share with the supreme God in the government of heaven and earth. In the same way, too, for some ages past, departed saints have been exalted to partnership with God, to be worshipped, invoked, and lauded in his stead. And yet we do not even think that the majesty of God is obscured by this abomination, whereas it is in a great measure suppressed and extinguished—all that we retain being a frigid opinion of his supreme power. At the same time, being deluded by these entanglements, we go astray after divers gods.

2. The distinction of what is called δυλια and λατρια was invented for the very purpose of permitting divine honours to be paid to angels and dead men with apparent impunity. For it is plain that the worship which Papists pay to saints differs in no respect from the worship of God: for this worship is paid without distinction; only when they are pressed they have recourse to the evasion, that what belongs to God is kept unimpaired, because they leave him λατρια. But since the question relates not to the word, but the thing, how can they be allowed to sport at will with a matter of the highest moment? But not to insist on this, the utmost they will obtain by their distinction is, that they give worship to God, and service to the others. For λατρεια in Greek has the same meaning as *worship* in Latin; whereas δουλεια properly means service, though the words are sometimes used in Scripture indiscriminately. But granting

that the distinction is invariably preserved, the thing to be inquired into is the meaning of each. Δουλεια unquestionably means service, and λατρεια worship. But no man doubts that to *serve* is something higher than to *worship*. For it were often a hard thing to serve him whom you would not refuse to reverence. It is, therefore, an unjust division to assign the greater to the saints and leave the less to God. But several of the ancient fathers observed this distinction. What if they did, when all men see that it is not only improper, but utterly frivolous?

3. Laying aside subtleties, let us examine the thing. When Paul reminds the Galatians of what they were before they came to the knowledge of Gods he says that they "did service unto them which by nature are no gods," (Gal. 4:8). Because he does not say λατρια, was their superstition excusable? This superstition, to which he gives the name of δυλια, he condemns as much as if he had given it the name of λατρια. When Christ repels Satan's insulting proposal with the words, "It is written, Thou shalt worship the Lord thy God, and him only shalt thou serve," (Mt. 4:10), there was no question of λατρια. For all that Satan asked was προσκυνεσις (obeisance). In like manners when John is rebuked by the angel for falling on his knees before him (Rev. 19:10; 22:8, 9), we ought not to suppose that John had so far forgotten himself as to have intended to transfer the honour due to God alone to an angel. But because it was impossible that a worship connected with religion should not savour somewhat of divine worship, he could not προσκυνειν (do obeisance to) the angel without derogating from the glory of God. True, we often read that men were worshipped; but that was, if I may so speak, civil honour. The case is different with religious honour, which, the moment it is conjoined with worship, carries profanation of the divine honour along with it. The same thing may be seen in the case of Cornelius (Acts 10:25). He had not made so little progress in piety as not to confine

supreme worship to God alone. Therefore, when he prostrates himself before Peter, he certainly does it not with the intention of adoring him instead of God. Yet Peter sternly forbids him. And why, but just because men never distinguish so accurately between the worship of God and the creatures as not to transfer promiscuously to the creature that which belongs only to God. Therefore, if we would have one God, let us remember that we can never appropriate the minutest portion of his glory without retaining what is his due. Accordingly, when Zechariah discourses concerning the repairing of the Church, he distinctly says not only that there would be one God, but also that he would have only one name—the reason being, that he might have nothing in common with idols. The nature of the worship which God requires will be seen in its own place (Book 2, c. 7 and 8). He has been pleased to prescribe in his Law what is lawful and right, and thus restrict men to a certain rule, lest any should allow themselves to devise a worship of their own. But as it is inexpedient to burden the reader by mixing up a variety of topics, I do not now dwell on this one. Let it suffice to remember, that whatever offices of piety are bestowed anywhere else than on God alone, are of the nature of sacrilege. First, superstition attached divine honours to the sun and stars, or to idols: afterwards ambition followed— ambition which, decking man in the spoils of God, dared to profane all that was sacred. And though the principle of worshipping a supreme Deity continued to be held, still the practice was to sacrifice promiscuously to genii and minor gods, or departed heroes: so prone is the descent to this vice of communicating to a crowd that which God strictly claims as his own peculiar right!

CHAPTER 13.

THE UNITY OF THE DIVINE ESSENCE IN THREE PERSONS TAUGHT, IN SCRIPTURE, FROM THE FOUNDATION OF THE WORLD.

This chapter consists of two parts. The former delivers the orthodox doctrine concerning the Holy Trinity. This occupies from sec. 1-21, and may be divided into four heads; the first, treating of the meaning of Person, including both the term and the thing meant by it, sec. 2-6; the second, proving the deity of the Son, sec. 7-13; the third, the deity of the Holy Spirit, sec. 14 and 15; and the fourth, explaining what is to be held concerning the Holy Trinity. The second part of the chapter refutes certain heresies which have arisen, particularly in our age, in opposition to this orthodox doctrine. This occupies from sec. 21 to the end.

Sections.

1. Scripture, in teaching that the essence of God is immense and spiritual, refutes not only idolaters and the foolish wisdom of the world, but also the Manichees and Anthropomorphites. These latter briefly refuted.

2. In this one essence are three persons, yet so that neither is there a triple God, nor is the simple essence of God divided. Meaning of the word Person in this discussion. Three hypostases in God, or the essence of God.

3. Objection of those who, in this discussion, reject the use of the word Person. Answer 1. That it is not a foreign term, but is employed for the explanation of sacred mysteries.

4. Answer continued, 2. The orthodox compelled to use the terms, Trinity, Subsistence, and Person. Examples from the case of the Arians and Sabellians.

5. Answer continued, 3. The ancient Church, though differing somewhat in the explanation of these terms, agree in substance. Proofs from Hilary, Jerome, Augustine, in their use of the words Essence, Substance, Hypostasis. 4. Provided the orthodox meaning is retained, there should be no dispute about mere terms. But those who object to the terms usually favour the Arian and Sabellian heresy.

6. After the definition of the term follows a definition and explanation of the thing meant by it. The distinction of Persons.

7. Proofs of the eternal Deity of the Son. The Son the λογος of the Eternal Father, and, therefore, the Son Eternal God. Objection. Reply.

8. Objection, that the Λογος began to be when the creating God spoke. Answer confirmed by Scripture and argument.

9. The Son called God and Jehovah. Other names of the Eternal Father applied to him in the Old Testament. He is, therefore, the Eternal God. Another objection refuted. Case of the Jews explained.

10. The angel who appeared to the fathers under the Law asserts that he is Jehovah. That angel was the Λογος of the Eternal Father. The Son being that Λογος is Eternal God. Impiety of Servetus refuted. Why the Son appeared in the form of an angel.

11. Passages from the New Testament in which the Son is acknowledged to be the Lord of Hosts, the Judge of the world, the God of glory, the Creator of the world, the Lord of angels, the King of the Church, the eternal Λογος, God blessed for ever, God manifest in the flesh, the equal of God, the true God and eternal life, the Lord and God of all believers. Therefore, the Eternal God.

12. Christ the Creator, Preserver, Redeemer, and Searcher of hearts. Therefore, the Eternal God.

13. Christ, by his own inherent power, wrought miracles, and bestowed the power of working them on

others. Out of the Eternal God there is no salvation, no righteousness, no life. All these are in Christ. Christ, consequently, is the Eternal God. He in whom we believe and hope, to whom we pray, whom the Church acknowledges as the Saviour of the faithful, whom to know is life eternal, in whom the pious glory, and through whom eternal blessings are communicated, is the Eternal God. All these Christ is, and, therefore, he is God.

14.The Divinity of the Spirit proved. I. He is the Creator and Preserver of the world. II. He sent the Prophets. III. He quickeneth all things. IV. He is everywhere present. V. He renews the saints, and fits them for eternal life. VI. All the offices of Deity belong to him.

15.The Divinity of the Spirit continued. VII. He is called God. VIII. Blasphemy against him is not forgiven.

16.What view to be taken of the Trinity. The form of Christian baptism proves that there are in one essence. The Arian and Macedonian heresies.

17.Of the distinction of Persons. They are distinct, but not divided. This proved.

18.Analogies taken from human affairs to be cautiously used. Due regard to be paid to those mentioned by Scripture.

19.How the Three Persons not only do not destroy, but constitute the most perfect unity

20. Conclusion of this part of the chapter, and summary of the true doctrine concerning the unity of Essence and the Three Persons.

21. Refutation of Arian, Macedonian, and Anti Trinitarian heresies. Caution to be observed.

22. The more modern Anti Trinitarians, and especially Servetus, refuted.

23. Other Anti Trinitarians refuted. No good objection

that Christ is called the Son of God, since he is also called God. Impious absurdities of some heretics.

24. The name of God sometimes given to the Son absolutely as to the Father. Same as to other attributes. Objections refuted. 25. Objections further refuted. Caution to be used.

26. Previous refutations further explained.

27. Reply to certain passages produced from Irenaeus. The meaning of Irenaeus.

28. Reply to certain passages produced from Tertullian. The meaning of Tertullian.

29. Anti Trinitarians refuted by ancient Christian writers; *e.g.*, Justin, Hilary. Objections drawn from writings improperly attributed to Ignatius. Conclusion of the whole discussion concerning the Trinity.

1. The doctrine of Scripture concerning the immensity and the spirituality of the essence of God, should have the effect not only of dissipating the wild dreams of the vulgar, but also of refuting the subtleties of a profane philosophy. One of the ancients thought he spake shrewdly when he said that everything we see and everything we do not see is God (Senec. Praef. lib. 1 Quaest. Nat.) In this way he fancied that the Divinity was transfused into every separate portion of the world. But although God, in order to keep us within the bounds of soberness, treats sparingly of his essence, still, by the two attributes which I have mentioned, he at once suppresses all gross imaginations, and checks the audacity of the human mind. His immensity surely ought to deter us from measuring him by our sense, while his spiritual nature forbids us to indulge in carnal or earthly speculation concerning him. With the same view he frequently represents heaven as his dwelling-place. It is true, indeed, that as he is incomprehensible, he fills the earth also, but knowing that our minds are heavy and grovel on the earth, he raises us above the worlds that he

157

may shake off our sluggishness and in- activity. And here we have a refutation of the error of the Manichees, who, by adopting two first principles, made the devil almost the equal of God. This, assuredly, was both to destroy his unity and restrict his immensity. Their attempt to pervert certain passages of Scripture proved their shameful ignorance, as the very nature of the error did their monstrous infatuation. The Anthropomorphites also, who dreamed of a corporeal God, because mouth, ears, eyes, hands, and feet, are often ascribed to him in Scripture, are easily refuted. For who is so devoid of intellect as not to understand that God, in so speaking, lisps with us as nurses are wont to do with little children? Such modes of expression, therefore, do not so much express what kind of a being God is, as accommodate the knowledge of him to our feebleness. In doing so, he must, of course, stoop far below his proper height.

2. But there is another special mark by which he designates himself, for the purpose of giving a more intimate knowledge of his nature. While he proclaims his unity, he distinctly sets it before us as existing in three persons. These we must hold, unless the bare and empty name of Deity merely is to flutter in our brain without any genuine knowledge. Moreover, lest any one should dream of a threefold God, or think that the simple essence is divided by the three Persons, we must here seek a brief and easy definition which may effectually guard us from error. But as some strongly inveigh against the term Person as being merely of human inventions let us first consider how far they have any ground for doing so.

When the Apostle calls the Son of God "the express image of his person," (Heb. 1:3), he undoubtedly does assign to the Father some subsistence in which he differs from the Son. For to hold with some interpreters that the term is equivalent to essence (as if Christ represented the substance of the Father like the impression of a seal upon wax), were not only harsh but absurd. For the essence of

God being simple and undivided, and contained in himself entire, in full perfection, without partition or diminution, it is improper, nay, ridiculous, to call it his express image (χαρακτερ). But because the Father, though distinguished by his own peculiar properties, has expressed himself wholly in the Son, he is said with perfect reason to have rendered his person (hypostasis) manifest in him. And this aptly ac- cords with what is immediately added—viz. that he is "the brightness of his glory." The fair inference from the Apostle's words is, that there is a proper subsistence (hypostasis) of the Father, which shines refulgent in the Son. From this, again it is easy to infer that there is a subsistence (hypostasis) of the Son which distinguishes him from the Father. The same holds in the case of the Holy Spirit; for we will immediately prove both that he is God, and that he has a separate subsistence from the Father. This, moreover, is not a distinction of essence, which it were impious to multiply. If credit, then, is given to the Apostle's testimony, it follows that there are three persons (hypostases) in God. The Latins having used the word *Persona* to express the same thing as the Greek υποστατις, it betrays excessive fastidiousness and even perverseness to quarrel with the term. The most literal translation would be *sub- sistence*. Many have used *substance* in the same sense. Nor, indeed, was the use of the term Person confined to the Latin Church. For the Greek Church in like manner, perhaps, for the purpose of testifying their consent, have taught that there are three προσωπα (*aspects*) in God. All these, however, whether Greeks or Latins, though differing as to the word, are perfectly agreed in substance.

3. Now, then, though heretics may snarl and the excessively fastidious carp at the word Person as inadmissible, in consequence of its human origin, since they cannot displace us from our position that three are named, each of whom is perfect God, and yet that there is no plurality of gods, it is most uncandid to attack the terms

which do nothing more than explain what the Scriptures declare and sanction. "It were better," they say, "to confine not only our meanings but our words within the bounds of Scripture, and not scatter about foreign terms to become the future seed-beds of brawls and dissensions. In this way, men grow tired of quarrels about words; the truth is lost in altercation, and charity melts away amid hateful strife." If they call it a *foreign* term, because it cannot be pointed out in Scripture in so many syllables, they certainly impose an unjust law—a law which would condemn every interpretation of Scripture that is not composed of other words of Scripture. But if by *foreign* they mean that which, after being idly devised, is superstitiously defended,—which tends more to strife than edification,—which is used either out of place, or with no benefit which offends pious ears by its harshness, and leads them away from the simplicity of God's Word, I embrace their soberness with all my heart. For I think we are bound to speak of God as reverently as we are bound to think of him. As our own thoughts respecting him are foolish, so our own language respecting him is absurd. Still, however, some medium must be observed. The unerring standard both of thinking and speaking must be derived from the Scriptures: by it all the thoughts of ours minds, and the words of our mouths, should he tested. But in regard to those parts of Scripture which, to our capacities, are dark and intricate, what forbids us to explain them in clearer terms—terms, however, kept in reverent and faithful subordination to Scripture truth, used sparingly and modestly, and not without occasion? Of this we are not without many examples. When it has been proved that the Church was impelled, by the strongest necessity, to use the words Trinity and Person, will not he who still inveighs against novelty of terms be deservedly suspected of taking offence at the light of truth, and of having no other ground for his invective, than that the truth is made plain and transparent?

4. Such novelty (if novelty it should be called) becomes most requisite, when the truth is to be maintained against calumniators who evade it by quibbling. Of this, we of the present day have too much experience in being constantly called upon to attack the enemies of pure and sound doctrine. These slippery snakes escape by their swift and tortuous windings, if not strenuously pursued, and when caught, firmly held. Thus the early Christians, when harassed with the disputes which heresies produced, were forced to declare their sentiments in terms most scrupulously exact in order that no indirect subterfuges might remain to ungodly men, to whom ambiguity of expression was a kind of hiding-place. Arius confessed that Christ was God, and the Son of God; because the passages of Scripture to this effect were too clear to be resisted, and then, as if he had done well, pretended to concur with others. But, meanwhile, he ceased not to give out that Christ was created, and had a beginning like other creatures. To drag this man of wiles out of his lurking-places, the ancient Church took a further step, and declared that Christ is the eternal Son of the Father, and consubstantial with the Father. The impiety was fully disclosed when the Arians began to declare their hatred and utter detestation of the term ομοουσιος. Had their first confession—viz. that Christ was God, been sincere and from the heart, they would not have denied that he was consubstantial with the Father. Who dare charge those ancient writers as men of strife and contention, for having debated so warmly, and disturbed the quiet of the Church for a single word? That little word distinguished between Christians of pure faith and the blasphemous Arians. Next Sabellius arose, who counted the names of Father, Son, and Holy Spirit, as al- most nonentities; maintaining that they were not used to mark out some distinction, but that they were different attributes of God, like many others of a similar kind. When the matter was debated, he

acknowledged his belief that the Father was God, the Son God, the Spirit God; but then he had the evasion ready, that he had said nothing more than if he had called God powerful, and just, and wise. Accordingly, he sung another note—viz. that the Father was the Son, and the Holy Spirit the Father, without order or distinction. The worthy doctors who then had the interests of piety at heart, in order to defeat it is man's dishonesty, proclaimed that three subsistence were to be truly acknowledged in the one God. That they might protect themselves against tortuous craftiness by the simple open truth, they affirmed that a Trinity of Persons subsisted in the one God, or (which is the same thing) in the unity of God.

5. Where names have not been invented rashly, we must beware lest we become chargeable with arrogance and rashness in rejecting them. I wish, indeed, that such names were buried, provided all would concur in the belief that the Father, Son, and Spirit, are one God, and yet that the Son is not the Father, nor the Spirit the Son, but that each has his peculiar subsistence. I am not so minutely precise as to fight furiously for mere words. For I observe, that the writers of the ancient Church, while they uniformly spoke with great reverence on these matters, neither agreed with each other, nor were always consistent with themselves. How strange the formula used by Councils, and defended by Hilary! How extravagant the view which Augustine sometimes takes! How unlike the Greeks are to the Latins! But let one example of variance suffice. The Latins, in translating ομοουσιος used consubstantialis (consubstantial), intimating that there was one substance of the Father and the Son, and thus using the word Substance for Essence. Hence Jerome, in his Letter to Damasus, says it is profane to affirm that there are three substances in God. But in Hilary you will find it said more than a hundred times that there are three substances in God. Then how greatly is Jerome perplexed with the word Hypostasis! He

suspects some lurking poison, when it is said that there are three Hypostases in God. And he does not disguise his belief that the expression, though used in a pious sense, is improper; if, indeed, he was sincere in saying this, and did not rather designedly endeavour, by an unfounded calumny, to throw odium on the Eastern bishops whom he hated. He certainly shows little candour in asserting, that in all heathen schools ουσια is equivalent to Hypostasis — an assertion completely refuted by trite and common use.

More courtesy and moderation is shown by Augustine (De Trinit. lib. 5 c. 8 and 9), who, although he says that Hypostasis in this sense is new to Latin ears, is still so far from objecting to the ordinary use of the term by the Greeks, that he is even tolerant of the Latins, who had imitated the Greek phraseology. The purport of what Socrates says of the term, in the Sixth Book of the Tripartite History, is, that it had been improperly applied to this purpose by the unskilful. Hilary (De Trinitat. lib. 2) charges it upon the heretics as a great crime, that their misconduct had rendered it necessary to subject to the peril of human utterance things which ought to have been reverently confined within the mind, not disguising his opinion that those who do so, do what is unlawful, speak what is ineffable, and pry into what is for- bidden. Shortly after, he apologises at great length for presuming to introduce new terms. For, after putting down the natural names of Father, Son, and Spirit, he adds, that all further inquiry transcends the significance of words, the discernment of sense, and the apprehension of intellect. And in another place (De Conciliis), he congratulates the Bishops of France in not having framed any other confession, but received, without alteration, the ancient and most simple confession received by all Churches from the days of the Apostles. Not unlike this is the apology of Augustine, that the term had been wrung from him by necessity from the poverty of human language in so high a matter: not that the reality could be thereby expressed, but that he might not pass on in silence without attempting to show how the Father, Son, and Spirit, are three.

The modesty of these holy men should be an admonition to us not instantly to dip our pen in gall, and sternly denounce those who may be unwilling to swear to the terms which we have devised, provided they do not in this betray pride, or petulance, or unbecoming heat, but are willing to ponder the necessity which compels us so to speak, and may thus become gradually accustomed to a useful form of expression. Let men also studiously beware, that in opposing the Arians on the one hand, and the Sabellians on the other, and eagerly endeavouring to deprive both of any handle for cavil, they do not bring themselves under some suspicion of being the disciples of either Arius or Sabellius. Arius says that *Christ is God*, and then mutters that *he was made and had a beginning.* He says, that *he is one with the Father*; but secretly whispers in the ears of his party, *made one*, like other believers, though with special privilege. Say, *he is consubstantial*, and you immediately pluck the mask from this chameleon, though you add nothing to Scripture. Sabellius says that *the Father, Son, and Spirit, indicate some distinction in God.* Say, *they are three*, and he will bawl out that you are making three Gods. Say, that *there is a Trinity of Persons in one Divine essence*, you will only express in one word what the Scriptures say, and stop his empty prattle. Should any be so superstitiously precise as not to tolerate these terms, still do their worst, they will not be able to deny that when *one* is spoken of, a unity of substance must be understood, and when *three* in one essence, the persons in this Trinity are denoted. When this is confessed without equivocations we dwell not on words. But I was long ago made aware, and, indeed, on more than one occasion, that those who contend pertinaciously about words are tainted with some hidden poison; and, therefore, that it is more expedient to provoke them purposely, than to court their favour by speaking obscurely.

6. But to say nothing more of words, let us now attend to the thing signified. By *person*, then, I mean a subsistence in the Divine essence,—a subsistence which, while related to the other two, is distinguished from them by incommunicable properties. By *subsistence* we wish something else to be understood than *essence*. For if the Word were God simply and had not some property peculiar to himself, John could not have said correctly that he had always been with God. When he adds immediately after, that the Word was God, he calls us back to the one essence. But because he could not be with God without dwelling in the Father, hence arises that subsistence, which, though connected with the essence by an indissoluble tie, being incapable of separation, yet has a special mark by which it is distinguished from it. Now, I say that each of the three subsistences while related to the others is distinguished by its own properties. Here relation is distinctly expressed, because, when God is mentioned simply and indefinitely the name belongs not less to the Son and Spirit than to the Father. But whenever the Father is compared with the Son, the peculiar property of each distinguishes the one from the other. Again, whatever is proper to each I affirm to be incommunicable, because nothing can apply or be transferred to the Son which is attributed to the Father as a mark of distinction. I have no objections to adopt the definition of Tertullian, provided it is properly understood, "that there is in God a certain arrangement or economy, which makes no change on the unity of essence."—Tertull. Lib. contra Praxeam.

7. Before proceeding farther, it will be necessary to prove the divinity of the Son and the Holy Spirit. Thereafter, we shall see how they differ from each other. When the Word of God is set before us in the Scriptures, it were certainly most absurd to imagine that it is only a

fleeting and evanescent voice, which is sent out into the air, and comes forth beyond God himself, as was the case with the communications made to the patriarchs, and all the prophecies. The reference is rather to the wisdom ever dwelling with God, and by which all oracles and prophecies were inspired. For, as Peter testifies (1 Pet. 1:11), the ancient prophets spake by the Spirit of Christ just as did the apostles, and all who after them were ministers of the heavenly doctrine. But as Christ was not yet manifested, we necessarily understand that the Word was begotten of the Father before all ages. But if that Spirit, whose organs the prophets were, belonged to the Word, the inference is irresistible, that the Word was truly God. And this is clearly enough shown by Moses in his account of the creation, where he places the Word as intermediate. For why does he distinctly narrate that God, in creating each of his works, said, Let there be this—let there be that, unless that the unsearchable glory of God might shine forth in his image? I know prattlers would easily evade this, by saying that *Word* is used for *order* or *command*; but the apostles are better expositors, when they tell us that the worlds were created by the Son, and that he sustains all things by his mighty word (Heb. 1:2). For we here see that *word* is used for the nod or command of the Son, who is himself the eternal and essential Word of the Father. And no man of sane mind can have any doubt as to Solomon's meaning, when he introduces Wisdom as begotten by God, and presiding at the creation of the world, and all other divine operations (Prov. 8:22). For it were trifling and foolish to imagine any temporary command at a time when God was pleased to execute his fixed and eternal counsel, and something more still mysterious. To this our Saviour's words refer, "My Father worketh hitherto, and I work," (John 5:17). In thus affirming, that from the foundation of the world he constantly worked with the Father, he gives a clearer explanation of what Moses simply touched. The meaning therefore is, that God spoke in such a manner as left the Word his peculiar part in the work, and thus made the operation common to both. But the clearest explanation is given by John, when he states that the Word—which was from the beginning, God and with God, was, together with God the Father, the maker of all things. For he both attributes a substantial and permanent essence to the Word, assigning to it a certain peculiarity, and distinctly showing how God spoke the world into being. Therefore, as all revelations from heaven are duly designated by the title of the Word of God, so the highest place must be assigned to that substantial Word, the source of all inspiration, which, as being liable to no variation, remains for ever one and the same with God, and is God.

8. Here an outcry is made by certain men, who, while they dare not openly deny his divinity, secretly rob him of his eternity. For they contend that the Word only began to be when God opened his sacred mouth in the creation of the world. Thus, with excessive temerity, they imagine some change in the essence of God. For as the names of God, which have respect to external work, began to be ascribed to him from the existence of the work (as when he is called the Creator of heaven and earth), so piety does not recognise or admit any name which might indicate that a change had taken place in God himself. For if any thing adventitious took place, the saying of James would cease to be true, that "every good gift, and every perfect gift, is from above, and cometh down from the Father of lights, with whom is no variableness, neither shadow of turning," (James 1:17). Nothing, therefore, is more intolerable than to fancy a beginning to that Word which was always God, and after- wards was the Creator of the world. But they think they argue acutely, in maintaining that Moses, when he says that God then spoke for the first time, must be held to intimate that till then no Word existed in him. This is the merest trifling. It does not surely follow,

that because a thing begins to be manifested at a certain time, it never existed previously. I draw a very different conclusion. Since at the very moment when God said, "Let there be light," the energy of the Word-was immediately exerted, it must have existed long before. If any inquire how long, he will find it was without beginning. No certain period of time is defined, when he himself says, "Now O Father, glorify thou me with thine own self with the glory which I had with thee before the world was," (John 17:5). Nor is this omitted by John: for before he descends to the creation of the world, he says, that "in the beginning was the Word, and the Word was with God." We, therefore, again conclude, that the Word was eternally begotten by God, and dwelt with him from everlasting. In this way, his true essence, his eternity, and divinity, are established.

9. But though I am not now treating of the office of the Mediator, having deferred it till the subject of redemption is considered, yet because it ought to be clear and incontrovertible to all, that Christ is that Word become incarnate, this seems the most appropriate place to introduce those passages which assert the Divinity of Christ. When it is said in the forty- fifth Psalm, "Thy throne, O God, is for ever and ever," the Jews quibble that the name Elohim is applied to angels and sovereign powers. But no passage is to be found in Scripture, where an eternal throne is set up for a creature. For he is not called God simply, but also the eternal Ruler. Besides, the title is not conferred on any man, without some addition, as when it is said that Moses would be a God to Pharaoh (Exod. 7:1). Some read as if it were in the genitive case, but this is too insipid. I admit, that anything possessed of singular excellence is often called divine, but it is clear from the context, that this meaning here were harsh and forced, and totally inapplicable. But if their perverseness still refuses to yield, surely there is no obscurity in Isaiah, where Christ is introduced both us God, and as possessed of supreme

powers one of the peculiar attributes of God, "His name shall be called the Mighty God, the Everlasting Father, the Prince of Peace," (Isa. 9:6). Here, too, the Jews object, and invert the passage thus, This is the name by which the mighty God, the Everlasting Father, will call him; so that all which they leave to the Son is, " Prince of Peace." But why should so many epithets be here accumulated on God the Father, seeing the prophet's design is to present the Messiah with certain distinguished properties which may induce us to put our faith in him? There can be no doubt, therefore, that he who a little before was called Emmanuel, is here called the Mighty God. Moreover, there can be nothing clearer than the words of Jeremiah, "This is the name whereby he shall be called, THE LORD OUR RIGHTEOUSNESS," (Jer. 23:6). For as the Jews themselves teach that the other names of God are mere epithets, whereas this, which they call the ineffable name, is substantive, and expresses his essence, we infer, that the only begotten Son is the eternal God, who elsewhere declares, "My glory will I not give to another," (Isa. 42:8). An attempt is made to evade this from the fact, that this name is given by Moses to the altar which he built, and by Ezekiel to the New Jerusalem. But who sees not that the altar was erected as a memorial to show that God was the exalter of Moses, and that the name of God was applied to Jerusalem, merely to testify the Divine presence? For thus the prophet speaks, "The name of the city from that day shall be, The Lord is there," (Ezek. 48:35). In the same way, "Moses built an altar, and called the name of it JEHOVAH-nissi," (Jehovah my exaltation). But it would seem the point is still more keenly disputed as to another passage in Jeremiah, where the same title is applied to Jerusalem in these words, "In those days shall Judah be saved, and Jerusalem shall dwell safely; and this is the name wherewith she shall be called, The Lord our Righteousness." But so far is this passage from being adverse to the truth which we defend, that it rather supports it. The prophet having formerly declared that Christ is the true Jehovah from whom righteousness flows, now declares that the Church would be made so sensible of this as to be able to glory in assuming his very name. In the former passage, therefore, the fountain and cause of righteousness is set down, in the latter, the effect is described.

10. But if this does not satisfy the Jews, I know not what cavils will enable them to evade the numerous passages in which Jehovah is said to have appeared in the form of an Angel (Judges 6:7; 13:16-23, &c). This Angel claims for himself the name of the Eternal God. Should it be alleged that this is done in respect of the office which he bears, the difficulty is by no means solved. No servant would rob God of his honour, by allowing sacrifice to be offered to himself. But the Angel, by refusing to eat bread, orders the sacrifice due to Jehovah to be offered to him. Thus the fact itself proves that he was truly Jehovah. Accordingly, Manoah and his wife infer from the sign, that they had seen not only an angel, but God. Hence Manoah's exclamation, "We shall die; for we have seen the Lord." When the woman replies, "If Jehovah had wished to slay us, he would not have received the sacrifice at our hand," she acknowledges that he who is previously called an angel was certainly God. We may add, that the angel's own reply removes all doubt, "Why do ye ask my name, which is wonderful?" Hence the impiety of Servetus was the more detestable, when he maintained that God was never manifested to Abraham and the Patriarchs, but that an angel was worshipped in his stead. The orthodox doctors of the Church have correctly and wisely expounded, that the Word of God was the supreme angel, who then began, as it were by anticipation, to perform the office of Mediator. For though he were not clothed with flesh, yet he descended as in an intermediate form, that he might have more familiar access to the faithful. This closer inter- course procured for

him the name of the Angel; still, however, he retained the character which justly belonged to him—that of the God of ineffable glory. The same thing is intimated by Hosea, who, after mentioning the wrestling of Jacob with the angel, says, "Even the Lord God of hosts; the Lord is his memorial," (Hosea 12:5). Servetus again insinuates that God personated an angel; as if the prophet did not confirm what had been said by Moses, "Wherefore is it that thou dost ask after my name?" (Gen. 32:29, 30). And the confession of the holy Patriarch sufficiently declares that he was not a created angel, but one in whom the fulness of the Godhead dwelt, when he says, "I have seen God face to face." Hence also Paul's statement, that Christ led the people in the wilderness (1 Cor. 10:4. See also Calvin on Acts 7:30, and *infra*, chap. 14, s. 9). Although the time of humiliation had not yet arrived, the eternal Word exhibited a type of the office which he was to fulfil. Again, if the first chapter of Zechariah (ver. 9, &c). and the second (ver. 3, &c). be candidly considered, it will be seen that the angel who sends the other angel is immediately after declared to be the Lord of hosts, and that supreme power is ascribed to him. I omit numberless passages in which our faith rests secure, though they may not have much weight with the Jews. For when it is said in Isaiah, "Lo, this is our God; we have waited for him, and he will save us; this is the Lord: we have waited for him, we will be glad and rejoice in his salvation," (Isa. 25:9), even the blind may see that the God referred to is he who again rises up for the deliverance of his people. And the emphatic description, twice repeated, precludes the idea that reference is made to any other than to Christ. Still clearer and stronger is the passage of Malachi, in which a promise is made that the messenger who was then expected would come to his own temple (Mal. 3:1). The temple certainly was dedicated to Almighty God only, and yet the prophet claims it for Christ. Hence it follows, that he is the God who was always worshipped by the Jews.

11. The New Testament teems with innumerable passages, and our object must therefore be, the selection of a few, rather than an accumulation of the whole. But though the Apostles spoke of him after his appearance in the flesh as Mediator, every passage which I adduce will be sufficient to prove his eternal Godhead. And the first thing deserving of special observation is that predictions concerning the eternal God are applied to Christ, as either already fulfilled in him, or to be fulfilled at some future period. Isaiah prophesies, that "the Lord of Hosts" shall be "for a stone of stumbling, and for a rock of offence," (Isa. 8:14). Paul asserts that this prophecy was fulfilled in Christ (Rom. 9:33), and, therefore, declares that Christ is that Lord of Hosts. In like manner, he says in another passage, "We shall all stand before the Judgment-seat of Christ. For it is written, As I live, saith the Lord, every knee shall bow to me, and every tongue shall confess to God." Since in Isaiah God predicts this of himself (Isa. 45:23), and Christ exhibits the reality fulfilled in himself, it follows that he is the very God, whose glory cannot be given to another. It is clear also, that the passage from the Psalms (Ps. 68:19) which he quotes in the Epistle to the Ephesians, is applicable only to God, "When he ascended up on high, he led captivity captive," (Eph. 4:8). Under- standing that such an ascension was shadowed forth when the Lord exerted his power, and gained a glorious victory over heathen nations, he intimates that what was thus shadowed was more fully manifested in Christ. So John testifies that it was the glory of the Son which was revealed to Isaiah in a vision (John 12:41; Isa. 6:4), though Isaiah himself expressly says that what he saw was the Majesty of God. Again, there can be no doubt that those qualities which, in the Epistle to the Hebrews, are applied to the Son, are the brightest attributes of God, "Thou, Lord, in the beginning

hast laid the foundation of the earth," &c., and, "Let all the angels of God worship him," (Heb. 1:10, 6). And yet he does not pervert the passages in thus applying them to Christ, since Christ alone performed the things which these passages celebrate. It was he who arose and pitied Zion— he who claimed for himself dominion over all nations and islands. And why should John have hesitated to ascribe the Majesty of God to Christ, after saying in his preface that the Word was God? (John 1:14). Why should Paul have feared to place Christ on the Judgment-seat of God (2 Cor. 5:10), after he had so openly proclaimed his divinity, when he said that he was God over all, blessed for ever? And to show how consistent he is in this respect, he elsewhere says that "God was manifest in the flesh," (1 Tim. 3:16). If he is God blessed for ever, he therefore it is to whom alone, as Paul affirms in another place, all glory and honour is due. Paul does not disguise this, but openly exclaims, that "being in the form of God (he) thought it not robbery to be equal with God, but made himself of no reputation," (Phil. 2:6). And lest the wicked should glamour and say that he was a kind of spurious God, John goes farther, and affirms, "This is the true God, and eternal life." Though it ought to be enough for us that he is called God, especially by a witness who distinctly testifies that we have no more gods than one, Paul says, "Though there be that are called gods, whether in heaven or in earth (as there be gods many, and lords many), but to us there is but one God," (1 Cor. 8:5, 6). When we hear from the same lips that God was manifest in the flesh, that God purchased the Church with his own blood, why do we dream of any second God, to whom he makes not the least allusion? And there is no room to doubt that all the godly entertained the same view. Thomas, by addressing him as his Lord and God, certainly professes that he was the only God whom he had ever adored (John 20:28).

173

12. The divinity of Christ, if judged by the works which are ascribed to him in Scripture, becomes still more evident. When he said of himself, "My Father worketh hitherto, and I work," the Jews, though most dull in regard to his other sayings, perceived that he was laying claim to divine power. And, therefore, as John relates (John 5:17), they sought the more to kill him, because he not only broke the Sabbath, but also said that God was his Father, making himself equal with God. What, then, will be our stupidity if we do not perceive from the same passage that his divinity is plainly instructed? To govern the world by his power and providence, and regulate all things by an energy inherent in himself (this an Apostle ascribes to him, Heb. 1:3), surely belongs to none but the Creator. Nor does he merely share the government of the world with the Father, but also each of the other offices, which cannot be communicated to creatures. The Lord proclaims by his prophets "I, even I, am he that blotteth out thy transgressions for mine own sake," (Is. 43:25). When, in accordance with this declaration, the Jews thought that injustice was done to God when Christ forgave sins, he not only asserted, in distinct terms, that this power belonged to him, but also proved it by a miracle (Mt. 9:6). We thus see that he possessed in himself not the ministry of forgiving sins, but the inherent power which the Lord declares he will not give to another. What! Is it not the province of God alone to penetrate and interrogate the secret thoughts of the heart? But Christ also had this power, and therefore we infer that Christ is God.

13. How clearly and transparently does this appear in his miracles? I admit that similar and equal miracles were performed by the prophets and apostles; but there is this very es- sential difference, that they dispensed the gifts of God as his ministers, whereas he exerted his own inherent might. Sometimes, indeed, he used prayer, that he might ascribe glory to the Father, but we see that for the most part

his own proper power is displayed. And how should not he be the true author of miracles, who, of his own authority, commissions others to perform them? For the Evangelist relates that he gave power to the apostles to cast out devils, cure the lepers, raise the dead, &c. And they, by the mode in which they performed this ministry, showed plainly that their whole power was derived from Christ. "In the name of Jesus Christ of Nazareth," says Peter (Acts 3:6), "rise up and walk." It is not surprising, then, that Christ appealed to his miracles in order to subdue the unbelief of the Jews, inasmuch as these were performed by his own energy, and therefore bore the most ample testimony to his divinity.

Again, if out of God there is no salvation, no righteousness, no life, Christ, having all these in himself, is certainly God. Let no one object that life or salvation is transfused into him by God. For it is said not that he received, but that he himself is salvation. And if there is none good but God, how could a mere man be pure, how could he be, I say not good and just, but goodness and justice? Then what shall we say to the testimony of the Evangelist, that from the very beginning of the creation "in him was life, and this life was the light of men?" Trusting to such proofs, we can boldly put our hope and faith in him, though we know it is blasphemous impiety to confide in any creature. "Ye believe in God," says he, "believe also in me," (John 14:1). And so Paul (Rom. 10:11, and 15:12) interprets two passages of Isaiah "Whose believeth in him shall not be confounded," (Isa. 28:16); and, "In that day there shall be a root of Jesse, which shall stand for an ensign of the people; to it shall the Gentiles seek," (Isa. 11:10). But why adduce more passages of Scripture on this head, when we so often meet with the expression, "He that believeth in me has eternal life?"

Again, the prayer of faith is addressed to him—prayer, which specially belongs to the divine majesty, if anything so belongs. For the Prophet Joel says, "And it shall come to pass, that whosoever shall call on the name of the Lord (Jehovah) shall be delivered" (Joel 2:32). And another says, "The name of the Lord (Jehovah) is a strong tower; the righteous runneth into it and is safe," (Prov. 18:10). But the name of Christ is invoked for salvation, and therefore it follows that he is Jehovah. Moreover, we have an example of invocation in Stephen, when he said, "Lord Jesus, receive my spirit;" and thereafter in the whole Church, when Ananias says in the same book, "Lord, I have heard by many of this man, how much evil he has done to thy saints at Jerusalem; and here he has authority from the chief priests to bind all that call on thy name," (Acts 9:13, 14). And to make it more clearly understood that in Christ dwelt the whole fulness of the Godhead bodily, the Apostle declares that the only doctrine which he professed to the Corinthians, the only doctrine which he taught, was the knowledge of Christ (1 Cor. 2:2). Consider what kind of thing it is, and how great, that the name of the Son alone is preached to us, though God command us to glory only in the knowledge of himself (Jer. 9:24). Who will dare to maintain that he, whom to know forms our only ground of glorying, is a mere creature? To this we may add, that the salutations prefixed to the Epistles of Paul pray for the same blessings from the Son as from the Father. By this we are taught, not only that the blessings which our heavenly Father bestows come to us through his intercession, but that by a partnership in power, the Son himself is their author. This practical knowledge is doubtless surer and more solid than any idle speculation. For the pious soul has the best view of God, and may almost be said to handle him, when it feels that it is quickened, enlightened, saved, justified, and sanctified by him.

14. In asserting the divinity of the Spirit, the proof must be derived from the same sources. And it is by no means an obscure testimony which Moses bears in the history of the creation, when he says that the Spirit of God was expanded

over the abyss or shapeless matter; for it shows not only that the beauty which the world displays is maintained by the invigorating power of the Spirit, but that even before this beauty existed the Spirit was at work cherishing the confused mass. Again, no cavils can explain away the force of what Isaiah says, "And now the Lord God, and his Spirit, has sent me," (Isa. 48:16), thus ascribing a share in the sovereign power of sending the prophets to the Holy Spirit. (Calvin in Acts 20:28). In this his divine majesty is clear.

But, as I observed, the best proof to us is our familiar experience. For nothing can be more alien from a creature, than the office which the Scriptures ascribe to him, and which the pious actually feel him discharging,—his being diffused over all space, sustaining, invigorating, and quickening all things, both in heaven and on the earth. The mere fact of his not being circumscribed by any limits raises him above the rank of creatures, while his transfusing vigour into all things, breathing into them being, life, and motion, is plainly divine. Again, if regeneration to incorruptible life is higher, and much more excellent than any present quickening, what must be thought of him by whose energy it is produced? Now, many passages of Scripture show that he is the author of regeneration, not by a borrowed, but by an intrinsic energy; and not only so, but that he is also the author of future immortality. In short, all the peculiar attributes of the Godhead are ascribed to him in the same way as to the Son. He searches the deep things of Gods and has no counsellor among the creatures; he bestows wisdom and the faculty of speech, though God declares to Moses (Exod. 4:11) that this is his own peculiar province. In like manner, by means of him we be- come partakers of the divine nature, so as in a manner to feel his quickening energy within us. Our justification is his work; from him is power, sanctification, truth, grace, and every good thought, since it is from the Spirit alone that all good gifts proceed. Particular attention is due to Paul's expression, that though there are diversities of gifts, "all these worketh that one and the self-same Spirit," (1 Cor. 12:11), he being not only the beginning or origin, but also the author; as is even more clearly expressed immediately after in these words "dividing to every man severally as he will." For were he not something subsisting in God, will and arbitrary disposal would never be ascribed to him. Most clearly, therefore does Paul ascribe divine power to the Spirit, and demonstrate that he dwells hypostatically in God.

15. Nor does the Scripture, in speaking of him, withhold the name of God. Paul infers that we are the temple of God, from the fact that "the Spirit of God dwelleth in us," (1 Cor. 3:16; 6:19; and 2 Cor. 6:16). Now it ought not to be slightly overlooked, that all the promises which God makes of choosing us to himself as a temple, receive their only fulfilment by his Spirit dwelling in us. Surely, as it is admirably expressed by Augustine (Ad Maximinum, Ep. 66), "were we ordered to make a temple of wood and stone to the Spirit, inasmuch as such worship is due to God alone, it would be a clear proof of the Spirit's divinity; how much clearer a proof in that we are not to make a temple to him, but to be ourselves that temple." And the Apostle says at one time that we are the temple of God, and at another time, in the same sense, that we are the temple of the Holy Spirit. Peter, when he rebuked Ananias for having lied to the Holy Spirit, said, that he had not lied unto men, but unto God. And when Isaiah had introduced the Lord of Hosts as speaking, Paul says, it was the Holy Spirit that spoke (Acts 28:25, 26). Nay, words uniformly said by the prophets to have been spoken by the Lord of Hosts, are by Christ and his apostles ascribed to the Holy Spirit. Hence it follows that the Spirit is the true Jehovah who dictated the prophecies. Again, when God complains that he was provoked to anger by the stubbornness of the people, in place of Him, Isaiah says that his Holy Spirit was

grieved (Isa. 63:10). Lastly, while blasphemy against the Spirit is not forgiven, either in the present life or that which is to come, whereas he who has blasphemed against the Son may obtain pardon, that majesty must certainly be divine which it is an inexpiable crime to offend or impair. I designedly omit several passages which the ancient fathers adduced. They thought it plausible to quote from David, "By the word of the Lord were the heavens made, and all the host of them by the breath (Spirit) of his mouth," (Ps. 33:6), in order to prove that the world was not less the work of the Holy Spirit than of the Son. But seeing it is usual in the Psalms to repeat the same thing twice, and in Isaiah the *spirit* (breath) of the mouth is equivalent to *word*, that proof was weak; and, accordingly, my wish has been to advert briefly to those proofs on which pious minds may securely rest.

16. But as God has manifested himself more clearly by the advent of Christ, so he has made himself more familiarly known in three persons. Of many proofs let this one suffice. Paul connects together these three, God, Faith, and Baptism, and reasons from the one to the other—viz. because there is one faith he infers that there is one God; and because there is one baptism he infers that there is one faith. Therefore, if by baptism we are initiated into the faith and worship of one God, we must of necessity believe that he into whose name we are baptised is the true God. And there cannot be a doubt that our Saviour wished to testify, by a solemn rehearsal, that the perfect light of faith is now exhibited, when he said, "Go and teach all nations, baptising them in the name of the Father, and of the Son, and of the Holy Spirit," (Mt. 28:19), since this is the same thing as to be baptised into the name of the one God, who has been fully manifested in the Father, the Son, and the Spirit. Hence it plainly appears, that the three persons, in whom alone God is known, subsist in the Divine essence. And since faith certainly ought not to look hither and

thither, or run up and down after various objects, but to look, refer, and cleave to God alone, it is obvious that were there various kinds of faith, there behaved also to be various gods. Then, as the baptism of faith is a sacrament, its unity assures us of the unity of God. Hence also it is proved that it is lawful only to be baptised into one God, because we make a profession of faith in him in whose name we are baptised. What, then, is our Saviour's meaning in commanding baptism to be administered in the name of the Father, and the Son, and the Holy Spirit, if it be not that we are to believe with one faith in the name of the Father, and the Son, and the Holy Spirit? But is this any thing else than to declare that the Father, Son, and Spirit, are one God? Wherefore, since it must be held certain that there is one God, not more than one, we conclude that the Word and Spirit are of the very essence of God. Nothing could be more stupid than the trifling of the Arians, who, while acknowledging the divinity of the Son, denied his divine essence. Equally extravagant were the ravings of the Macedonians, who insisted that by the Spirit were only meant the gifts of grace poured out upon men. For as wisdom understanding, prudence, fortitude, and the fear of the Lord, proceed from the Spirit, so he is the one Spirit of wisdom, prudence, fortitude, and piety. He is not divided according to the distribution of his gifts, but, as the Apostle assures us (1 Cor. 12:11), however they be divided, he remains one and the same.

17. On the other hand, the Scriptures demonstrate that there is some distinction between the Father and the Word, the Word and the Spirit; but the magnitude of the mystery reminds us of the great reverence and soberness which ought to he employed in discussing it. It seems to me, that nothing can be more admirable than the words of Gregory Nanzianzen: " Ου φθανω το ει νοησαι, και τοις τρισι περιλαμπομαι ου φθανω τα τρια διελειν και εις το εν αναφερομαι" (Greg. Nanzian. in Serm. de Sacro Baptis.).

"I cannot think of the unity without being irradiated by the Trinity: I cannot distinguish between the Trinity without being carried up to the unity." Therefore, let us beware of imagining such a Trinity of persons as will distract our thoughts, instead of bringing them instantly back to the unity. The words Father, Son, and Holy Spirit, certainly indicate a real distinction, not allowing us to suppose that they are merely epithets by which God is variously designated from his works. Still they indicate distinction only, not division. The passages we have already quoted show that the Son has a distinct subsistence from the Father, because the Word could not have been with God unless he were distinct from the Father; nor but for this could he have had his glory with the Father. In like manner, Christ distinguishes the Father from himself when he says that there is another who bears witness of him (John 5:32; 8:16). To the same effect is it elsewhere said, that the Father made all things by the Word. This could not be, if he were not in some respect distinct from him. Besides, it was not the Father that descended to the earth, but he who came forth from the Father; nor was it the Father that died and rose again, but he whom the Father had sent. This distinction did not take its beginning at the incarnation: for it is clear that the only begotten Son previously existed in the bosom of the Father (John 1:18). For who will dare to affirm that the Son entered his Father's bosom for the first time, when he came down from heaven to assume human nature? Therefore, he was previously in the bosom of the Father, and had his glory with the Father. Christ intimates the distinction between the Holy Spirit and the Father, when he says that the Spirit proceedeth from the Father, and between the Holy Spirit and himself, when he speaks of him as another as he does when he declares that he will send another Comforter; and in many other passages besides (John 14:6; 15:26; 14:16).

18. I am not sure whether it is expedient to borrow analogies from human affairs to express the nature of this distinction. The ancient fathers sometimes do so, but they at the same time admits that what they bring forward as analogous is very widely different. And hence it is that I have a great dread of any thing like presumption here, lest some rash saying may furnish an occasion of calumny to the malicious, or of delusion to the unlearned. It were unbecoming, however, to say nothing of a distinction which we observe that the Scriptures have pointed out. This distinction is, that to the Father is attributed the beginning of action, the fountain and source of all things; to the Son, wisdom, counsel, and arrangement in action, while the energy and efficacy of action is assigned to the Spirit. Moreover, though the eternity of the Father is also the eternity of the Son and Spirit, since God never could be without his own wisdom and energy; and though in eternity there can be no room for first or last, still the distinction of order is not unmeaning or superfluous, the Father being considered first, next the Son from him, and then the Spirit from both. For the mind of every man naturally inclines to consider, first, God, secondly, the wisdom emerging from him, and, lastly, the energy by which he executes the purposes of his counsel. For this reason, the Son is said to be of the Father only; the Spirit of both the Father and the Son. This is done in many passages, but in none more clearly than in the eighth chapter to the Romans, where the same Spirit is called indiscriminately the Spirit of Christ, and the Spirit of him who raised up Christ from the dead. And not improperly. For Peter also testifies (1 Pet. 1:21), that it was the Spirit of Christ which inspired the prophets, though the Scriptures so often say that it was the Spirit of God the Father.

19. Moreover, this distinction is so far from interfering with the most perfect unity of God, that the Son may thereby be proved to be one God with the Father, inasmuch

as he constitutes one Spirit with him, and that the Spirit is not different from the Father and the Son, inasmuch as he is the Spirit of the Father and the Son. In each hypostasis the whole nature is understood the only difference being that each has his own peculiar subsistence. The whole Father is in the Son, and the whole Son in the Father, as the Son himself also declares (John 14:10), "I am in the Father, and the Father in me;" nor do ecclesiastical writers admit that the one is separated from the other by any difference of essence. "By those names which denote distinctions" says Augustine "is meant the relation which they mutually bear to each other, not the very substance by which they are one." In this way, the sentiments of the Fathers, which might sometimes appear to be at variance with each other, are to be reconciled. At one time they teach that the Father is the beginning of the Son, at another they assert that the Son has both divinity and essence from himself, and therefore is one beginning with the Father. The cause of this discrepancy is well and clearly explained by Augustine, when he says, "Christ, as to himself, is called God, as to the Father he is called Son." And again, "The Father, as to himself, is called God, as to the Son he is called Father. He who, as to the Son, is called Father, is not Son; and he who, as to himself, is called Father, and he who, as to himself, is called Son, is the same God." Therefore, when we speak of the Son simply, without reference to the Father, we truly and properly affirm that he is of himself, and, accordingly, call him the only beginning; but when we denote the relation which he bears to the Father, we correctly make the Father the beginning of the Son. Augustine's fifth book on the Trinity is wholly devoted to the explanation of this subject. But it is far safer to rest contented with the relation as taught by him, than get bewildered in vain speculation by subtle prying into a sublime mystery.

20. Let those, then, who love soberness, and are contented with the measure of faith, briefly receive what is

useful to be known. It is as follows: — When we profess to believe in one God, by the name God is understood the one simple essence, comprehending three persons or hypostases; and, accordingly, whenever the name of God is used indefinitely, the Son and Spirit, not less than the Father, is meant. But when the Son is joined with the Father, relation comes into view, and so we distinguish between the Persons. But as the Personal subsistence carry an order with them, the principle and origin being in the Father, whenever mention is made of the Father and Son, or of the Father and Spirit together, the name of God is specially given to the Father. In this way the unity of essence is retained, and respect is had to the order, which, however derogates in no respect from the divinity of the Son and Spirit. And surely since we have already seen how the apostles declare the Son of God to have been He whom Moses and the prophets declared to be Jehovah, we must always arrive at a unity of essence. We, therefore, hold it detestable blasphemy to call the Son a different God from the Father, because the simple name God admits not of relation, nor can God, considered in himself, be said to be this or that. Then, that the name Jehovah, taken indefinitely, may be applied to Christ, is clear from the words of Paul, "For this thing I besought the Lord thrice." After giving the answer, "My grace is sufficient for thee," he subjoins, "that the power of Christ may rest upon me," (2 Cor. 12:8, 9). For it is certain that the name of Lord (Κύριος) is there put for Jehovah, and, therefore, to restrict it to the person of the Mediator were puerile and frivolous, the words being used absolutely, and not with the view of comparing the Father and the Son. And we know that, in accordance with the received usage of the Greeks, the apostles uniformly substitute the word Κύριος for Jehovah. Not to go far for an example, Paul besought the Lord in the same sense in which Peter quotes the passage of Joel, "Whosoever shall call upon the name of the Lord shall be saved," (Acts 2:21;

Joel 2:28). Where this name is specially applied to the Son, there is a different ground for it, as will be seen in its own place; at present it is sufficient to remember, that Paul, after praying to God absolutely, immediately subjoins the name of Christ. Thus, too, the Spirit is called God absolutely by Christ himself. For nothing prevents us from holding that he is the entire spiritual essence of God, in which are comprehended Father, Son, and Spirit. This is plain from Scripture. For as God is there called a Spirit, so the Holy Spirit also, in so far as he is a hypostasis of the whole essence, is said to be both of God and from God.

21. But since Satan, in order to pluck up our faith by the roots, has always provoked fierce disputes, partly concerning the divine essence of the Son and Spirit, and partly concerning the distinction of persons; since in almost every age he has stirred up impious spirits to vex the orthodox doctors on this head, and is attempting in the present day to kindle a new flame out of the old embers, it will be proper here to dispose of some of these perverse dreams. Hitherto our chief object has been to stretch out our hand for the guidance of such as are disposed to learn, not to war with the stubborn and contentious; but now the truth which was calmly demonstrated must be vindicated from the calumnies of the ungodly. Still, however it will be our principal study to provide a sure footing for those whose ears are open to the word of God. Here, if any where, in considering the hidden mysteries of Scripture, we should speculate soberly and with great moderation, cautiously guarding against allowing either our mind or our tongue to go a step beyond the confines of God's word. For how can the human minds which has not yet been able to ascertain of what the body of the sun consists, though it is daily presented to the eye, bring down the boundless essence of God to its little measure? Nay, how can it, under its own guidance, penetrate to a knowledge of the substance of God while unable to understand its own? Wherefore, let

us willingly leave to God the knowledge of himself. In the words of Hilary (De Trinit. lib. 1), "He alone is a fit witness to himself who is known only by himself." This knowledge, then, if we would leave to God, we must conceive of him as he has made himself known, and in our inquiries make application to no other quarter than his word. On this subject we have five homilies of Chrysostom against the Anomoei (De Incomprehensit. Dei Natura), in which he endeavoured, but in vain, to check the presumption of the sophists, and curb their garrulity. They showed no more modesty here than they are wont to do in everything else. The very unhappy results of their temerity should be a warning to us to bring more docility than acumen to the discussion of this question, never to attempt to search after God anywhere but in his sacred word, and never to speak or think of him farther than we have it for our guide. But if the distinction of Father, Son, and Spirit, subsisting in the one Godhead (certainly a subject of great difficulty), gives more trouble and annoyance to some intellects than is meet, let us remember that the human mind enters a labyrinth whenever it indulges its curiosity, and thus submit to be guided by the divine oracles, how much soever the mystery may be beyond our reach.

22. It were tedious, and to no purpose toilsome, to form a catalogue of the errors by which, in regard to this branch of doctrine, the purity of the faith has been assailed. The greater part of heretics have with their gross deliriums made a general attack on the glory of God, deeming it enough if they could disturb and shake the unwary. From a few individuals numerous sects have sprung up, some of them rending the divine essence, and others con- founding the distinction of Persons. But if we hold, what has already been demonstrated from Scripture, that the essence of the one God, pertaining to the Father, Son, and Spirit, is simple and indivisible, and again, that the Father differs in some special property from the Son, and the Son from the Spirit,

the door will be shut against Arius and Sabellius, as well as the other ancient authors of error. But as in our day have arisen certain frantic men, such as Servetus and others, who, by new devices, have thrown every thing into confusion, it may be worthwhile briefly to discuss their fallacies.

The name of Trinity was so much disliked, nay detested, by Servetus, that he charged all whom he called Trinitarians with being Atheists. I say nothing of the insulting terms in which he thought proper to make his charges. The sum of his speculations was, that a threefold Deity is introduced wherever three Persons are said to exist in his essence, and that this Triad was imaginary, inasmuch as it was inconsistent with the unity of God. At the same time, he would have it that the Persons are certain external ideas which do not truly subsist in the Divine essence, but only figure God to us under this or that form: that at first, indeed, there was no distinction in God, because originally the Word was the same as the Spirit, but ever since Christ came forth God of God, another Spirit, also a God, had proceeded from him. But although he sometimes cloaks his absurdities in allegory, as when he says that the eternal Word of God was the Spirit of Christ with God, and the reflection of the idea, likewise that the Spirit was a shadow of Deity, he at last reduces the divinity of both to nothing; maintaining that, according to the mode of distribution, there is a part of God as well in the Son as in the Spirit, just as the same Spirit substantially is a portion of God in us, and also in wood and stone. His absurd babbling concerning the person of the Mediator will be seen in its own place.

The monstrous fiction that a Person is nothing else than a visible appearance of the glory of God, needs not a long refutation. For when John declares that before the world was created the Logos was God (John 1:1), he shows that he was something very different from an idea. But if even then, and from the remotest eternity, that Logos, who was God, was with the Father, and had his own distinct and peculiar glory with the Father (John 17:5), he certainly could not be an external or figurative splendour, but must necessarily have been a hypostasis which dwelt inherently in God himself. But although there is no mention made of the Spirit antecedent to the account of the creation, he is not there introduced as a shadow, but as the essential power of God, where Moses relates that the shapeless mass was unborn by him (Gen. 1:2). It is obvious that the eternal Spirit always existed in God, seeing he cherished and sustained the confused materials of heaven and earth before they possessed order or beauty. Assuredly he could not then be an image or representation of God, as Ser- vetus dreams. But he is elsewhere forced to make a more open disclosure of his impiety when he says, that God by his eternal reason decreeing a Son to himself, in this way assumed a visible appearance. For if this be true, no other Divinity is left to Christ than is implied in his having been ordained a Son by God's eternal decree. Moreover, those phantoms which Servetus substitutes for the hypostases he so transforms as to make new changes in God. But the most execrable heresy of all is his confounding both the Son and Spirit promiscuously with all the creatures. For he distinctly asserts, that there are parts and partitions in the es- sence of God, and that every such portion is God. This he does especially when he says, that the spirits of the faithful are co-eternal and consubstantial with God, although he elsewhere assigns a substantial divinity, not only to the soul of man, but to all created things.

23. This pool has bred another monster not unlike the former. For certain restless spirits, unwilling to share the disgrace and obloquy of the impiety of Servetus, have confessed that there were indeed three Persons, but added, as a reason, that the Father, who alone is truly and properly God, transfused his Divinity into the Son and Spirit when

he formed them. Nor do they refrain from expressing themselves in such shocking terms as these: that the Father is essentially distinguished from the Son and Spirit by this; that he is the only *essentiator*. Their first pretext for this is, that Christ is uniformly called the Son of God. From this they infer, that there is no proper God but the Father. But they forget, that although the name of God is common also to the Son, yet it is sometimes, by way of excellence, ascribed to the Father, as being the source and principle of Divinity; and this is done in order to mark the simple unity of essence. They object, that if the Son is truly God, he must be deemed the Son of a person: which is absurd. I answer, that both are true; namely, that he is the Son of God, because he is the Word, begotten of the Father before all ages; (for we are not now speaking of the Person of the Mediator), and yet, that for the purpose of explanation, regard must be had to the Person, so that the name God may not be understood in its absolute sense, but as equivalent to Father. For if we hold that there is no other God than the Fathers this rank is clearly denied to the Son.

In every case where the Godhead is mentioned, we are by no means to admit that there is an antithesis between the Father and the Son, as if to the former only the name of God could competently be applied. For assuredly, the God who appeared to Isaiah was the one true God, and yet John declares that he was Christ (Isa. 6; John 12:41). He who declared, by the mouth of Isaiah, that he was to be "for a stone of stumbling" to the Jews, was the one God; and yet Paul declares that he was Christ (Isa. 8:14; Rom. 9:33). He who proclaims by Isaiah, "Unto me every knee shall bow," is the one God; yet Paul again explains that he is Christ (Isa. 45:23; Rom. 14:11). To this we may add the passages quoted by an Apostle, "Thou, Lord, hast laid the foundations of the earth;" "Let all the angels of God worship him," (Heb. 1:10; 10:6; Ps. 102:26; 97:7). All these apply to the one God; and yet the Apostle con- tends that they are the proper attributes of Christ. There is nothing in the cavil, that what properly applies to God is transferred to Christ, because he is the brightness of his glory. Since the name of Jehovah is everywhere applied to Christ, it follows that, in regard to Deity, he is of himself. For if he is Jehovah, it is impossible to deny that he is the same God who elsewhere proclaims by Isaiah, "I am the first, and I am the last; and beside me there is no God," (Is. 44:6). We would also do well to ponder the words of Jeremiah, "The gods that have not made the heavens and the earth, even they shall perish from the earth and from under these heavens," (Jer. 10:11); whence it follows conversely, that He whose divinity Isaiah repeatedly proves from the creation of the world, is none other than the Son of God. And how is it possible that the Creator, who gives to all should not be of himself, but should borrow his essence from another? Whosoever says that the Son was *essentiated* by the Father, denies his selfexistence. Against this, however, the Holy Spirit protests, when he calls him Jehovah. On the supposition, then, that the whole essence is in the Father only, the essence becomes divisible, or is denied to the Son, who, being thus robbed of his essences will be only a titular God. If we are to believe these triflers, divine essence belongs to the Father only, on the ground that he is sole God, and *essentiator* of the Son. In this way, the divinity of the Son will be something abstracte from the essence of God, or the derivation of a part from the whole. On the same principle it must also be conceded, that the Spirit belongs to the Father only. For if the derivation is from the primary essence which is proper to none but the Father, the Spirit cannot justly be deemed the Spirit of the Son. This view, however, is refuted by the testimony of Paul, when he makes the Spirit common both to Christ and the Father. Moreover, if the Person of the Father is expunged from the Trinity, in what will he differ from the Son and Spirit, except in being the only God? They confess that Christ is God, and that he differs from the Father. If he differs, there must be some mark of distinction between them. Those who place it in the essence, manifestly reduce the true divinity of Christ to nothing, since divinity cannot exist without essence, and indeed without entire essence. The Father certainly cannot differ from the Son, unless he have something peculiar to himself, and not common to him with the Son. What, then, do these men show as the mark of distinction? If it is in the essence, let them tell whether or not he communicated essence to the Son. This he could not do in part merely, for it were impious to think of a divided God. And besides, on this supposition, there would be a rending of the Divine essence. The whole entire essence must therefore be common to the Father and the Son; and if so, in respect of essence there is no distinction between them. If they reply that the Father, while essentiating, still remains the only God, being the possessor of the essence, then Christ will be a figurative God, one in name or semblance only, and not in reality, be- cause no property can be more peculiar to God than essence, according to the words, "I Am hath sent me unto you," (Ex. 3:4).

24. The assumption, that whenever God is mentioned absolutely, the Father only is meant, may be proved erroneous by many passages. Even in those which they quote in support of their views they betray a lamentable inconsistency because the name of Son occurs there by way of contrast, showing that the other name God is used relatively, and in that way confined to the person of the Father. Their objection may be disposed of in a single word. Were not the Father alone the true God, he would, say they, be his own Father. But there is nothing absurd in the name of God being specially applied, in respect of order and degree, to him who not only of himself begat his own wisdom, but is the God of the Mediator, as I will more fully show in its own place. For ever since Christ was manifested

in the flesh he is called the Son of God, not only because begotten of the Father before all worlds he was the Eternal Word, but because he undertook the person and office of the Mediator that he might unite us to God. Seeing they are so bold in excluding the Son from the honour of God, I would fain know whether, when he declares that there is "none good but one, that is, God," he deprives himself of goodness. I speak not of his human nature, lest perhaps they should object, that whatever goodness was in it was derived by gratuitous gift: I ask whether the Eternal Word of God is good, yes or no? If they say no, their impiety is manifest; if yes, they refute themselves. Christ's seeming at the first glance to disclaim the name of good (Mt. 19:17), rather confirms our view. Goodness. being the special property of God alone, and yet being at the time applied to him in the ordinary way of salutation, his rejection of false honour intimates that the goodness in which he excels is Divine. Again, I ask whether, when Paul affirms. that God alone is "immortal," "wise, and true," (1 Tim. 1:17), he reduces Christ to the rank of beings mortal, foolish, and false. Is not he immortal, who, from the beginning, had life so as to bestow immortality on angels? Is not he wise who is the eternal wisdom of God? Is not he true who is truth itself?

I ask, moreover, whether they think Christ should be worshipped. If he claims justly, that every knee shall bow to him, it follows that he is the God who, in the law, forbade worship to be offered to any but himself. If they insist on applying to the Father only the words of Isaiah, "I am, and besides me there is none else," (Is. 44:6), I turn the passage against themselves, since we see that every property of God is attributed to Christ. There is no room for the cavil that Christ was exalted in the flesh in which he humbled himself, and in respect of which all power is given to him in heaven and on earth. For although the majesty of King and Judge extends to the whole person of the

Mediator, yet had he not been God manifested in the flesh, he could not have been exalted to such a height without coming into collision with God. And the dispute is admirably settled by Paul, when he declares that he was equal with God before he humbled himself, and assumed the form of a servants (Phil. 2:6, 7). Moreover, how could such equality exist, if he were not that God whose name is Jah and Jehovah, who rides upon the cherubim, is King of all the earth, and King of ages? Let them glamour as they may, Christ cannot be robbed of the honour described by Isaiah, "Lo, this is our God; we have waited for him," (Is. 25:9); for these words describe the advent of God the Redeemer, who was not only to bring back the people from Babylonish captivity, but restore the Church, and make her completely perfect.

Nor does another cavil avail them, that Christ was God in his Father. For though we admit that, in respect of order and gradation, the beginning of divinity is in the Father, we hold it a detestable fiction to maintain that essence is proper to the Father alone, as if he were the deifier of the Son. On this view either the essence is manifold, or Christ is God only in name and imagination. If they grant that the Son is God, but only in subordination to the Father, the essence which in the Father is unformed and unbegotten will in him be formed and begotten. I know that many who would be thought wise deride us for extracting the distinction of persons from the words of Moses when he introduces God as saying, "Let us make man in our own image," (Gen. 1:26). Pious readers, however, see how frigidly and absurdly the colloquy were introduced by Moses, if there were not several persons in the Godhead. It is certain that those whom the Father addresses must have been untreated. But nothing is untreated except the one God. Now then, unless they concede that the power of creating was common to the Father, Son, and Spirit, and the power of commanding common, it will follow that God did not speak

thus inwardly with himself, but addressed other ex-
traneous architects. In fine, there is a single passage which
will at once dispose of these two objections. The
declaration of Christ that "God is a Spirit," (John 4:24),
cannot be confined to the Father only, as if the Word were
not of a spiritual nature. But if the name Spirit applies
equally to the Son as to the Father, I infer that under the
indefinite name of God the Son is included. He adds
immediately after, that the only worshipers approved by the
Father are those who worship him in spirit and in truth; and
hence I also infer, that because Christ performs the office of
teacher under a head, he applies the name God to the
Father, not for the purpose of destroying his own Divinity,
but for the purpose of raising us up to it as it were step by
step.

25. The hallucination consists in dreaming of
individuals, each of whom possesses a part of the essence.
The Scriptures teach that there is essentially but one God,
and, therefore, that the essence both of the Son and Spirit is
unbegotten; but inasmuch as the Father is first in order, and
of himself begat his own Wisdom, he, as we lately
observed, is justly regarded as the principle and fountain of
all the Godhead. Thus God, taken indefinitely, is
unbegotten, and the Father, in respect of his person, is
unbegotten. For it is absurd to imagine that our doctrine
gives any ground for alleging that we establish a quaternion
of gods. They falsely and calumniously ascribe to us the
figment of their own brain, as if we virtually held that three
persons emanate from one essence, whereas it is plain,
from our writings, that we do not disjoin the persons from
the essence, but interpose a distinction between the persons
residing in it. If the persons were separated from the
essence, there might be some plausibility in their argument;
as in this way there would be a trinity of Gods, not of
persons comprehended in one God. This affords an answer
to their futile question—whether or not the essence concurs

in forming the Trinity; as if we imagined that three Gods were derived from it. Their objection, that there would thus be a Trinity without a God, originates in the same absurdity. Although the essence does not contribute to the distinction, as if it were a part or member, the persons are not without it, or external to it; for the Father, if he were not God, could not be the Father; nor could the Son possibly be Son unless he were God. We say, then, that the Godhead is absolutely of itself. And hence also we hold that the Son, regarded as God, and without reference to person, is also of himself; though we also say that, regarded as Son, he is of the Father. Thus his essence is without beginning, while his person has its beginning in God. And, indeed, the orthodox writers who in former times spoke of the Trinity, used this term only with reference to the Persons. To have included the essence in the distinction, would not only have been an absurd error, but gross impiety. For those who class the three thus—Essence, Son, and Spirit—plainly do away with the essence of the Son and Spirit; otherwise the parts being intermingled would merge into each other—a circumstance which would vitiate any distinction. In short, if God and Father were synonymous terms, the Father would be deifier in a sense which would leave the Son nothing but a shadow; and the Trinity would be nothing more than the union of one God with two creatures.

26. To the objection, that if Christ be properly God, he is improperly called the Son of God, it has been already answered, that when one person is compared with another, the name God is not used indefinitely, but is restricted to the Father, regarded as the beginning of the Godhead, not by *essentiating*, as fanatics absurdly express it, but in respect of order. In this sense are to be understood the words which Christ addressed to the Father, "This is life eternal, that they might know thee the only true God, and Jesus Christ whom thou hast sent," (John 17:3). For speaking in the person of the Mediator, he holds a middle

place between God and man; yet so that his majesty is not diminished thereby. For though he humbled (emptied) himself, he did not lose the glory which he had with the Father, though it was concealed from the world. So in the Epistle to the Hebrews (Heb. 1:10; 2:9), though the apostle confesses that Christ was made a little lower than the angels, he at the same time hesitates not to assert that he is the eternal God who founded the earth. We must hold, therefore, that as often as Christ, in the character of Mediator, addresses the Father, he, under the term God, includes his own divinity also. Thus, when he says to the apostles, "It is expedient for you that I go away," "My Father is greater than I," he does not attribute to himself a secondary divinity merely, as if in regard to eternal essence he were inferior to the Father; but having obtained celestial glory, he gathers together the faithful to share it with him. He places the Father in the higher degree, inasmuch as the full perfection of brightness conspicuous in heaven, differs from that measure of glory which he himself displayed when clothed in flesh. For the same reason Paul says, that Christ will restore "the kingdom to God, even the Father," "that God may be all in all," (1 Cor. 15:24, 28). Nothing can be more absurd than to deny the perpetuity of Christ's divinity. But if he will never cease to be the Son of God, but will ever remain the same that he was from the beginning, it follows that under the name of Father the one divine essence common to both is comprehended. And assuredly Christ descended to us for the very purpose of raising us to the Father, and thereby, at the same time, raising us to himself, inasmuch as he is one with the Father. It is therefore erro- neous and impious to confine the name of God to the Father, so as to deny it to the Son. Accordingly, John, declaring that he is the true God, has no idea of placing him beneath the Father in a subordinate rank of divinity. I wonder what these fabricators of new gods mean, when they confess that Christ is truly God, and yet exclude him from the godhead of the Father, as if there could be any true God but the one God, or as if transfused divinity were not a mere modern fiction.

27. In the many passages which they collect from Irenæus, in which he maintains that the Father of Christ is the only eternal God of Israel, they betray shameful ignorance, or very great dishonesty. For they ought to have observed, that that holy man was contending against certain frantic persons, who, denying that the Father of Christ was that God who had in old times spoken by Moses and the prophets, held that he was some phantom or other produced from the pollution of the world. His whole object, therefore, is to make it plain, that in the Scriptures no other God is announced but the Father of Christ; that it is wicked to imagine any other. Accordingly, there is nothing strange in his so often concluding that the God of Israel was no other than he who is celebrated by Christ and the apostles. Now, when a different heresy is to be resisted, we also say with truth, that the God who in old times appeared to the fathers, was no other than Christ. Moreover, if it is objected that he was the Father, we have the answer ready, that while we contend for the divinity of the Son, we by no means exclude the Father. When the reader attends to the purpose of Irenæus, the dispute is at an end. Indeed, we have only to look to lib. 3 c. 6, where the pious writer insists on this one point, "that he who in Scripture is called God absolutely and indefinitely, is truly the only God; and that Christ is called God absolutely." Let us remember (as appears from the whole work, and especially from lib. 2 c. 46), that the point under discussion was, that the name of Father is not applied enigmatically and parabolically to one who was not truly God. We may adds that in lib. 3 c. 9, he contends that the Son as well as the Father united was the God proclaimed by the prophets and apostles. He afterwards explains (lib. 3 c. 12) how Christ, who is Lord of all, and King and Judge, received power from him who is God of

all, namely, in respect of the humiliation by which he humbled himself, even to the death of the cross. At the same time he shortly after affirms (lib. 3 c. 16), that the Son is the maker of heaven and earth, who delivered the law by the hand of Moses, and appeared to the fathers. Should any babbler now insist that, according to Irenaeus, the Father alone is the God of Israel, I will refer him to a passage in which Irenaeus distinctly says (lib. 3 c. 18, 23), that Christ is ever one and the same, and also applies to Christ the words of the prophecy of Habakkuk, "God cometh from the south." To the same effect he says (lib. 4 c. 9), "Therefore, Christ himself, with the Father, is the God of the living." And in the 12th chapter of the same book he explains that Abraham believed God, because Christ is the maker of heaven and earth, and very God.

28. With no more truth do they claim Tertullian as a patron. Though his style is some- times rugged and obscure, he delivers the doctrine which we maintain in no ambiguous manner, namely, that while there is one God, his Word, however, is with dispensation or economy; that there is only one God in unity of substance; but that, nevertheless, by the mystery of dispensation, the unity is arranged into Trinity; that there are three, not in state, but in degree — not in substance, but in form — not in power, but in order. He says indeed that he holds the Son to be second to the Father; but he means that the only difference is by distinction. In one place he says the Son is visible; but after he has discoursed on both views, he declares that he is invisible regarded as the Word. In fine, by affirming that the Father is characterised by his own Person, he shows that he is very far from countenancing the fiction which we refute. And although he does not acknowledge any other God than the Father, yet, explaining himself in the immediate context, he shows that he does not speak exclusively in respect of the Son, because he denies that he is a different God from the Father; and, ac- cordingly, that the one

supremacy is not violated by the distinction of Person. And it is easy to collect his meaning from the whole tenor of his discourse. For he contends against Praxeas, that although God has three distinct Persons, yet there are not several gods, nor is unity divided. According to the fiction of Praxeas, Christ could not be God without being the Father also; and this is the reason why Tertullian dwells so much on the distinction. When he calls the Word and Spirit a portion of the whole, the expression, though harsh, may be allowed, since it does not refer to the substance, but only (as Tertullian himself testifies) denotes arrangement and economy which applies to the persons only. Accordingly, he asks, "How many persons, Praxeas, do you think there are, but just as many as there are names for?" In the same way, he shortly after says, "That they may believe the Father and the Son, each in his own name and person." These things, I think, sufficiently refute the effrontery of those who endeavour to blind the simple by pretending the authority of Tertullian.

29. Assuredly, whosoever will compare the writings of the ancient fathers with each other, will not find any thing in Irenaeus different from what is taught by those who come after him. Justin is one of the most ancient, and he agrees with us out and out. Let them object that, by him and others, the Father of Christ is called the one God. The same thing is taught by Hilary, who uses the still harsher expression, that Eternity is in the Father. Is it that he may withhold divine essence from the Son? His whole work is a defence of the doc- trine which we maintain; and yet these men are not ashamed to produce some kind of mu- tilated excerpts for the purpose of persuading us that Hilary is a patron of their heresy. With regard to what they pretend as to Ignatius, if they would have it to be of the least importance, let them prove that the apostles enacted laws concerning Lent, and other corruptions. Nothing can be more nauseating, than the absurdities which have been

published under the name of Ignatius; and therefore, the conduct of those who provide themselves with such masks for deception is the less entitled to toleration.

Moreover, the consent of the ancient fathers clearly appears from this, that in the Council of Nice, no attempt was made by Arius to cloak his heresy by the authority of any approved author; and no Greek or Latin writer apologises as dissenting from his predecessors. It cannot be necessary to observe how carefully Augustine, to whom all these miscreants are most violently opposed, examined all ancient writings, and how reverently he embraced the doctrine taught by them (August. lib. de Trinit. &c). He is most scrupulous in stating the grounds on which he is forced to differ from them, even in the minutest point. On this subject, too, if he finds any thing ambiguous or obscure in other writers, he does not disguise it. And he assumes it as an acknowledged fact, that the doctrine opposed by the Arians was received without dispute from the earliest antiquity. At the same time, he was not ignorant of what some others had previously taught. This is obvious from a single expression. When he says (De Doct. Christ. lib. 1). that "unity is in the Father," will they pretend that he then forgot himself? In another passage, he clears away every such charge, when he calls the Father the beginning of the Godhead, as being from none—thus wisely inferring that the name of God is specially ascribed to the Father, because, unless the beginning were from him, the simple unity of essence could not be maintained. I hope the pious reader will admit that I have now disposed of all the calumnies by which Satan has hitherto attempted to pervert or obscure the pure doctrine of faith. The whole substance of the doctrine has, I trust, been faithfully expounded, if my readers will set bounds to their curiosity, and not long more eagerly than they ought for perplexing disputation. I did not undertake to satisfy those who delight in speculate views, but I have not designedly omitted any thing which I thought adverse to me. At the same time, studying the edification of the Church, I have thought it better not to touch on various topics, which could have yielded little profit, while they must have needlessly burdened and fatigued the reader. For instance, what avails it to discuss, as Lombard does at length (lib. 1 dist. 9), Whether or not the Father always generates? This idea of continual generation becomes an absurd fiction from the moment it is seen, that from eternity there were three persons in one God.

CHAPTER 14.

IN THE CREATION OF THE WORLD, AND ALL THINGS IN IT, THE TRUE GOD DISTINGUISHED BY CERTAIN MARKS FROM FICTITIOUS GODS.

In this chapter commences the second part of Book First—viz. the knowledge of man. Certain things premised. I. The creation of the world generally (s. 1 and 2). II. The subject of angels considered (s. 3-13). III. Of bad angels or devils (s. 13-20); and, IV. The practical use to be made of the history of the creation (s. 20-22).

Sections.

1. The mere fact of creation should lead us to acknowledge God, but to prevent our falling away to Gentile fictions, God has been pleased to furnish a history of the creation. An impious objection, Why the world was not created sooner? Answer to it. Shrewd saying of an old man.

2. For the same reason, the world was created, not in an instant, but in six days. The order of creation described, showing that Adam was not created until God had, with infinite goodness made ample provision for him.

3. The doctrine concerning angels expounded. 1. That we may learn from them also to acknowledge God. 2. That we may be put on our guard against the errors of the worshippers of angels and the Manichees. Manicheeism refuted. Rule of piety.

4. The angels created by God. At what time and in what order it is inexpedient to inquire. The garrulity of the Pseudo- Dionysius.

5. The nature, offices, and various names of angels.

6. Angels the dispensers of the divine beneficence to us.

7. A kind of prefects over kingdoms and provinces, but specially the guardians of the elect. Not certain that every believer is under the charge of a single angel. Enough, that all angels watch over the safety of the Church.

8. The number and orders of angels not defined. Why angels said to be winged.

9. Angels are ministering spirits and spiritual essences.

10. The heathen error of placing angels on the throne of God refuted. 1. By passages of Scripture.

11. Refutation continued. 2. By inferences from other passages. Why God employs the ministry of angels.

12. Use of the doctrine of Scripture concerning the holy angels.

13. The doctrine concerning bad angels or devils reduced to four heads. 1. That we may guard against their wiles and assaults.

14. That we may be stimulated to exercises of piety. Why one angel in the singular number often spoken of.

15. The devil being described as the enemy of man, we should perpetually war against him.

16. The wickedness of the devil not by creation but by corruption. Vain and useless to inquire into the mode, time, and character of the fall of angels.

17. Though the devil is always opposed in will and endeavour to the will of God, he can do nothing without his permission and consent.

18. God so overrules wicked spirits as to permit them to try the faithful, and rule over the wicked.

19. The nature of bad angels. They are spiritual essences endued with sense and intelligence.

20. The latter part of the chapter briefly embracing the history of creation, and showing what it is of importance for us to know concerning God.

21. The special object of this knowledge is to prevent us, through ingratitude or thoughtlessness, from overlooking the perfections of God. Example of this primary

knowledge.

22. Another object of this knowledge—viz. that perceiving how these things were created for our use, we may be excited to trust in God, pray to him, and love him.

1. Although Isaiah justly charges the worshipers of false gods with stupidity, in not learning from the foundations of the earth, and the circle of the heavens, who the true God is (Isa. 40:21); yet so sluggish and grovelling is our intellect, that it was necessary he should be more clearly depicted, in order that the faithful might not fall away to Gentile fictions. the idea that God is the soul of the world, though the most tolerable that philosophers have suggested, is absurd; and, therefore, it was of importance to furnish us with a more intimate knowledge in order that we might not wander to and fro in uncertainty. Hence God was pleased that a history of the creation should exist—a history on which the faith of the Church might lean without seeking any other God than Him whom Moses sets forth as the Creator and Architect of the world. First, in that history, the period of time is marked so as to enable the faithful to ascend by an unbroken succession of years to the first origin of their race and of all things. This knowledge is of the highest use not only as an antidote to the monstrous fables which anciently prevailed both in Egypt and the other regions of the world, but also as a means of giving a clearer manifestation of the eternity of God as contrasted with the birth of creation, and thereby inspiring us with higher admiration. We must not be moved by the profane jeer, that it is strange how it did not sooner occur to the Deity to create the heavens and the earth, instead of idly allowing an infinite period to pass away, during which thousands of generations might have existed, while the present world is drawing to a close before it has completed its six thousandth year. Why God delayed so long it is

neither fit nor lawful to inquire. Should the human mind presume to do it, it could only fail in the at- tempt, nor would it be useful for us to know what God, as a trial of the modesty of our faith, has been pleased purposely to conceal. It was a shrewd saying of a good old man, who when some one pertly asked in derision what God did before the world was created, answered he made a hell for the inquisitive (August. Confess., lib. 11 c. 12). This reproof, not less weighty than severe, should repress the tickling wantonness which urges many to indulge in vicious and hurtful speculation.

In fine, let us remember that that invisible God, whose wisdom, power, and justice, are incomprehensible, is set before us in the history of Moses as in a mirror, in which his living image is reflected. For as an eye, either dimmed by age or weakened by any other cause, sees nothing distinctly without the aid of glasses, so (such is our imbecility) if Scripture does not direct us in our inquiries after God, we immediately turn vain in our imaginations. Those who now indulge their petulance, and refuse to take warning, will learn, when too late, how much better it had been reverently to regard the secret counsels of God, than to belch forth blasphemies which pollute the face of heaven. Justly does Augustine complain that God is insulted whenever any higher reason than his will is demanded. (Lib. de Gent.). He also in another place wisely reminds us that it is just as improper to raise questions about infinite periods of time as about infinite space. (De Civit. Dei.). However wide the circuit of the heavens may be, it is of some definite extent. But should any one expostulate with God that vacant space remains exceeding creation by a hundred-fold, must not every pious mind detest the presumption? Similar is the madness of those who charge God with idleness in not having pleased them by creating the world countless ages sooner than he did create it. In their cupidity they affect to go beyond the world, as if the ample circumference of heaven and earth did not contain objects numerous and resplendent enough to absorb all our senses; as if, in the period of six thousand years, God had not furnished facts enough to exercise our minds in ceaseless meditation. Therefore, let us willingly remain hedged in by those boundaries within which God has been pleased to confine our persons, and, as it were, enclose our minds, so as to prevent them from losing themselves by wandering unrestrained.

2. With the same view Moses relates that the work of creation was accomplished not in one moment, but in six days. By this statement we are drawn away from fiction to the one God who thus divided his work into six days, that we may have no reluctance to devote our whole lives to the contemplation of it. For though our eyes, in what direction soever they turn, are forced to behold the works of God, we see how fleeting our attention is, and holy quickly pious thoughts, if any arise, vanish away. Here, too, objection is taken to these progressive steps as inconsistent with the power of God, until human reason is subdued to the obedience of faith, and learns to welcome the calm quiescence to which the sanctification of the seventh day invited us. In the very order of events, we ought diligently to ponder on the paternal goodness of God toward the human race, in not creating Adam until he had liberally enriched the earth with all good things. Had he placed him on an earth barren and unfurnished; had he given life before light, he might have seemed to pay little regard to his interest. But now that he has arranged the motions of the sun and stars for man's use, has replenished the air, earth, and water, with living creatures, and produced all kinds of fruit in abundance for the supply of food, by performing the office of a provident and industrious head of a family, he has shown his wondrous goodness toward us. These subjects, which I only briefly touch, if more attentively pondered, will make it manifest that Moses was a sure

witness and herald of the one only Creator. I do not repeat what I have already explained—viz. that mention is here made not of the bare essence of God, but that his eternal Wisdom and Spirit are also set before us, in order that we may not dream of any other God than Him who desires to be recognised in that express image.

3. But before I begin to treat more fully of the nature of man (chap. 15 and B. 2 c. 1), it will be proper to say something of angels. For although Moses, in accommodation to the ignorance of the generality of men, does not in the history of the creation make mention of any other works of God than those which meet our eye, yet, seeing he afterwards introduces angels as the ministers of God, we easily infer that he for whom they do service is their Creator. Hence, though Moses, speaking in popular language, did not at the very commencement enumerate the angels among the creatures of God, nothing prevents us from treating distinctly and explicitly of what is delivered by Scripture concerning them in other places. For if we desire to know God by his works, we surely cannot overlook this noble and illustrious specimen. We may add that this branch of doctrine is very necessary for the refutation of numerous errors. The minds of many are so struck with the excellence of angelic natures, that they would think them insulted in being subjected to the authority of God, and so made subordinate. Hence a fancied divinity has been assigned them. Manes, too, has arisen with his sect, fabricating to himself two principles— God and the devil, attributing the origin of good things to God, but assigning all bad natures to the devil as their author. Were this delirium to take possession of our minds, God would be denied his glory in the creation of the world. For, seeing there is nothing more peculiar to God than eternity and αυτουσια, *i.e.* self-existence, or existence of himself, if I may so speak, do not those who attribute it to the devil in some degree invest him with the honour of

divinity? And where is the omnipotence of God, if the devil has the power of executing whatever he pleases against the will, and notwithstanding of the opposition of God? But the only good ground which the Manichees have—viz. that it were impious to ascribe the creation of any thing bad to a good God, militates in no degree against the orthodox faith, since it is not admitted that there is any thing naturally bad throughout the universe; the depravity and wickedness whether of man or of the devil, and the sins thence resulting, being not from nature, but from the corruption of nature; nor, at first, did anything whatever exist that did not exhibit some manifestation of the divine wisdom and justice. To obviate such perverse imaginations, we must raise our minds higher than our eyes can penetrate. It was probably with this view that the Nicene Creed, in calling God the creator of all things, makes express mention of things invisible. My care, however, must be to keep within the bounds which piety prescribes, lest by indulging in speculations beyond my reach, I bewilder the reader, and lead him away from the simplicity of the faith. And since the Holy Spirit always instructs us in what is useful, but altogether omits, or only touches cursorily on matters which tend little to edification, of all such matters, it certainly is our duty to remain in willing ignorance.

4. Angels being the ministers appointed to execute the commands of God, must, of course, be admitted to be his creatures, but to stir up questions concerning the time or order in which they were created (see Lombard, lib. 2 dist. 2, sqq.), bespeaks more perverseness than industry. Moses relates that the heavens and the earth were finished, with all their host; what avails it anxiously to inquire at what time other more hidden celestial hosts than the stars and planets also began to be? Not to dwell on this, let us here remember that on the whole subject of religion one rule of modesty and soberness is to be observed, and it is this, in obscure matters not to speak or think, or even long to know,

more than the Word of God has delivered. A second rule is, that in reading the Scriptures we should constantly direct our inquiries and meditations to those things which tend to edification, not indulge in curiosity, or in studying things of no use. And since the Lord has been pleased to instruct us, not in frivolous questions, but in solid piety, in the fear of his name, in true faith, and the duties of holiness, let us rest satisfied with such knowledge. Wherefore, if we would be duly wise, we must renounce those vain babblings of idle men, concerning the nature, ranks, and number of angels, without any authority from the Word of God. I know that many fasten on these topics more eagerly, and take greater pleasure in them than in those relating to daily practice. But if we decline not to be the disciples of Christ, let us not decline to follow the method which he has prescribed. In this way, being contented with him for our master, we will not only refrain from, but even feel averse to, superfluous speculations which he discourages. None can deny that Dionysus (whoever he may have been) has many shrewd and subtle disquisitions in his Celestial Hierarchy, but on looking at them more closely, every one must see that they are merely idle talk. The duty of a Theologian, however, is not to tickle the ear, but confirm the conscience, by teaching what is true, certain, and useful. When you read the work of Dionysus, you would think that the man had come down from heaven, and was relating, not what he had learned, but what he had actually seen. Paul, however, though he was carried to the third heaven, so far from delivering any thing of the kind, positively declares, that it was not lawful for man to speak the secrets which he had seen. Bidding adieu, therefore, to that nugatory wisdom, let us endeavour to ascertain from the simple doctrine of Scripture what it is the Lord's pleasure that we should know concerning angels.

5. In Scripture, then, we uniformly read that angels are heavenly spirits, whose obedience and ministry God

employs to execute all the purposes which he has decreed, and hence their name as being a kind of intermediate messengers to manifest his will to men. The names by which several of them are distinguished have reference to the same office. They are called hosts, because they surround their Prince as his court,—adorn and display his majesty,—like soldiers, have their eyes always turned to their leader's standard, and are so ready and prompt to execute his orders, that the moment he gives the nod, they prepare for, or rather are actually at work. In declaring the magnificence of the divine throne, similar representations are given by the prophets, and especially by Daniel, when he says, that when God stood up to Judgment, "thousand thousands ministered unto him, and ten thousand times ten thousand stood before him," (Dan. 7:10). As by these means the Lord wonderfully exerts and declares the power and might of his hand, they are called virtues. Again, as his government of the world is exercised and administered by them, they are called at one time Principalities, at another Powers, at another Dominions (Col. 1:16; Eph. 1:21). Lastly, as the glory of God in some measure dwells in them, they are also termed Thrones; though as to this last designation I am unwilling to speak positively, as a different interpretation is equally, if not more congruous. To say nothing, therefore, of the name of Thrones, the former names are often employed by the Holy Spirit in commendation of the dignity of angelic service. Nor is it right to pass by unhonoured those instruments by whom God specially manifests the presence of his power. Nay, they are more than once called Gods, because the Deity is in some measure represented to us in their service, as in a mirror. I am rather inclined, however, to agree with ancient writers, that in those passages wherein it is stated that the angel of the Lord appeared to Abraham, Jacob, and Moses, Christ was that angel. Still it is true, that when mention is made of all the angels, they are frequently so designated.

Nor ought this to seem strange. For if princes and rulers have this honour given them, because in their office they are vicegerents of God, the supreme King and Judge, with far greater reason may it be given to angels, in whom the brightness of the divine glory is much more conspicuously displayed.

6. But the point on which the Scriptures specially insist is that which tends most to our comfort, and to the confirmation of our faith, namely, that angels are the ministers and dispensers of the divine bounty towards us. Accordingly, we are told how they watch for our safety, how they undertake our defence, direct our path, and take heed that no evil befall us. There are whole passages which relate, in the first instance, to Christ, the Head of the Church, and after him to all believers. "He shall give his angels charge over thee, to keep thee in all thy ways. They shall bear thee up in their hands, lest thou dash thy foot against a stone." Again, "The angel of the Lord encampeth round about them that fear him, and delivereth them." By these passages the Lord shows that the protection of those whom he has undertaken to defend he has delegated to his angels. Accordingly, an angel of the Lord consoles Hagar in her flight, and bids her be reconciled to her mistress. Abraham promises to his servant that an angel will be the guide of his journey. Jacob, in blessing Ephraim and Manasseh, prays "The angel which redeemed me from all evil bless the lads." So an angel was appointed to guard the camp of the Israelites; and as often as God was pleased to deliver Israel from the hands of his enemies, he stirred up avengers by the ministry of angels. Thus, in fine (not to mention more), angels ministered to Christ, and were present with him in all straits. To the women they announced his resurrection; to the disciples they foretold his glorious advent. In discharging the office of our protectors, they war against the devil and all our enemies, and execute vengeance upon those who afflict us. Thus we

read that an angel of the Lord, to deliver Jerusalem from siege, slew one hundred and eighty-five thousand men in the camp of the king of Assyria in a single night.

7. Whether or not each believer has a single angel assigned to him for his defence, I dare not positively affirm. When Daniel introduces the angel of the Persian and the angel of the Greeks, he undoubtedly intimates that certain angels are appointed as a kind of presidents over kingdoms and provinces. Again, when Christ says that the angels of children always behold the face of his Father, he insinuates that there are certain angels to whom their safety has been entrusted. But I know not if it can be inferred from this, that each believer has his own angel. This, indeed, I hold for certain, that each of us is cared for, not by one angel merely, but that all with one consent watch for our safety. For it is said of all the angels collectively, that they rejoice "over one sinner that repenteth, more than over ninety and nine just persons which need no repentance." It is also said, that the angels (meaning more than one) carried the soul of Lazarus into Abraham's bosom. Nor was it to no purpose that Elisha showed his servant the many chariots of fire which were specially allotted him.

There is one passage which seems to intimate somewhat more clearly that each individual has a separate angel. When Peter, after his deliverance from prison, knocked at the door of the house where the brethren were assembled, being unable to think it could be himself, they said that it was his angel. This idea seems to have been suggested to them by a common belief that every believer has a single angel assigned to him. Here, however, it may be alleged, that there is nothing to prevent us from understanding it of any one of the angels to whom the Lord might have given the charge of Peter at that particular time, without implying that he was to be his, perpetual guardian, according to the vulgar imagination (see Calvin on Mark 5:9), that two angels a good and a bad, as a kind of genii, are assigned to each individual. After all, it is not worthwhile anxiously to investigate a point which does not greatly concern us. If any one does not think it enough to know that all the orders of the heavenly host are perpetually watching for his safety, I do not see what he could gain by knowing that he has one angel as a special guardian. Those, again, who limit the care which God takes of each of us to a single angel, do great injury to themselves and to all the members of the Church, as if there were no value in those promises of auxiliary troops, who on every side encircling and defending us, embolden us to fight more manfully.

8. Those who presume to dogmatize on the ranks and numbers of angels, would do well to consider on what foundation they rest. As to their rank, I admit that Michael is described by David as a mighty Prince, and by Jude as an Archangel. Paul also tells us, that an archangel will blow the trumpet which is to summon the world to Judgment. But how is it possible from such passages to ascertain the gradations of honour among the angels to determine the insignia, and assign the place and station of each? Even the two names, Michael and Gabriel, mentioned in Scripture, or a third, if you choose to add it from the history of Tobit, seem to intimate by their meaning that they are given to angels in accommodation to the weakness of our capacity, though I rather choose not to speak positively on the point. As to the number of angels, we learn from the mouth of our Saviour that there are many legions, and from Daniel that there are many myriads. Elisha's servant saw a multitude of chariots, and their vast number is declared by the fact, that they encamp round about those that fear the Lord. It is certain that spirits have no bodily shape, and yet Scripture, in accommodation to us, describes them under the form of winged Cherubim and Seraphim; not without cause, to assure us that when occasion requires, they will hasten to our aid with incredible swiftness, winging their way to us with the speed of lightning. Farther than this, in regard both

to the ranks and numbers of angels, let us class them among those mysterious subjects, the full revelation of which is deferred to the last day, and accordingly refrain from inquiring too curiously, or talking presumptuously.

9. There is one point, however, which though called into doubt by certain restless individuals, we ought to hold for certain—viz. that angels are ministering spirits (Heb. 1:14); whose service God employs for the protection of his people, and by whose means he distributes his favours among men, and also executes other works. The Sadducees of old maintained, that by angels nothing more was meant than the movements which God impresses on men, or manifestations which he gives of his own power (Acts 23:8). But this dream is contradicted by so many passages of Scriptures that it seems strange how such gross ignorance could have had any countenance among the Jews. To say nothing of the passages I have already quoted, passages which refer to thousands and legions of angels, speak of them as rejoicing, as bearing up the faithful in their hands, carrying their souls to rest, beholding the face of their Father, and so forth: there are other passages which most clearly prove that they are real beings possessed of spiritual essence. Stephen and Paul say that the Law was enacted in the hands of angels. Our Saviour, moreover says that at the resurrection the elect will be like angels; that the day of Judgment is known not even to the angels; that at that time he himself will come with the holy angels. However much such passages may be twisted, their meaning is plain. In like manner, when Paul beseeches Timothy to keep his precepts as before Christ and his elect angels, it is not qualities or inspirations without substance that he speaks of, but true spirits. And when it is said, in the Epistle to the Hebrews, that Christ was made more excellent than the angels, that the world was not made subject to them, that Christ assumed not their nature, but that of man, it is impossible to give a meaning to the

passages without understanding that angels are blessed spirits, as to whom such comparisons may competently be made. The author of that Epistle declares the same thing when he places the souls of believers and the holy angels together in the kingdom of heaven. Moreover, in the passages we have already quoted, the angels of children are said to behold the face of God, to defend us by their protection, to rejoice in our salvation, to admire the manifold grace of God in the Church, to be under Christ their head. To the same effect is their frequent appearance to the holy patriarchs in human form, their speaking, and consenting to be hospitably entertained. Christ, too, in consequence of the supremacy which he obtains as Mediator, is called the Angel (Mal. 3:1). It was thought proper to touch on this subject in passing, with the view of putting the simple upon their guard against the foolish and absurd imaginations which, suggested by Satan many centuries ago, are ever and anon starting up anew

10. It remains to give warning against the superstition which usually begins to creep in, when it is said that all blessings are ministered and dispensed to us by angels. For the human mind is apt immediately to think that there is no honour which they ought not to receive, and hence the peculiar offices of Christ and God are bestowed upon them. In this ways the glory of Christ was for several former ages greatly obscured, extravagant eulogiums being pronounced on angels without any authority from Scripture. Among the corruptions which we now oppose, there is scarcely any one of greater antiquity. Even Paul appears to have had a severe contest with some who so exalted angels as to make them almost the superiors of Christ. Hence he so anxiously urges in his Epistle to the Colossians (Col. 1:16, 20), that Christ is not only superior to all angels, but that all the endowments which they possess are derived from him; thus warning us against forsaking him, by turning to those who are not sufficient for themselves, but must draw with us at a

common fountain. As the refulgence of the Divine glory is manifested in them, there is nothing to which we are more prone than to prostrate ourselves before them in stupid adoration, and then ascribe to them the blessings which we owe to God alone. Even John confesses in the Apocalypse (Rev. 19:10; 22:8, 9), that this was his own case, but he immediately adds the answer which was given to him, "See thou do it not; I am thy fellow servant: worship God."

11. This danger we will happily avoid, if we consider why it is that Gods instead of acting directly without their agency, is wont to employ it in manifesting his power, providing for the safety of his people, and imparting the gifts of his beneficence. This he certainly does not from necessity, as if he were unable to dispense with them. Whenever he pleases, he passes them by, and performs his own work by a single nod: so far are they from relieving him of any difficulty. Therefore, when he employs them it is as a help to our weakness, that nothing may be wanting to elevate our hopes or strengthen our confidence. It ought, indeed, to be sufficient for us that the Lord declares himself to be our protector. But when we see ourselves beset by so many perils, so many injuries, so many kinds of enemies, such is our frailty and effeminacy, that we might at times be filled with alarm, or driven to despair, did not the Lord proclaim his gracious presence by some means in accordance with our feeble capacities. For this reason, he not only promises to take care of us, but assures us that he has numberless attendants, to whom he has committed the charge of our safety, that whatever dangers may impend, so long as we are encircled by their protection and guardianship, we are placed beyond all hazard of evil. I admit that after we have a simple assurance of the divine protection, it is improper in us still to look round for help. But since for this our weakness the Lord is pleased, in his infinite goodness and indulgence, to provide, it would ill become us to overlook the favour. Of this we have an

example in the servant of Elisha (2 Kings 6:17), who, seeing the mountain encompassed by the army of the Assyrians, and no means of escape, was completely overcome with terror, and thought it all over with himself and his master. Then Elisha prayed to God to open the eyes of the servant, who forthwith beheld the mountain filled with horses and chariots of fire; in other words, with a multitude of angels, to whom he and the prophet had been given in charge. Confirmed by the vision he received courage, and could boldly defy the enemy, whose appearance previously filled him with dismay.

12. Whatever, therefore, is said as to the ministry of angels, let us employ for the purpose of removing all distrust, and strengthening our confidence in God. Since the Lord has provided us with such protection, let us not be terrified at the multitude of our enemies as if they could prevail notwithstanding of his aid, but let us adopt the sentiment of Elisha, that more are for us than against us. How preposterous, therefore, is it to allow ourselves to be led away from God by angels who have been appointed for the very purpose of assuring us of his more immediate presence to help us? But we are so led away, if angels do not conduct us directly to him—making us look to him, invoke and celebrate him as our only defender—if they are not regarded merely as hands moving to our assistance just as he directs—if they do not direct us to Christ as the only Mediator on whom we must wholly depend and recline, looking towards him, and resting in him. Our minds ought to give thorough heed to what Jacob saw in his vision (Gen. 28:12),—angels descending to the earth to men, and again mounting up from men to heaven, by means of a ladder, at the head of which the Lord of Hosts was seated, intimating that it is solely by the intercession of Christ that the ministry of angels extends to us, as he himself declares, "Hereafter ye shall see heaven open, and the angels of God ascending and descending upon the Son of man," (John

1:51). Accordingly, the servant of Abraham, though he had been commended to the guardianship of an angel (Gen. 24:7), does not therefore invoke that angel to be present with him, but trusting to the commendation, pours out his prayers before the Lord, and entreats him to show mercy to Abraham. As God does not make angels the ministers of his power and goodness, that he may share his glory with them, so he does not promise his assistance by their instrumentality, that we may divide our confidence between him and them. Away, then, with that Platonic philosophy of seeking access to God by means of angels and courting them with the view of making God more propitious (*Plat. in Epinomide et Cratylo*),—a philosophy which presumptuous and superstitious men attempted at first to introduce into our religion, and which they persist in even to this day.

13. The tendency of all that Scripture teaches concerning devils is to put us on our guard against their wiles and machinations, that we may provide ourselves with weapons strong enough to drive away the most formidable foes. For when Satan is called the god and ruler of this world, the strong man armed, the prince of the power of the air, the roaring lion, the object of all these descriptions is to make us more cautious and vigilant, and more pre- pared for the contest. This is sometimes stated in distinct terms. For Peter, after describing the devil as a roaring lion going about seeking whom he may devour, immediately adds the exhortation, "whom resist steadfast in the faith," (1 Pet. 5:9). And Paul, after reminding us that we wrestle not against flesh and blood, but against principalities, against powers, against the rulers of the darkness of this world, against spiritual wickedness in high places, immediately enjoins us to put on armour equal to so great and perilous a contest (Ephes. 6:12). Wherefore, let this be the use to which we turn all these statements. Being forewarned of the constant presence of an enemy the most

daring, the most powerful, the most crafty, the most indefatigable, the most completely equipped with all the engines and the most expert in the science of war, let us not allow ourselves to be overtaken by sloth or cowardice, but, on the contrary, with minds aroused and ever on the alert, let us stand ready to resist; and, knowing that this warfare is terminated only by death, let us study to persevere. Above all, fully conscious of our weakness and want of skill, let us invoke the help of God, and attempt nothing without trusting in him, since it is his alone to supply counsel, and strength, and courage, and arms.

14. That we may feel the more strongly urged to do so, the Scripture declares that the enemies who war against us are not one or two, or few in number, but a great host. Mary Magdalene is said to have been delivered from seven devils by which she was possessed; and our Saviour assures us that it is an ordinary circumstance, when a devil has been expelled, if access is again given to it, to take seven other spirits, more wicked than itself, and resume the vacant possession. Nay, one man is said to have been possessed by a whole legion. By this, then, we are taught that the number of enemies with whom we have to war is almost infinite, that we may not, from a contemptuous idea of the fewness of their numbers, be more remiss in the contest, or from imagining that an occasional truce is given us, indulge in sloth. In one Satan or devil being often mentioned in the singular number, the thing denoted is that domination of iniquity which is opposed to the reign of righteousness. For, as the Church and the communion of saints has Christ for its head, so the faction of the wicked and wickedness itself, is portrayed with its prince exercising supremacy. Hence the expression, "Depart, ye cursed, into everlasting fire, prepared for the devil and his angels," (Mt. 25:41).

15. One thing which ought to animate us to perpetual contest with the devil is, that he is everywhere called both our adversary and the adversary of God. For, if the glory of

God is dear to us, as it ought to be, we ought to struggle with all our might against him who aims at the extinction of that glory. If we are animated with proper zeal to maintain the Kingdom of Christ, v. e must wage irreconcilable war with him who conspires its ruin. Again, if we have any anxiety about our own salvation, we ought to make no peace nor truce with him who is continually laying schemes for its destruction. But such is the character given to Satan in the third chapter of Genesis, where he is seen seducing man from his allegiance to God, that he may both deprive God of his due honour, and plunge man headlong in destruction. Such, too, is the description given of him in the Gospels (Mt. 13:28), where he is called the enemy, and is said to sow tares in order to corrupt the seed of eternal life. In one word, in all his actions we experience the truth of our Saviour's description, that he was "a murderer from the beginning, and abode not in the truth," (John 8:44). Truth he assails with lies, light he obscures with darkness. The minds of men he involves in error; he stirs up hatred, inflames strife and war, and all in order that he may overthrow the kingdom of God, and drown men in eternal perdition with himself. Hence it is evident that his whole nature is depraved, mischievous, and malignant. There must be extreme depravity in a mind bent on assailing the glory of God and the salvation of man. This is intimated by John in his Epistle, when he says that he "sinneth from the beginning," (1 John 3:8), implying that he is the author, leader, and contriver of all malice and wickedness.

16. But as the devil was created by God, we must remember that this malice which we attribute to his nature is not from creation, but from depravation. Every thing damnable in him he brought upon himself, by his revolt and fall. Of this Scripture reminds us, lest, by believing that he was so created at first, we should ascribe to God what is most foreign to his nature. For this reason, Christ declares (John 8:44), that Satan, when he lies, "speaketh of his

own," and states the reason, "because he abode not in the truth." By saying that he abode not in the truth, he certainly intimates that he once was in the truth, and by calling him the father of lies, he puts it out of his power to charge God with the depravity of which he was himself the cause. But although the expressions are brief and not very explicit, they are amply sufficient to vindicate the majesty of God from every calumny. And what more does it concern us to know of devils? Some murmur because the Scripture does not in various passages give a distinct and regular exposition of Satan's fall, its cause, mode, date, and nature. But as these things are of no consequence to us, it was better, if not entirely to pass them in silence, at least only to touch lightly upon them. The Holy Spirit could not deign to feed curiosity with idle, unprofitable histories. We see it was the Lord's purpose to deliver nothing in his sacred oracles which we might not learn for edification. Therefore, instead of dwelling on superfluous matters, let it be sufficient for us briefly to hold, with regard to the nature of devils, that at their first creation they were the angels of God, but by revolting they both ruined themselves, and became the instruments of perdition to others. As it was useful to know this much, it is clearly taught by Peter and Jude; "God," they say, "spared not the angels that sinned, but cast them down to hell, and delivered them into chains of darkness to be reserved unto Judgment," (2 Pet. 2:4; Jude ver. 6). And Paul, by speaking of the elect angels, obviously draws a tacit contrast between them and reprobate angels.

17. With regard to the strife and war which Satan is said to wage with God, it must be understood with this qualification, that Satan cannot possibly do anything against the will and consent of God. For we read in the history of Job, that Satan appears in the presence of God to receive his commands, and dares not proceed to execute any enterprise until he is authorised. In the same way, when

Ahab was to be deceived, he undertook to be a lying spirit in the mouth of all the prophets; and on being commissioned by the Lord, proceeds to do so. For this reason, also, the spirit which tormented Saul is said to be an evil spirit from the Lord, because he was, as it were, the scourge by which the misdeeds of the wicked king were punished. In another place it is said that the plagues of Egypt were inflicted by God through the instrumentality of wicked angels. In conformity with these particular examples, Paul declares generally that unbelievers are blinded by God, though he had previously described it as the doing of Satan. It is evident, therefore, that Satan is under the power of God, and is so ruled by his authority, that he must yield obedience to it. Moreover, though we say that Satan resists God, and does works at variance with His works, we at the same time maintain that this contrariety and opposition depend on the permission of God. I now speak not of Satan's will and endeavour, but only of the result. For the disposition of the devil being wicked, he has no inclination whatever to obey the divine will, but, on the contrary, is wholly bent on contumacy and rebellion. This much, therefore, he has of himself, and his own iniquity, that he eagerly, and of set purpose, opposes God, aiming at those things which he deems most contrary to the will of God. But as God holds him bound and fettered by the curb of his power, he executes those things only for which permission has been given him, and thus, however unwilling, obeys his Creator, being forced, whenever he is required, to do Him service.

18. God thus turning the unclean spirits hither and thither at his pleasure, employs them in exercising believers by warring against them, assailing them with wiles, urging them with solicitations, pressing close upon them, disturbing, alarming, and occasionally wounding, but never conquering or oppressing them; whereas they hold the wicked in thraldom, exercise dominion over their minds

and bodies, and employ them as bond-slaves in all kinds of iniquity. Because believers are disturbed by such enemies, they are addressed in such exhortations as these: "Neither give place to the devil;" "Your adversary the devil, as a roaring lion, walketh about seeking whom he may devour; whom resist steadfast in the faith," (Eph. 4:27; 1 Pet. 5:8). Paul acknowledges that he was not exempt from this species of contest when he says, that for the purpose of subduing his pride, a messenger of Satan was sent to buffet him (2 Cor. 12:7). This trial, therefore, is common to all the children of God. But as the promise of bruising Satan's head (Gen. 3:15) applies alike to Christ and to all his members, I deny that believers can ever be oppressed or vanquished by him. They are often, indeed, thrown into alarm, but never so thoroughly as not to recover themselves. They fall by the violence of the blows, but they get up again; they are wounded, but not mortally. In fine, they labour on through the whole course of their lives, so as ultimately to gain the victory, though they meet with occasional defeats. We know how David, through the just anger of God, was left for a time to Satan, and by his instigation numbered the people (2 Sam. 24:1); nor without cause does Paul hold out a hope of pardon in case any should have become ensnared by the wiles of the devil (2 Tim. 2:26). Accordingly, he elsewhere shows that the promise above quoted commences in this life where the struggle is carried on, and that it is completed after the struggle is ended. His words are, "The God of peace shall bruise Satan under your feet shortly," (Rom. 16:20). In our Head, indeed, this victory was always perfect, because the prince of the world "had nothing" in him (John 14:30); but in us, who are his members, it is now partially obtained, and will be perfected when we shall have put off our mortal flesh, through which we are liable to infirmity, and shall have been filled with the energy of the Holy Spirit. In this way, when the kingdom of Christ is raised up and established, that of Satan falls, as our Lord himself expresses it, "I beheld Satan as lightning fall from heaven," (Luke 10:18). By these words, he confirmed the report which the apostles gave of the efficacy of their preaching. In like manner he says, "When a strong man armed keepeth his palace, his goods are in peace. But when a stronger than he shall come upon him, and overcome him, he taketh from him all his armour wherein he trusted, and divideth his spoils," (Luke 11:21, 22). And to this end, Christ, by dying, overcame Satan, who had the power of death (Heb. 2:14), and triumphed over all his hosts that they might not injure the Church, which otherwise would suffer from them every moment. For (such being our weakness, and such his raging fury), how could we withstand his manifold and unintermitted assaults for any period, however short, if we did not trust to the victory of our leader? God, therefore, does not allow Satan to have dominion over the souls of believers, but only gives over to his sway the impious and unbelieving, whom he deigns not to number among his flock. For the devil is said to have undisputed possession of this world until he is dispossessed by Christ. In like manner, he is said to blind all who do not believe the Gospel, and to do his own work in the children of disobedience. And justly; for all the wicked are vessels of wrath, and, accordingly, to whom should they be subjected but to the minister of the divine vengeance? In fine, they are said to be of their father the devil. For as believers are recognised to be the sons of God by bearing his image, so the wicked are properly regarded as the children of Satan, from having degenerated into his image.

19. Having above refuted that nugatory philosophy concerning the holy angels, which teaches that they are nothing but good motions or inspirations which God excites in the minds of men, we must here likewise refute those who foolishly allege that devils are nothing but bad affections or perturbations suggested by our carnal nature.

The brief refutation is to be found in passages of Scripture on this subject, passages neither few nor obscure. First, when they are called unclean spirits and apostate angels (Mt. 12:43; Jude, verse 6), who have degenerated from their original, the very terms sufficiently declare that they are not motions or affections of the mind, but truly, as they are called, minds or spirits endued with sense and intellect. In like manner, when the children of God are contrasted by John, and also by our Saviour, with the children of the devil, would not the contrast be absurd if the term devil meant nothing more than evil inspirations? And John adds still more emphatically, that the devil sinneth from the beginning (1 John 3:8). In like manner, when Jude introduces the archangel Michael contending with the devil (Jude, verse 9), he certainly contrasts a wicked and rebellious with a good angel. To this corresponds the account given in the Book of Job, that Satan appeared in the presence of God with the holy angels. But the clearest passages of all are those which make mention of the punishment which, from the Judgment of God, they already begin to feel, and are to feel more especially at the resurrection, "What have we to do with thee, Jesus, thou Son of God? art thou come hither to torment us before the time?" (Mt. 8:29); and again, "Depart, ye cursed, into everlasting fire, prepared for the devil and his angels," (Mt. 25:41). Again, "If God spared not the angels that sinned, but cast them down to hell, and delivered them into chains of darkness to be reserved unto Judgment," &c. (2 Pet. 2:4). How absurd the expressions, that devils are doomed to eternal punishment, that fire is prepared for them, that they are even now excruciated and tormented by the glory of Christ, if there were truly no devils at all? But as all discussion on this subject is superfluous for those who give credit to the Word of God, while little is gained by quoting Scripture to those empty speculators whom nothing but novelty can please, I believe I have already done enough for my purpose, which was to put the pious on their guard against the delirious dreams with which restless men harass themselves and the simple. The subject, however, deserved to be touched upon, lest any, by embracing that errors should imagine they have no enemy and thereby be more remiss or less cautious in resisting.

20. Meanwhile, being placed in this most beautiful theatre, let us not decline to take a pious delight in the clear and manifest works of God. For, as we have elsewhere observed, though not the chief, it is, in point of order, the first evidence of faith, to remember to which side soever we turn, that all which meets the eye is the work of God, and at the same time to meditate with pious care on the end which God had in view in creating it. Wherefore, in order that we may apprehend with true faith what it is necessary to know concerning God, it is of importance to attend to the history of the creation, as briefly recorded by Moses and afterwards more copiously illustrated by pious writers, more especially by Basil and Ambrose. From this history we learn that God, by the power of his Word and his Spirit, created the heavens and the earth out of nothing; that thereafter he produced things inanimate and animate of every kind, arranging an innumerable variety of objects in admirable order, giving each kind its proper nature, office, place, and station; at the same time, as all things were liable to corruption, providing for the perpetuation of each single species, cherishing some by secret methods, and, as it were, from time to time instilling new vigour into them, and bestowing on others a power of continuing their race, so preventing it from perishing at their own death. Heaven and earth being thus most richly adorned, and copiously supplied with all things, like a large and splendid mansion gorgeously constructed and exquisitely furnished, at length man was made—man, by the beauty of his person and his many noble endowments, the most glorious specimen of the works of God. But, as I have no intention to give the

history of creation in detail, it is sufficient to have again thus briefly touched on it in passing. I have already reminded my reader, that the best course for him is to derive his knowledge of the subject from Moses and others who have carefully and faithfully transmitted an account of the creation.

21. It is unnecessary to dwell at length on the end that should be aimed at in considering the works of God. The subject has been in a great measure explained elsewhere, and in so far as required by our present work, may now be disposed of in a few words. Undoubtedly were one to attempt to speak in due terms of the inestimable wisdom, power, justice, and goodness of God, in the formation of the world, no grace or splendour of diction could equal the greatness of the subject. Still there can be no doubt that the Lord would have us constantly occupied with such holy meditation, in order that, while we contemplate the immense treasures of wisdom and goodness exhibited in the creatures as in so many mirrors, we may not only run our eye over them with a hasty, and, as it were, evanescent glance, but dwell long upon them, seriously and faithfully turn them in our minds, and every now and then bring them to recollection. But as the present work is of a didactic nature, we cannot fittingly enter on topics which require lengthened discourse. Therefore, in order to be compendious, let the reader understand that he has a genuine apprehension of the character of God as the Creator of the world; first, if he attends to the general rule, never thoughtlessly or obliviously to overlook the glorious perfections which God displays in his creatures; and, secondly, if he makes a self application of what he sees, so as to fix it deeply on his heart. The former is exemplified when we consider how great the Architect must be who framed and ordered the multitude of the starry host so admirably, that it is impossible to imagine a more glorious sight, so stationing some, and fixing them to particular

spots that they cannot move; giving a freer course to others yet setting limits to their wanderings; so tempering the movement of the whole as to measure out day and night, months, years, and seasons, and at the same time so regulating the inequality of days as to prevent every thing like confusion. The former course is, moreover, exemplified when we attend to his power in sustaining the vast mass, and guiding the swift revolutions of the heavenly bodies, &c. These few examples sufficiently explain what is meant by recognising the divine perfections in the creation of the world. Were we to attempt to go over the whole subject we should never come to a conclusion, there being as many miracles of divine power, as many striking evidences of wisdom and goodness, as there are classes of objects, nay, as there are individual objects, great or small, throughout the universe.

22. The other course which has a closer relation to faith remains to be considered—viz. that while we observe how God has destined all things for our good and salvation, we at the same time feel his power and grace, both in ourselves and in the great blessings which he has bestowed upon us; thence stirring up ourselves to confidence in him, to invocation, praise, and love. Moreover, as I lately observed, the Lord himself, by the very order of creation, has demonstrated that he created all things for the sake of man. Nor is it unimportant to observe, that he divided the formation of the world into six days, though it had been in no respect more difficult to complete the whole work, in all its parts, in one moment than by a gradual progression. But he was pleased to display his providence and paternal care towards us in this, that before he formed man, he provided whatever he foresaw would be useful and salutary to him. How ungrateful, then, were it to doubt whether we are cared for by this most excellent Parent, who we see cared for us even before we were born! How impious were it to tremble in distrust, lest we should one day be abandoned in

our necessity by that kindness which, antecedent to our existence, displayed itself in a complete supply of all good things! Moreover, Moses tells us that everything which the world contains is liberally placed at our disposal. This God certainly did not that he might delude us with an empty form of donation. Nothing, therefore, which concerns our safety will ever be wanting. To conclude, in one word; as often as we call God the Creator of heaven and earth, let us remember that the distribution of all the things which he created are in his hand and power, but that we are his sons, whom he has undertaken to nourish and bring up in allegiance to him, that we may expect the substance of all good from him alone, and have full hope that he will never suffer us to be in want of things necessary to salvation, so as to leave us dependent on some other source; that in everything we desire we may address our prayers to him, and, in every benefit we receive, acknowledge his hand, and give him thanks; that thus allured by his great goodness and beneficence, we may study with our whole heart to love and serve him.

CHAPTER 15.

STATE IN WHICH MAN WAS CREATED. THE FACULTIES OF THE SOUL—THE IMAGE OF GOD—FREE WILL—ORIGINAL RIGHTEOUSNESS.

This chapter is thus divided:—I. The necessary rules to be observed in considering the state of man before the fall being laid down, the point first considered is the creation of the body, and the lesson taught by its being formed out of the earth, and made alive, sec. 1. II. The immortality of the human soul is proved by various solid arguments, sec. 2. III. The image of God (the strongest proof of the soul's immortality) is considered, and various absurd fancies are refuted, sec. 3. IV. Several errors which obscure the light of truth being dissipated, follows a philosophical and theological consideration of the faculties of the soul before the fall.

Sections.

1. A twofold knowledge of God—viz. before the fall and after it. The former here considered. Particular rules or precautions to be observed in this discussion. What we are taught by a body formed ant of the dust, and tenanted by a spirit.

2. The immortality of the soul proved from, 1. The testimony of conscience. 2. The knowledge of God. 3. The noble faculties with which it is endued. 4. Its activity and wondrous fancies in sleep. 5. Innumerable passages of Scripture.

3. The image of God one of the strongest proofs of the immortality of the soul. What meant by this image. The dreams of Osiander concerning the image of God refuted. Whether any difference between "image" and "likeness."

Another objection of Osiander refuted. The image of God conspicuous in the whole Adam.

4. The image of God is in the soul. Its nature may be learnt from its renewal by Christ. What comprehended under this renewal. What the image of God in man before the fall. In what things it now appears. When and where it will be seen in perfection.

5. The dreams of the Manichees and of Servetus, as to the origin of the soul, refuted. Also of Osiander, who denies that there is any image of God in man without essential righteousness.

6. The doctrine of philosophers as to the faculties of the soul generally discordant, doubtful, and obscure. The excellence of the soul described. Only one soul in each man. A brief review of the opinion of philosophers as to the faculties of the soul. What to be thought of this opinion.

7. The division of the faculties of the soul into intellect and will, more agreeable to Christian doctrine.

8. The power and office of the intellect and will in man before the fall. Man's free will. This freedom lost by the fall—a fact unknown to philosophers. The delusion of Pelagians and Papists. Objection as to the fall of man when free, refuted.

1. We have now to speak of the creation of man, not only because of all the works of God it is the noblest, and most admirable specimen of his justice, wisdom, and goodness, but, as we observed at the outset, we cannot clearly and properly know God unless the knowledge of ourselves be added. This knowledge is twofold,—relating, first, to the condition in which we were at first created; and, secondly to our condition such as it began to be immediately after Adam's fall. For it would little avail us to know how we were created if we remained ignorant of the corruption and degradation of our nature in consequence of the fall. At present, however, we confine ourselves to a

consideration of our nature in its original integrity. And, certainly, before we descend to the miserable condition into which man has fallen, it is of importance to consider what he was at first. For there is need of caution, lest we attend only to the natural ills of man, and thereby seem to ascribe them to the Author of nature; impiety deeming it a sufficient defence if it can pretend that everything vicious in it proceeded in some sense from God, and not hesitating, when accused, to plead against God, and throw the blame of its guilt upon Him. Those who would be thought to speak more reverently of the Deity catch at an excuse for their depravity from nature, not considering that they also, though more obscurely, bring a charge against God, on whom the dishonour would fall if anything vicious were proved to exist in nature. Seeing, therefore, that the flesh is continually on the alert for subterfuges, by which it imagines it can remove the blame of its own wickedness from itself to some other quarter, we must diligently guard against this depraved procedure, and accordingly treat of the calamity of the human race in such a way as may cut off every evasion, and vindicate the justice of God against all who would impugn it. We shall afterwards see, in its own place (Book 2 chap. 1 sec. 3), how far mankind now are from the purity originally conferred on Adam. And, first, it is to be ob- served, that when he was formed out of the dust of the ground a curb was laid on his pride — nothing being more absurd than that those should glory in their excellence who not only dwell in tabernacles of clay, but are themselves in part dust and ashes. But God having not only deigned to animate a vessel of clay, but to make it the habitation of an immortal spirit, Adam might well glory in the great liberality of his Maker.

2. Moreover, there can be no question that man consists of a body and a soul; meaning by soul, an immortal though created essence, which is his nobler part. Sometimes he is called a spirit. But though the two terms, while they are

used together differ in their meaning, still, when spirit is used by itself it is equivalent to soul, as when Solomon speaking of death says, that the spirit returns to God who gave it (Eccles. 12:7). And Christ, in commending his spirit to the Father, and Stephen his to Christ, simply mean, that when the soul is freed from the prison-house of the body, God becomes its perpetual keeper. Those who imagine that the soul is called a spirit because it is a breath or energy divinely infused into bodies, but devoid of essence, err too grossly, as is shown both by the nature of the thing, and the whole tenor of Scripture. It is true, indeed, that men cleaving too much to the earth are dull of apprehension, nay, being alienated from the Father of Lights, are so immersed in darkness as to imagine that they will not survive the grave; still the light is not so completely quenched in darkness that all sense of immortality is lost. Conscience, which, distinguishing, between good and evil, responds to the Judgment of God, is an undoubted sign of an immortal spirit. How could motion devoid of essence penetrate to the Judgment-seat of God, and under a sense of guilt strike itself with terror? The body cannot be affected by any fear of spiritual punishment. This is competent only to the soul, which must therefore be endued with essence. Then the mere knowledge of a God sufficiently proves that souls which rise higher than the world must be immortal, it being impossible that any evanescent vigour could reach the very fountain of life. In fine, while the many noble faculties with which the human mind is endued proclaim that something divine is engraven on it, they are so many evidences of an immortal essence. For such sense as the lower animals possess goes not beyond the body, or at least not beyond the objects actually presented to it. But the swiftness with which the human mind glances from heaven to earth, scans the secrets of nature, and, after it has embraced all ages, with intellect and memory digests each in its proper order, and reads the future in the past, clearly demonstrates that there lurks in man a something separated from the body. We have intellect by which we are able to conceive of the invisible God and angels—a thing of which body is altogether incapable. We have ideas of rectitude, justice, and honesty—ideas which the bodily senses cannot reach. The seat of these ideas must therefore be a spirit. Nay, sleep itself, which stupefying the man, seems even to deprive him of life, is no obscure evidence of immortality; not only suggesting thoughts of things which never existed, but foreboding future events. I briefly touch on topics which even profane writers describe with a more splendid eloquence. For pious readers, a simple reference is sufficient. Were not the soul some kind of essence separated from the body, Scripture would not teach that we dwell in houses of clay, and at death remove from a tabernacle of flesh; that we put off that which is corruptible, in order that, at the last day, we may finally receive according to the deeds done in the body. These, and similar passages which every- where occur, not only clearly distinguish the soul from the body, but by giving it the name of man, intimate that it is his principal part. Again, when Paul exhorts believers to cleanse themselves from all filthiness of the flesh and the spirit, he shows that there are two parts in which the taint of sin resides. Peter, also, in calling Christ the Shepherd and Bishop of souls, would have spoken absurdly if there were no souls towards which he might discharge such an office. Nor would there be any ground for what he says concerning the eternal salvation of souls, or for his injunction to purify our souls, or for his assertion that fleshly lusts war against the soul; neither could the author of the Epistle to the Hebrews say, that pastors watch as those who must give an account for our souls, if souls were devoid of essence. To the same effect Paul calls God to witness upon his soul, which could not be brought to trial before God if incapable of suffering punishment. This is still more clearly expressed by our

Saviour, when he bids us fear him who, after he has killed the body, is able also to cast into hell fire. Again when the author of the Epistle to the Hebrews distinguishes the fathers of our flesh from God, who alone is the Father of our spirits, he could not have asserted the essence of the soul in clearer terms. Moreover, did not the soul, when freed from the fetters of the body, continue to exist, our Saviour would not have represented the soul of Lazarus as enjoying blessedness in Abraham's bosom, while, on the contrary, that of Dives was suffering dreadful torments. Paul assures us of the same thing when he says, that so long as we are present in the body, we are absent from the Lord. Not to dwell on a matter as to which there is little obscurity, I will only add, that Luke mentions among the errors of the Sadducees that they believed neither angel nor spirit.

3. A strong proof of this point may be gathered from its being said, that man was created in the image of God. For though the divine glory is displayed in man's outward appearance, it cannot be doubted that the proper seat of the image is in the soul. I deny not, indeed, that external shape, in so far as it distinguishes and separates us from the lower animals, brings us nearer to God; nor will I vehemently oppose any who may choose to include under the image of God that

"While the mute creation downward bend Their sight, and to their earthly mother tend, Man looks aloft, and with erected eyes, Beholds his own hereditary skies."

Only let it be understood, that the image of God which is beheld or made conspicuous by these external marks, is spiritual. For Osiander (whose writings exhibit a perverse ingenuity in futile devices), extending the image of God indiscriminately as well to the body as to the soul, confounds heaven with earth. He says, that the Father, the Son, and the Holy Spirit, placed their image in man, because, even though Adam had stood entire, Christ would still have become man. Thus, according to him, the body which was destined for Christ was a model and type of that corporeal figure which was then formed. But where does he find that Christ is an image of the Spirit? I admit, indeed, that in the person of the Mediator, the glory of the whole Godhead is displayed: but how can the eternal Word, who in order precedes the Spirit, be called his image? In short, the distinction between the Son and the Spirit is destroyed when the former is represented as the image of the latter. Moreover, I should like to know in what respect Christ in the flesh in which he was clothed resembles the Holy Spirit, and by what marks, or lineaments, the likeness is expressed. And since the expression, "Let us make man in our own image," is used in the person of the Son also, it follows that he is the image of himself—a thing utterly absurd. Add that, according to the figment of Osiander, Adam was formed after the model or type of the man Christ. Hence Christ, in as much as he was to be clothed with flesh, was the idea according to which Adam was formed, whereas the Scriptures teach very differently—viz. that he was formed in the image of God. There is more plausibility in the imagination of those who interpret that Adam was created in the image of God, because it was conformable to Christ, who is the only image of God; but not even for this is there any solid foundation. The "image" and "likeness" has given rise to no small discussion; interpreters searching without cause for a difference between the two terms, since "likeness" is merely added by way of exposition. First, we know that repetitions are common in Hebrew, which often gives two words for one thing; And, secondly, there is no ambiguity in the thing itself, man being called the image of God because of his likeness to God. Hence there is an obvious absurdity in those who indulge in philosophical speculation as to these names, placing the *Zelem*, that is the image, in the substance of the soul, and the *Demuth*, that is the likeness, in its qualities, and so forth. God having determined to create man in his own image, to remove the obscurity which was in this terms adds, by way of explanation, in *his likeness*, as if he had said, that he would make man, in whom he would, as it were, image himself by means of the marks of resemblance impressed upon him. Accordingly, Moses, shortly after repeating the account, puts down the image of God twice, and makes no mention of the likeness. Osiander frivolously objects that it is not a part of the man, or the soul with its faculties, which is called the image of God, but the whole Adam, who received his name from the dust out of which he was taken. I call the objection frivolous, as all sound readers will judge. For though the whole man is called mortal, the soul is not therefore liable to death, nor when he is called a rational animal is reason or intelligence thereby attributed to the body. Hence, although the soul is not the man, there is no absurdity in holding that he is called the image of God in respect of the soul; though I retain the principle which I lately laid down, that the image of God extends to everything in which the nature of man surpasses that of all other species of animals. Accordingly, by this term is denoted the integrity with which Adam was endued when his intellect was clear, his affections subordinated to reason, all his senses duly regulated, and when he truly ascribed all his excellence to the admirable gifts of his Maker. And though the primary seat of the divine image was in the mind and the heart, or in the soul and its powers, there was no part even of the body in which some rays of glory did not shine. It is certain that in every part of the world some lineaments of divine glory are beheld and hence we may infer, that when his image is placed in man, there is a kind of tacit antithesis, as it were, setting man apart from the crowd, and exalting him above all the other creatures. But it cannot be denied that the angels also were created in the likeness of God, since, as Christ declares (Mt. 22:30), our highest perfection will consist in being like them. But it is not without good cause that Moses commends the favour of God towards us by giving us this peculiar title, the more especially that he was only comparing man with the visible creation.

4. But our definition of the image seems not to be complete until it appears more clearly what the faculties are in which man excels, and in which he is to be regarded as a mirror of the divine glory. This, however, cannot be better known than from the remedy provided for the corruption of nature. It cannot be doubted that when Adam lost his first estate he became alienated from God. Wherefore, although we grant that the image of God was not utterly effaced and destroyed in him, it was, however, so corrupted, that any thing which remains is fearful deformity; and, therefore, our deliverance begins with that renovation which we obtain from Christ, who is, therefore, called the second Adam, because he restores us to true and substantial integrity. For although Paul, contrasting the quickening Spirit which believers receive from Christ, with the living soul which Adam was created (1 Cor. 15:45), commends the richer measure of grace bestowed in regeneration, he does not, however, contradict the statement, that the end of regeneration is to form us anew in the image of God. Accordingly, he elsewhere shows that the new man is renewed after the image of him that created him (Col. 3:19). To this corresponds another passage, "Put ye on the new man, who after God is created," (Eph. 4:24). We must now see what particulars Paul comprehends under this renovation. In the first place, he mentions knowledge, and in the second, true righteousness and holiness. Hence we infer, that at the beginning the image of God was manifested by light of intellect, rectitude of heart, and the soundness of every part. For though I admit that the forms of expression are elliptical, this principle cannot be overthrown — viz. that the leading feature in the renovation of the divine image must also have held the highest place in its creation. To the same effect Paul elsewhere says, that be-

holding the glory of Christ with unveiled face, we are transformed into the same image. We now see how Christ is the most perfect image of God, into which we are so renewed as to bear the image of God in knowledge, purity, righteousness, and true holiness. This being established, the imagination of Osiander, as to bodily form, vanishes of its own accord. As to that passage of St Paul (1 Cor. 11:7), in which the man alone to the express exclusion of the woman, is called the image and glory of God, it is evident from the context, that it merely refers to civil order. I presume it has already been sufficiently proved, that the image comprehends everything which has any relation to the spiritual and eternal life. The same thing, in different terms, is declared by St John when he says, that the light which was from the beginning, in the eternal Word of God, was the light of man (John 1:4). His object being to extol the singular grace of God in making man excel the other animals, he at the same time shows how he was formed in the image of God, that he may separate him from the common herd, as possessing not ordinary animal existence, but one which combines with it the light of intelligence. Therefore, as the image of God constitutes the entire excellence of human nature, as it shone in Adam before his fall, but was afterwards vitiated and almost destroyed, nothing remaining but a ruin, confused, mutilated, and tainted with impurity, so it is now partly seen in the elect, in so far as they are regenerated by the Spirit. Its full lustre, however, will be displayed in heaven. But in order to know the particular properties in which it consists, it will be proper to treat of the faculties of the soul. For there is no solidity in Augustine's speculation, that the soul is a mirror of the Trinity, inasmuch as it comprehends within itself, intellect, will, and memory. Nor is there probability in the opinion of those who place likeness to God in the dominion bestowed upon man, as if he only resembled God in this, that he is appointed lord and master of all things. The likeness must be within, in himself. It must be something which is not external to him but is properly the internal good of the soul.

5. But before I proceed further, it is necessary to advert to the dream of the Manichees, which Servetus has attempted in our day to revive. Because it is said that God breathed into man's nostrils the breath of life (Gen. 2:7), they thought that the soul was a transmission of the substance of God; as if some portion of the boundless divinity had passed into man. It cannot take long time to show how many gross and foul absurdities this devilish error carries in its train. For if the soul of man is a portion transmitted from the essence of God, the divine nature must not only be liable to passion and change, but also to ignorance, evil desires, infirmity, and all kinds of vice. There is nothing more inconstant than man, contrary movements agitating and distracting his soul. He is ever and anon deluded by want of skill, and overcome by the slightest temptations; while every one feels that the soul itself is a receptacle for all kinds of pollution. All these things must be attributed to the divine nature, if we hold that the soul is of the essence of God, or a secret influx of divinity. Who does not shudder at a thing so monstrous? Paul, indeed, quoting from Aratus, tells us we are his off-spring (Acts 17:28); not in substance, however, but in quality, in as much as he has adorned us with divine endowments. Meanwhile, to lacerate the essence of the Creator, in order to assign a portion to each individual, is the height of madness. It must, therefore, be held as certain, that souls, notwithstanding of their having the divine image engraven on them, are created just as angels are. Creation, however, is not a transfusion of essence, but a commencement of it out of nothing. Nor, though the spirit is given by God, and when it quits the flesh again returns to him, does it follow that it is a portion withdrawn from his essence.72 Here, too, Osiander, carried away by his

illusions entangled himself in an impious error, by denying that the image of God could be in man without his essential righteousness; as if God were unable, by the mighty power of his Spirit, to render us conformable to himself, unless Christ were substantially transfused into us. Under whatever colour some attempt to gloss these delusions, they can never so blind the eyes of intelligent readers as to prevent them from discerning in them a revival of Manicheism. But from the words of Paul, when treating of the renewal of the image (2 Cor. 3:18), the inference is obvious, that man was conformable to God, not by an influx of substance, but by the grace and virtue of the Spirit. He says, that by beholding the glory of Christ, we are transformed into the same image as by the Spirit of the Lord; and certainly the Spirit does not work in us so as to make us of the same substance with God.

6. It were vain to seek a definition of the soul from philosophers, not one of whom, with the exception of Plato, distinctly maintained its immortality. Others of the school of Socrates, indeed, lean the same way, but still without teaching distinctly a doctrine of which they were not fully persuaded. Plato, however, advanced still further, and regarded the soul as an image of God. Others so attach its powers and faculties to the present life, that they leave nothing external to the body. Moreover, having already shown from Scripture that the substance of the soul is incorporeal, we must now add, that though it is not properly enclosed by space, it however occupies the body as a kind of habitation, not only animating all its parts, and rendering the organs fit and useful for their actions, but also holding the first place in regulating the conduct. This it does not merely in regard to the offices of a terrestrial life, but also in regard to the service of God. This, though not clearly seen in our corrupt state, yet the impress of its remains is seen in our very vices. For whence have men such a thirst for glory but from a sense of shame? And whence this

sense of shame but from a respect for what is honourable? Of this, the first principle and source is a consciousness that they were born to cultivate righteousness,—a consciousness akin to religion. But as man was undoubtedly created to meditate on the heavenly life, so it is certain that the knowledge of it was engraven on the soul. And, indeed, man would want the principal use of his understand- ing if he were unable to discern his felicity, the perfection of which consists in being united to God. Hence, the principal action of the soul is to aspire thither, and, accordingly, the more a man studies to approach to God, the more he proves himself to be endued with reason.

Though there is some plausibility in the opinion of those who maintain that man has more than one soul, namely, a sentient and a rational, yet as there is no soundness in their arguments, we must reject it, unless we would torment ourselves with things frivolous and useless. They tell us (see chap. 5 sec. 4), there is a great repugnance between organic movements and the rational part of the soul. As if reason also were not at variance with herself, and her counsels sometimes conflicting with each other like hostile armies. But since this disorder results from the depravation of nature, it is erroneous to infer that there are two souls, because the faculties do not accord so harmoniously as they ought. But I leave it to philosophers to discourse more subtilely of these faculties. For the edification of the pious, a simple definition will be sufficient. I admit, indeed, that what they ingeniously teach on the subject is true, and not only pleasant, but also useful to be known; nor do I forbid any who are inclined to prosecute the study. First, I admit that there are five senses, which Plato (in Theæteto) prefers calling organs, by which all objects are brought into a common sensorium, as into a kind of receptacle: Next comes the imagination (*phantasia*), which distinguishes between the objects brought into the sensorium: Next, reason, to which the general power of Judgment belongs: And, lastly, intellect, which contemplates with fixed and quiet look whatever reason discursively revolves. In like manner, to intellect, fancy, and reason, the three cognitive faculties of the soul, correspond three appetite faculties—viz. will—whose office is to choose whatever reason and intellect propound; irascibility, which seizes on what is set before it by reason and fancy; and concupiscence, which lays hold of the objects presented by sense and fancy.

Though these things are true, or at least plausible, still, as I fear they are more fitted to entangle, by their obscurity, than to assist us, I think it best to omit them. If any one chooses to distribute the powers of the mind in a different manner, calling one appetive, which, though devoid of reason, yet obeys reason, if directed from a different quarter, and another intellectual, as being by itself participant of reason, I have no great objection. Nor am I dis- posed to quarrel with the view, that there are three principles of action—viz. sense, intellect, and appetite. But let us rather adopt a division adapted to all capacities—a thing which certainly is not to be obtained from philosophers. For they, when they would speak most plainly, divide the soul into appetite and intellect, but make both double. To the latter they sometimes give the name of *contemplative*, as being contented with mere knowledge and having no active powers (which circumstance makes Cicero designate it by the name of intellect, *ingenii*) (De Fin. lib. 5). At other times they give it the name of *practical*, because it variously moves the will by the apprehension of good or evil. Under this class is included the art of living well and justly. The former—viz. appetite —they divide into will and concupiscence, calling it βουλεσις, so whenever the appetite, which they call ορμη, obeys the reason. But when appetite, casting off the yoke of reason, runs to intemperance, they call it πατηος. Thus they always presuppose in man a reason by which he is able to guide himself aright.

7. From this method of teaching we are forced somewhat to dissent. For philosophers, being unacquainted with the corruption of nature, which is the punishment of revolt, erroneously confound two states of man which are very different from each other. Let us therefore hold, for the purpose of the present work, that the soul consists of two parts, the intellect and the will (Book 2 chap. 2 sec. 2, 12), —the office of the intellect being to distinguish between objects, according as they seem deserving of being approved or disapproved; and the office of the will, to choose and follow what the intellect declares to be good, to reject and shun what it declares to be bad (Plato, in Phædro). We dwell not on the subtlety of Aristotle, that the mind has no motion of itself; but that the moving power is choice, which he also terms the appetite intellect. Not to lose ourselves in superfluous questions, let it be enough to know that the intellect is to us, as it were, the guide and ruler of the soul; that the will always follows its beck, and waits for its decision, in matters of desire. For which reason Aristotle truly taught, that in the appetite there is a pursuit and rejection corresponding in some degree to affirmation and negation in the intellect (Aristot. Ethic. lib. 6 sec. 2). Moreover, it will be seen in another place (Book 2 c. 2 see. 12-26), how surely the intellect governs the will. Here we only wish to observe, that the soul does not possess any faculty which may not be duly referred to one or other of these members. And in this way we comprehend sense under intellect. Others distinguish thus: They say that sense inclines to pleasure in the same way as the intellect to good; that hence the appetite of sense becomes concupiscence and lust, while the affection of the intellect becomes will. For the term appetite, which they prefer, I use that of will, as being more common.

8. Therefore, God has provided the soul of man with intellect, by which he might discern good from evil, just from unjust, and might know what to follow or to shun, reason going before with her lamp; whence philosophers, in reference to her directing power, have called her το εγεμονικον. To this he has joined will, to which choice belongs. Man excelled in these noble endowments in his primitive condition, when reason, intelligence, prudence, and Judgment, not only sufficed for the government of his earthly life, but also enabled him to rise up to God and eternal happiness. Thereafter choice was added to direct the appetites, and temper all the organic motions; the will being thus perfectly submissive to the authority of reason. In this upright state, man possessed freedom of will, by which, if he chose, he was able to obtain eternal life. It were here unseasonable to introduce the question concerning the secret predestination of God, because we are not considering what might or might not happen, but what the nature of man truly was. Adam, therefore, might have stood if he chose, since it was only by his own will that he fell; but it was because his will was pliable in either directions and he had not received constancy to persevere, that he so easily fell. Still he had a free choice of good and evil; and not only so, but in the mind and will there was the highest rectitude, and all the organic parts were duly framed to obedience, until man corrupted its good properties, and destroyed himself. Hence the great darkness of philosophers who have looked for a complete building in a ruin, and fit arrangement in disorder. The principle they set out with was, that man could not be a rational animal unless he had a free choice of good and evil. They also imagined that the distinction between virtue and vice was destroyed, if man did not of his own counsel arrange his life. So far well, had there been no change in man. This being unknown to them, it is not surprising that they throw every thing into confusion. But those who, while they profess to

be the disciples of Christ, still seek for free-will in man, notwithstanding of his being lost and drowned in spiritual destruction, labour under manifold delusion, making a heterogeneous mixture of inspired doctrine and philosophical opinions, and so erring as to both. But it will be better to leave these things to their own place (see Book 2 chap. 2) At present it is necessary only to remember, that man, at his first creation, was very different from all his posterity; who, deriving their origin from him after he was corrupted, received a hereditary taint. At first every part of the soul was formed to rectitude. There was soundness of mind and freedom of will to choose the good. If any one objects that it was placed, as it were, in a slippery position, because its power was weak, I answer, that the degree conferred was sufficient to take away every excuse. For surely the Deity could not be tied down to this condition,— to make man such, that he either could not or would not sin. Such a nature might have been more excellent; but to expostulate with God as if he had been bound to confer this nature on man, is more than unjust, seeing he had full right to determine how much or how little He would give. Why He did not sustain him by the virtue of perseverance is hidden in his counsel; it is ours to keep within the bounds of soberness. Man had received the power, if he had the will, but he had not the will which would have given the power; for this will would have been followed by perseverance. Still, after he had received so much, there is no excuse for his having spontaneously brought death upon himself. No necessity was laid upon God to give him more than that intermediate and even transient will, that out of man's fall he might extract materials for his own glory.

CHAPTER 16.

THE WORLD, CREATED BY GOD, STILL CHERISHED AND PROTECTED BY HIM. EACH AND ALL OF ITS PARTS GOVERNED BY HIS PROVIDENCE.

The divisions of this chapter are, I. The doctrine of the special providence of God over all the creatures, singly and collectively, as opposed to the dreams of the Epicureans about fortune and fortuitous causes. II. The fiction of the Sophists concerning the omnipotence of God, and the error of philosophers, as to a confused and equivocal government of the world, sec. 1-5. All animals, but especially mankind, from the peculiar superintendence exercised over them, are proofs, evidences, and examples of the providence of God, sec. 6, 7. III. A consideration of fate, fortune, chance, contingence, and uncertain events (on which the matter here under discussion turns).

Sections.

1. Even the wicked, under the guidance of carnal sense, acknowledge that God is the Creator. The godly acknowledge not this only, but that he is a most wise and powerful governor and preserver of all created objects. In so doing, they lean on the Word of God, some passages from which are produced.

2. Refutation of the Epicureans, who oppose fortune and fortuitous causes to Divine Providence, as taught in Scripture. The sun, a bright manifestation of Divine Providence.

3. Figment of the Sophists as to an indolent Providence refuted. Consideration of the Omnipotence as combined with the Providence of God. Double benefit resulting from

a proper acknowledgement of the Divine Omnipotence. Cavils of Infidelity.

4. A definition of Providence refuting the erroneous dogmas of Philosophers. Dreams of the Epicureans and Peripatetics. 5. Special Providence of God asserted and proved by arguments founded on a consideration of the Divine Justice and Mercy. Proved also by passages of Scripture, relating to the sky, the earth, and animals.
6. Special Providence proved by passages relating to the human race, and the more especially that for its sake the world was created.
7. Special Providence proved, lastly, from examples taken from the history of the Israelites, of Jonah, Jacob, and from daily experience.
8. Erroneous views as to Providence refuted:—I. The sect of the Stoics. II. The fortune and chance of the Heathen.
9. How things are said to be fortuitous to us, though done by the determinate counsel of God. Example. Error of separating contingency and event from the secret, but just, and most wise counsel of God. Two examples.

1. It were cold and lifeless to represent God as a momentary Creator, who completed his work once for all, and then left it. Here, especially, we must dissent from the profane, and maintain that the presence of the divine power is conspicuous, not less in the perpetual condition of the world then in its first creation. For, although even wicked men are forced, by the mere view of the earth and sky, to rise to the Creator, yet faith has a method of its own in assigning the whole praise of creation to God. To this effect is the passage of the Apostle already quoted that by faith we understand that the worlds were framed by the Word of God (Heb. 11:3); because, without proceeding to his Providence, we cannot under- stand the full force of what is meant by God being the Creator, how much soever we may

seem to comprehend it with our mind, and confess it with our tongue. The carnal mind, when once it has perceived the power of God in the creation, stops there, and, at the farthest, thinks and ponders on nothing else than the wisdom, power, and goodness displayed by the Author of such a work (matters which rise spontaneously, and force themselves on the notice even of the unwilling), or on some general agency on which the power of motion depends, exercised in preserving and governing it. In short, it imagines that all things are sufficiently sustained by the energy divinely infused into them at first. But faith must penetrate deeper. After learning that there is a Creator, it must forthwith infer that he is also a Governor and Preserver, and that, not by producing a kind of general motion in the machine of the globe as well as in each of its parts, but by a special providence sustaining, cherishing, superintending, all the things which he has made, to the very minutest, even to a sparrow. Thus David, after briefly premising that the world was created by God, immediately descends to the continual course of Providence, "By the word of the Lord were the heavens framed, and all the host of them by the breath of his mouth;" immediately adding, "The Lord looketh from heaven, he beholdeth the children of men," (Ps. 33:6, 13, &c). He subjoins other things to the same effect. For although all do not reason so accurately, yet because it would not be credible that human affairs were superintended by God, unless he were the maker of the world, and no one could seriously believe that he is its Creator without feeling convinced that he takes care of his works; David with good reason, and in admirable order, leads us from the one to the other. In general, indeed, philosophers teach, and the human mind conceives, that all the parts of the world are invigorated by the secret inspiration of God. They do not, however reach the height to which David rises taking all the pious along with him, when he says, "These wait all upon thee, that thou mayest give them their meat in due season. That thou givest them they gather: thou openest thine hand, they are filled with good. Thou hidest thy face, they are troubled: thou takest away their breath, they die, and return to their dust. Thou sendest forth thy Spirit, they are created, and thou renewest the face of the earth," (Ps. 104:27-30). Nay, though they subscribe to the sentiment of Paul, that in God "we live, and move, and have our being," (Acts 17:28), yet they are far from having a serious apprehension of the grace which he commends, because they have not the least relish for that special care in which alone the paternal favour of God is discerned.

2. That this distinction may be the more manifest, we must consider that the Providence of God, as taught in Scripture, is opposed to fortune and fortuitous causes. By an erroneous opinion prevailing in all ages, an opinion almost universally prevailing in our own day — viz. that all things happen fortuitously, the true doctrine of Providence has not only been obscured, but almost buried. If one falls among robbers, or ravenous beasts; if a sudden gust of wind at sea causes shipwreck; if one is struck down by the fall of a house or a tree; if an- other, when wandering through desert paths, meets with deliverance; or, after being tossed by the waves, arrives in port, and makes some wondrous hair-breadth escape from death — all these occurrences, prosperous as well as adverse, carnal sense will attribute to fortune. But whose has learned from the mouth of Christ that all the hairs of his head are numbered (Mt. 10:30), will look farther for the cause, and hold that all events whatsoever are governed by the secret counsel of God. With regard to inanimate objects again we must hold that though each is possessed of its peculiar properties, yet all of them exert their force only in so far as directed by the immediate hand of God. Hence they are merely instruments, into which God constantly infuses what energy he sees meet, and turns and converts to any purpose at his

pleasure. No created object makes a more wonderful or glorious display than the sun. For, besides illuminating the whole world with its brightness, how admirably does it foster and invigorate all animals by its heat, and fertilise the earth by its rays, warming the seeds of grain in its lap, and thereby calling forth the verdant blade! This it supports, increases, and strengthens with additional nurture, till it rises into the stalk; and still feeds it with perpetual moisture, till it comes into flower; and from flower to fruit, which it continues to ripen till it attains maturity. In like manner, by its warmth trees and vines bud, and put forth first their leaves, then their blossom, then their fruit. And the Lord, that he might claim the entire glory of these things as his own, was pleased that light should exist, and that the earth should be replenished with all kinds of herbs and fruits before he made the sun. No pious man, therefore, will make the sun either the necessary or principal cause of those things which existed before the creation of the sun, but only the instrument which God employs, because he so pleases; though he can lay it aside, and act equally well by himself: Again, when we read, that at the prayer of Joshua the sun was stayed in its course (Josh. 10:13); that as a favour to Hezekiah, its shadow receded ten degrees (2 Kings 20:11); by these miracles God declared that the sun does not daily rise and set by a blind instinct of nature, but is governed by Him in its course, that he may renew the remembrance of his paternal favour toward us. Nothing is more natural than for spring, in its turns to succeed winter, summer spring, and autumn summer; but in this series the variations are so great and so unequal as to make it very apparent that every single year, month, and day, is regulated by a new and special providence of God.

3. And truly God claims omnipotence to himself, and would have us to acknowledge it,—not the vain, indolent, slumbering omnipotence which sophists feign, but vigilant, efficacious, energetic, and ever active,—not an

omnipotence which may only act as a general principle of confused motion, as in ordering a stream to keep within the channel once pre- scribed to it, but one which is intent on individual and special movements. God is deemed omnipotent, not because he can act though he may cease or be idle, or because by a general instinct he continues the order of nature previously appointed; but because, governing heaven and earth by his providence, he so overrules all things that nothing happens without his counsel. For when it is said in the Psalms, "He has done whatsoever he has pleased," (Ps. 115:3), the thing meant is his sure and deliberate purpose. It were insipid to interpret the Psalmist's words in philosophic fashion, to mean that God is the primary agent, because the beginning and cause of all motion. This rather is the solace of the faithful, in their adversity, that every thing which they endure is by the ordination and command of God, that they are under his hand. But if the government of God thus extends to all his works, it is a childish cavil to confine it to natural influx. Those moreover who confine the providence of God within narrow limits, as if he allowed all things to be borne along freely according to a perpetual law of nature, do not more defraud God of his glory than themselves of a most useful doctrine; for nothing were more wretched than man if he were exposed to all possible movements of the sky, the air, the earth, and the water. We may add, that by this view the singular goodness of God towards each individual is unbecomingly impaired. David exclaims (Ps. 8:3), that infants hanging at their mothers breasts are eloquent enough to celebrate the glory of God, because, from the very moment of their births they find an aliment prepared for them by heavenly care. Indeed, if we do not shut our eyes and senses to the fact, we must see that some mothers have full provision for their infants, and others almost none, according as it is the pleasure of God to nourish one child more liberally, and another more sparingly. Those who attribute due praise to the omnipotence of God thereby derive a double benefit. He to whom heaven and earth belong, and whose nod all creatures must obey, is fully able to reward the homage which they pay to him, and they can rest secure in the protection of Him to whose control everything that could do them harm is subject, by whose authority, Satan, with all his furies and engines, is curbed as with a bridle, and on whose will everything adverse to our safety depends. In this way, and in no other, can the immoderate and superstitious fears, excited by the dangers to which we are exposed, be calmed or subdued. I say superstitious fears. For such they are, as often as the dangers threatened by any created objects inspire us with such terror, that we tremble as if they had in themselves a power to hurt us, or could hurt at random or by chance; or as if we had not in God a sufficient protection against them. For example, Jeremiah forbids the children of God " to be dismayed at the signs of heaven, as the heathen are dismayed at them," (Jer. 10:2). He does not, indeed, condemn every kind of fear. But as unbelievers transfer the government of the world from God to the stars, imagining that happiness or misery depends on their decrees or presages, and not on the Divine will, the consequence is, that their fear, which ought to have reference to him only, is diverted to stars and comets. Let him, therefore, who would beware of such unbelief, always bear in mind, that there is no random power, or agency, or motion in the creatures, who are so governed by the secret counsel of God, that nothing happens but what he has knowingly and willingly decreed.

4. First, then, let the reader remember that the providence we mean is not one by which the Deity, sitting idly in heaven, looks on at what is taking place in the world, but one by which he, as it were, holds the helms and overrules all events. Hence his providence extends not less to the hand than to the eye. When Abraham said to his son,

God will provide (Gen. 22:8), he meant not merely to assert that the future event was foreknown to Gods but to resign the management of an unknown business to the will of Him whose province it is to bring perplexed and dubious matters to a happy result. Hence it appears that providence consists in action. What many talk of bare prescience is the merest trifling. Those do not err quite so grossly who attribute government to God, but still, as I have observed, a confused and promiscuous government which consists in giving an impulse and general movement to the machine of the globe and each of its parts, but does not specially direct the action of every creature. It is impossible, however, to tolerate this error. For, according to its abettors, there is nothing in this providence, which they call universal, to prevent all the creatures from being moved contingently, or to prevent man from turning himself in this direction or in that, according to the mere freedom of his own will. In this ways they make man a partner with God,—God, by his energy, impressing man with the movement by which he can act, agreeably to the nature conferred upon him while man voluntarily regulates his own actions. In short, their doctrine is, that the world, the affairs of men, and men themselves, are governed by the power, but not by the decree of God. I say nothing of the Epicureans (a pest with which the world has always been plagued), who dream of an inert and idle God, and others, not a whit sounder, who of old feigned that God rules the upper regions of the air, but leaves the inferior to Fortune. Against such evident madness even dumb creatures lift their voice.

My intention now is, to refute an opinion which has very generally obtained—an opinion which, while it concedes to God some blind and equivocal movement, withholds what is of principal moment—viz. the disposing and directing of every thing to its proper end by incomprehensible wisdom. By withholding government, it makes God the ruler of the world in name only, not in reality. For what, I ask, is meant by government, if it be not to preside so as to regulate the destiny of that over which you preside? I do not, however, totally repudiate what is said of an universal providence, provided, on the other hand, it is conceded to me that the world is governed by God, not only because he maintains the order of nature appointed by him, but because he takes a special charge of every one of his works. It is true, indeed, that each species of created objects is moved by a secret instinct of nature, as if they obeyed the eternal command of God, and spontaneously followed the course which God at first appointed. And to this we may refer our Saviour's words, that he and his Father have always been at work from the beginning (John 5:17); also the words of Paul, that "in him we live, and move, and have our being," (Acts 17:28); also the words of the author of the Epistle to the Hebrews, who, when wishing to prove the divinity of Christ, says, that he upholdeth "all things by the word of his power," (Heb. 1:3). But some, under pretext of the general, hide and obscure the special providence, which is so surely and clearly taught in Scripture, that it is strange how any one can bring himself to doubt of it. And, indeed, those who interpose that disguise are themselves forced to modify their doctrine, by adding that many things are done by the special care of God. This, however, they erroneously confine to particular acts. The thing to be proved, therefore, is, that single events are so regulated by God, and all events so proceed from his determinate counsel, that nothing happens fortuitously.

5. Assuming that the beginning of motion belongs to God, but that all things move spontaneously or casually, according to the impulse which nature gives, the vicissitudes of day and nights summer and winter, will be the work of God; inasmuch as he, in assigning the office of each, appointed a certain law, namely, that they should always with uniform tenor observe the same course, day

succeeding night, month succeeding month, and year succeeding year. But, as at one time, excessive heat, combined with drought, burns up the fields; at another time excessive rains rot the crops, while sudden devastation is produced by tempests and storms of hail, these will not be the works of God, unless in so far as rainy or fair weather, heat or cold, are produced by the concourse of the stars, and other natural causes. According to this view, there is no place left either for the paternal favour, or the Judgments of God. If it is said that God fully manifests his beneficence to the human race, by furnishing heaven and earth with the ordinary power of producing food, the explanation is meagre and heathenish: as if the fertility of one year were not a special blessing, the penury and dearth of another a special punishment and curse from God. But as it would occupy too much time to enumerate all the arguments, let the authority of God himself suffice. In the Law and the Prophets he repeatedly declares, that as often as he waters the earth with dew and rain, he manifests his favour, that by his command the heaven becomes hard as iron, the crops are destroyed by mildew and other evils, that storms and hail, in devastating the fields, are signs of sure and special vengeance. This being admitted, it is certain that not a drop of rain falls without the express command of God. David, indeed (Ps. 146:9), extols the general providence of God in supplying food to the young ravens that cry to him but when God himself threatens living creatures with famine, does he not plainly declare that they are all nourished by him, at one time with scanty, at another with more ample measure? It is childish, as I have already said, to confine this to particular acts, when Christ says, without reservation, that not a sparrow falls to the ground without the will of his Father (Mt. 10:29). Surely, if the flight of birds is regulated by the counsel of God, we must acknowledge with the prophet, that while he "dwelleth on high," he "humbleth himself to behold the things that are in heaven and in the earth," (Ps. 113:5, 6).

6. But as we know that it was chiefly for the sake of mankind that the world was made, we must look to this as the end which God has in view in the government of it. The prophet Jeremiah exclaims, "O Lord, I know that the way of man is not in himself: it is not in man that walketh to direct his steps," (Jer. 10:23). Solomon again says, "Man's goings are of the Lord: how can a man then understand his own way?" (Prov. 20:24). Will it now be said that man is moved by God according to the bent of his nature, but that man himself gives the movement any direction he pleases? Were it truly so, man would have the full disposal of his own ways. To this it will perhaps be answered, that man can do nothing without the power of God. But the answer will not avail, since both Jeremiah and Solomon attribute to God not power only, but also election and decree. And Solomon, in another place, elegantly rebukes the rashness of men in fixing their plans without reference to God, as if they were not led by his hand. "The preparations of the heart in man, and the answer of the tongue, is from the Lord," (Prov. 16:1). It is a strange infatuation, surely for miserable men, who cannot even give utterance except in so far as God pleases, to begin to act without him! Scriptures moreover, the better to show that every thing done in the world is according to his decree, declares that the things which seem most fortuitous are subject to him. For what seems more attributable to chance than the branch which falls from a tree, and kills the passing traveller? But the Lord sees very differently, and declares that He delivered him into the hand of the slayer (Exod. 21:13). In like manners who does not attribute the lot to the blindness of Fortune? Not so the Lord, who claims the decision for himself (Prov. 16:33). He says not, that by his power the lot is thrown into the lap, and taken out, but declares that the only thing which could be attributed to chance is from him.

To the same effect are the words of Solomon, "The poor and the deceitful man meet together; the Lord lighteneth both their eyes," (Prov. 29:13). For although rich and poor are mingled together in the world, in saying that the condition of each is divinely appointed, he reminds us that God, Who en- lightens all, has his own eye always open, and thus exhorts the poor to patient endurance, seeing that those who are discontented with their lot endeavour to shake off a burden which God has imposed upon them. Thus, too, another prophet upbraids the profane, who ascribe it to human industry, or to fortune, that some grovel in the mire while others rise to honour. "Promotion cometh neither from the east, nor from the west, nor from the south. But God is the judge: he putteth down ones and setteth up another," (Ps. 75:6, 7). Because God cannot divest himself of the office of judge, he infers that to his secret counsel it is owing that some are elevated, while others remain without honour.

7. Nay, I affirm in general, that particular events are evidences of the special providence of God. In the wilderness God caused a south wind to blow, and brought the people a plentiful supply of birds (Exod. 19:13). When he desired that Jonah should be thrown into the sea, he sent forth a whirlwind. Those who deny that God holds the reins of government will say that this was contrary to ordinary practice, whereas I infer from it that no wind ever rises or rages without his special command. In no way could it be true that "he maketh the winds his messengers, and the flames of fire his ministers;" that "he maketh the clouds his chariot, and walketh upon the wings of the wind," (Ps. 104:3, 4), did he not at pleasure drive the clouds and winds and therein manifest the special presence of his power. In like manner, we are elsewhere taught, that whenever the sea is raised into a storm, its billows attest the special presence of God. "He commandeth and raiseth the stormy wind, which lifteth up the waves." "He maketh the storm a calm,

so that the waves thereof are still," (Ps. 107:25, 29) He also elsewhere declares, that he had smitten the people with blasting and mildew (Amos 4:9). Again while man naturally possesses the power of continuing his species, God describes it as a mark of his special favour, that while some continue childless, others are blessed with offspring: for the fruit of the womb is his gift. Hence the words of Jacob to Rachel, "Am I in God's stead, who has withheld from thee the fruit of the womb?" (Gen. 30:2). To conclude in one word. Nothing in nature is more ordinary than that we should be nourished with bread. But the Spirit declares not only that the produce of the earth is God's special gift, but "that man does not live by bread only," (Deut. 8:3), because it is not mere fulness that nourishes him but the secret blessing of God. And hence, on the other hand, he threatens to take away "the stay and the staff, the whole stay of bread, and the whole stay of water," (Is. 3:1). Indeed, there could be no serious meaning in our prayer for daily bread, if God did not with paternal hand supply us with food. Accordingly, to convince the faithful that God, in feeding them, fulfils the office of the best of parents, the prophet reminds them that he "giveth food to all flesh," (Ps. 136:25). In fine, when we hear on the one hand, that "the eyes of the Lord are upon the righteous, and his ears are open unto their cry," and, on the other hand, that "the face of the Lord is against them that do evil, to cut off the remembrance of them from the earth," (Ps. 34:15, 16), let us be assured that all creatures above and below are ready at his service, that he may employ them in whatever way he pleases. Hence we infer, not only that the general providence of God, continuing the order of nature, extends over the creatures, but that by his wonderful counsel they are adapted to a certain and special purpose.

8. Those who would cast obloquy on this doctrine, calumniate it as the dogma of the Stoics concerning fate. The same charge was formerly brought against Augustine

(lib. ad Bonifac. 2, c. 6 et alibi). We are unwilling to dispute about words; but we do not admit the term Fate, both because it is of the class which Paul teaches us to shun, as profane novelties (1 Tim. 6:20), and also because it is attempted, by means of an odious term, to fix a stigma on the truth of God. But the dogma itself is falsely and maliciously imputed to us. For we do not with the Stoics imagine a necessity consisting of a perpetual chain of causes, and a kind of involved series contained in nature, but we hold that God is the disposer and ruler of all things, —that from the remotest eternity, according to his own wisdom, he decreed what he was to do, and now by his power executes what he decreed. Hence we maintain, that by his providence, not heaven and earth and inanimate creatures only, but also the counsels and wills of men are so governed as to move exactly in the course which he has destined. What, then, you will say, does nothing happen fortuitously, nothing contingently? I answer, it was a true saying of Basil the Great, that Fortune and Chance are heathen terms; the meaning of which ought not to occupy pious minds. For if all success is blessing from God, and calamity and adversity are his curse, there is no place left in human affairs for fortune and chance. We ought also to be moved by the words of Augustine (Retract. lib. 1 cap. 1), "In my writings against the Academics," says he, "I regret having so often used the term Fortune; although I intended to denote by it not some goddess, but the fortuitous issue of events in external matters, whether good or evil. Hence, too, those words, Perhaps, Per- chance, Fortuitously, which no religion forbids us to use, though everything must be referred to Divine Providence. Nor did I omit to observe this when I said, Although, perhaps, that which is vulgarly called Fortune, is also regulated by a hidden order, and what we call Chance is nothing else than that the reason and cause of which is secret. It is true, I so spoke, but I repent of having mentioned Fortune there as I did, when I see the very bad custom which men have of saying, not as they ought to do, 'So God pleased,' but, 'So Fortune pleased.' " In short, Augustine everywhere teaches, that if anything is left to fortune, the world moves at random. And although he elsewhere declares (Quæstionum, lib. 83). that all things are carried on, partly by the free will of man, and partly by the Providence of God, he shortly after shows clearly enough that his meaning was, that men also are .ruled by Providence, when he assumes it as a principle, that there cannot be a greater absurdity than to hold that anything is done without the ordination of God; because it would happen at random. For which reason, he also excludes the contingency which depends on human will, maintaining a little further on, in clearer terms, that no cause must be sought for but the will of God. When he uses the term permission, the meaning which he attaches to it will best appear from a single passage (De Trinity. lib. 3 cap. 4), where he proves that the will of God is the supreme and primary cause of all things, because nothing happens without his order or permission. He certainly does not figure God sitting idly in a watch-tower, when he chooses to permit anything. The will which he represents as interposing is, if I may so express it, active (*actualis*), and but for this could not be regarded as a cause.

9. But since our sluggish minds rest far beneath the height of Divine Providence, we must have recourse to a distinction which may assist them in rising. I say then, that though all things are ordered by the counsel and certain arrangement of God, to us, however, they are fortuitous,— not because we imagine that Fortune rules the world and mankind, and turns all things upside down at random (far be such a heartless thought from every Christian breast); but as the order, method, end, and necessity of events, are, for the most part, hidden in the counsel of God, though it is certain that they are produced by the will of God, they have the appearance of being fortuitous, such being the form

under which they present themselves to us, whether considered in their own nature, or estimated according to our knowledge and Judgment. Let us suppose, for example, that a merchant, after entering a forest in company with trust-worthy individuals, imprudently strays from his companions and wanders bewildered till he falls into a den of robbers and is murdered. His death was not only foreseen by the eye of God, but had been fixed by his decree. For it is said, not that he foresaw how far the life of each individual should extend, but that he determined and fixed the bounds which could not be passed (Job 14:5). Still, in relation to our capacity of discernment, all these things appear fortuitous. How will the Christian feel? Though he will consider that every circumstance which occurred in that person's death was indeed in its nature fortuitous, he will have no doubt that the Providence of God overruled it and guided fortune to his own end. The same thing holds in the case of future contingencies. All future events being uncertain to us, seem in suspense as if ready to take either direction. Still, however, the impression remains seated in our hearts, that nothing will happen which the Lord has not provided. In this sense the term event is repeatedly used in Ecclesiastes, because, at the first glance, men do not penetrate to the primary cause which lies concealed. And yet, what is taught in Scripture of the secret providence of God was never so completely effaced from the human heart, as that some sparks did not always shine in the darkness. Thus the soothsayers of the Philistine, though they waver in uncertainty, attribute the adverse event partly to God and partly to chance. If the ark, say they, "Goes up by the way of his own coast to Bethshemish, then he has done us this great evil; but if not, then we shall know that it is not his hand that smote us, it was a chance that happened to us." (1 Sam. 6:9). Foolishly, indeed, when divination fails them they flee to fortune. Still we see them constrained, so as not to venture to regard their disaster as fortuitous. But the mode in which God, by the curb of his Providence, turns events in whatever direction he pleases, will appear from a remark- able example. At the very same moment when David was discovered in the wilderness of Maon, the Philistines make an inroad into the country, and Saul is forced to depart (1 Sam. 23:26, 27). If God, in order to provide for the safety of his servant, threw this obstacle in the way of Saul, we surely cannot say, that though the Philistine took up arms contrary to human expectation, they did it by chance. What seems to us contingence, faith will recognise as the secret impulse of God. The reason is not always equally apparent, but we ought undoubtedly to hold that all the changes which take place in the world are produced by the secret agency of the hand of God. At the same time, that which God has determined, though it must come to pass, is not, however, precisely, or in its own nature, necessary. We have a familiar example in the case of our Saviour's bones. As he assumed a body similar to ours, no sane man will deny that his bones were capable of being broken and yet it was impossible that they should be broken (John 19:33, 36). Hence, again, we see that there was good ground for the distinction which the Schoolmen made between necessity, *secundum quid*, and necessity absolute, also between the necessity of *consequent* and of *consequence*. God made the bones of his Son frangible, though he exempted them from actual fracture; and thus, in reference to the necessity of his counsel, made that impossible which might have naturally taken place.

CHAPTER 17.

USE TO BE MADE OF THE DOCTRINE OF PROVIDENCE.

This chapter may be conveniently divided into two parts:—I. A general explanation is given of the doctrine of Divine Providence, in so far as conducive to the solid instruction and consolation of the godly, sect. 1, and specially sect. 2-12. First, however, those are refuted who deny that the world is governed by the secret and incomprehensible counsel of God; those also who throw the blame of all wickedness upon God, and absurdly pretend that exercises of piety are useless, sect. 2-5. Thereafter is added a holy meditation on Divine Providence, which, in the case of prosperity, is painted to the life, sect. 6-11.

II. A solution of two objections from passages of Scripture, which attribute repentance to God, and speak of something like an abrogation of his decrees.

Sections.

1. Summary of the doctrine of Divine Providence. 1. It embraces the future and the past. 2. It works by means, without means, and against means. 3. Mankind, and particularly the Church, the object of special care. 4. The mode of ad- ministration usually secret, but always just. This last point more fully considered.

2. The profane denial that the world is governed by the secret counsel of God, refuted by passages of Scripture. Salutary counsel.

3. This doctrine, as to the secret counsel of God in the government of the world, gives no countenance either to the impiety of those who throw the blame of their wickedness upon God, the petulance of those who reject

means, or the error of those who neglect the duties of religion.

4. As regards future events, the doctrine of Divine Providence not inconsistent with deliberation on the part of man.

5. In regard to past events, it is absurd to argue that crimes ought not to be punished, because they are in accordance with the divine decrees. 1. The wicked resist the declared will of God. 2. They are condemned by conscience. 3. The essence and guilt of the crime is in themselves, though God uses them as instruments.

6. A holy meditation on Divine Providence. 1. All events happen by the ordination of God. 2. All things contribute to the advantage of the godly. 3. The hearts of men and all their endeavours are in the hand of God. 4. Providence watches for the safety of the righteous. 5. God has a special care of his elect.

7. Meditation on Providence continued. 6. God in various ways curbs and defeats the enemies of the Church. 7. He overrules all creatures, even Satan himself, for the good of his people.

8. Meditation on Providence continued. 8. He trains the godly to patience and moderation. Examples. Joseph, Job, and David. 9. He shakes off their lethargy, and urges them to repentance.

9. Meditation continued. 10. The right use of inferior causes explained. 11. When the godly become negligent or imprudent in the discharge of duty, Providence reminds them of their fault. 12. It condemns the iniquities of the wicked. 13. It produces a right consideration of the future, rendering the servants of God prudent, diligent, and active. 14. It causes them to resign themselves to the wisdom and omnipotence of God, and, at the same time, makes them diligent in their calling.

10. Meditation continued. 15. Though human life is beset with innumerable evils, the righteous, trusting to Divine Providence, feel perfectly secure.

11. The use of the foregoing meditation.

12. The second part of the chapter, disposing of two objections. 1. That Scripture represents God as changing his purpose, or repenting, and that, therefore, his Providence is not fixed. Answer to this first objection. Proof from Scripture that God cannot repent.

13. Why repentance attributed to God.

14. Second objection, that Scripture speaks of an annulment of the divine decrees. Objection answered. Answer confirmed by an example.

1. Moreover, such is the proneness of the human mind to indulge in vain subtleties, that it becomes almost impossible for those who do not see the sound and proper use of this doctrine, to avoid entangling themselves in perplexing difficulties. It will, therefore, be proper here to advert to the end which Scripture has in view in teaching that all things are divinely ordained. And it is to be observed, first, that the Providence of God is to be considered with reference both to the past and the future; and, secondly, that in overruling all things, it works at one time with means, at another without means, and at another against means. Lastly, the design of God is to show that He takes care of the whole human race, but is especially vigilant in governing the Church, which he favours with a closer inspection. Moreover, we must add, that although the paternal favour and beneficence, as well as the judicial severity of God, is often conspicuous in the whole course of his Providence, yet occasionally as the causes of events are concealed, the thought is apt to rise, that human affairs are whirled about by the blind impulse of Fortune, or our carnal nature inclines us to speak as if God were amusing himself by tossing men up and down like balls. It is true,

indeed, that if with sedate and quiet minds we were disposed to learn, the issue would at length make it manifest, that the counsel of God was in accordance with the highest reason, that his purpose was either to train his people to patience, correct their depraved affections, tame their wantonness, inure them to self-denial, and arouse them from torpor; or, on the other hand, to cast down the proud, defeat the craftiness of the ungodly, and frustrate all their schemes. How much soever causes may escape our notice, we must feel assured that they are deposited with him, and accordingly exclaim with David, "Many, O Lord my God, are thy wonderful works which thou hast done, and thy thoughts which are to us-ward: if I would declare and speak of them, they are more than can be numbered," (Ps. 40:5). For while our adversities ought always to remind us of our sins, that the punishment may incline us to repentance, we see, moreover, how Christ declares there is something more in the secret counsel of his Father than to chastise every one as he deserves. For he says of the man who was born blind, "Neither has this man sinned, nor his parents: but that the works of God should be made manifest in him," (John 9:3). Here, where calamity takes precedence even of birth, our carnal sense murmurs as if God were unmerciful in thus afflicting those who have not offended. But Christ declares that, provided we had eyes clear enough, we should perceive that in this spectacle the glory of his Father is brightly displayed. We must use modesty, not as it were compelling God to render an account, but so revering his hidden Judgments as to account his will the best of all reasons. When the sky is overcast with dense clouds, and a violent tempest arises, the darkness which is presented to our eye, and the thunder which strikes our ears, and stupefies all our senses with terror, make us imagine that every thing is thrown into confusion, though in the firmament itself all continues quiet and serene. In the same way, when the tumultuous aspect of human affairs unfits us for judging, we should still hold, that God, in the pure light of his justice and wisdom, keeps all these commotions in due subordination, and conducts them to their proper end. And certainly in this matter many display monstrous infatuation, presuming to subject the works of God to their calculation, and discuss his secret counsels, as well as to pass a precipitate Judgment on things unknown, and that with greater license than on the doings of mortal men. What can be more preposterous than to show modesty toward our equals, and choose rather to suspend our Judgment than incur the blame of rashness, while we petulantly insult the hidden Judgments of God, Judgments which it becomes us to look up to and revere.

2. No man, therefore, will duly and usefully ponder on the providence of God save he who recollects that he has to do with his own Maker, and the Maker of the world, and in the exercise of the humility which becomes him, manifests both fear and reverence. Hence it is, that in the present day so many dogs tear this doctrine with envenomed teeth, or, at least, assail it with their bark, refusing to give more license to God than their own reason dictates to themselves. With what petulance, too, are we assailed for not being contented with the precepts of the Law, in which the will of God is comprehended, and for maintaining that the world is governed by his secret counsels? As if our doctrine were the figment of our own brain, and were not distinctly declared by the Spirit, and repeated in innumerable forms of expression! Since some feeling of shame restrains them from daring to belch forth their blasphemies against heaven, that they may give the freer vent to their rage, they pretend to pick a quarrel with us. But if they refuse to admit that every event which happens in the world is governed by the incomprehensible counsel of God, let them explain to what effect Scripture declares, that "his Judgments are a great deep," (Ps. 36:7). For when Moses exclaims that the will of God "is not in heaven that thou shouldest say, Who

shall go up for us to heaven, and bring it unto us? Neither is it beyond the sea that thou shouldest say, Who shall go over the sea and bring it unto us?" (Deut. 30:12, 13), because it was familiarly expounded in the law, it follows that there must be another hidden will which is compared to " a great deep." It is of this will Paul exclaims, "O! the depths of the riches of the wisdom and know- ledge of God! How unsearchable are his Judgments, and his ways past finding out! For who has known the mind of the Lord, or who has been his counsellor?" (Rom. 11:33, 34). It is true, indeed, that in the law and the gospel are comprehended mysteries which far transcend the measure of our sense; but since God, to enable his people to understand those mysteries which he has deigned to reveal in his word, enlightens their minds with a spirit of under- standing, they are now no longer a deep, but a path in which they can walk safely—a lamp to guide their feet—a light of life—a school of clear and certain truth. But the admirable method of governing the world is justly called a deep, because, while it lies hid from us, it is to be reverently adored. Both views Moses has beautifully expressed in a few words. "Secret things," saith he, "belong unto the Lord our God, but those things which are revealed belong unto us and to our children for ever," (Deut. 29:29). We see how he enjoins us not only studiously to meditate on the law, but to look up with reverence to the secret Providence of God. The Book of Job also, in order to keep our minds humble, contains a description of this lofty theme. The author of the Book, after taking an ample survey of the universe, and discoursing magnificently on the works of God, at length adds, "Lo, these are parts of his ways: but how little a portion is heard of him?" (Job 26:14). For which reason he, in another passage, distinguishes between the wisdom which dwells in God, and the measure of wisdom which he has assigned to man (Job 28:21, 28). After discoursing of the secrets of nature, he says that wisdom "is hid from the eyes of all living;" that "God understandeth the way thereof." Shortly after he adds, that it has been divulged that it might be investigated; for "unto man he said, Behold the fear of the Lord, that is wisdom." To this the words of Augustine refer, "As we do not know all the things which God does respecting us in the best order, we ought, with good intention, to act according to the Law, and in some things be acted upon according to the Law, his Providence being a Law immutable," (August. Quest. lib. 83 c. 27). Therefore, since God claims to himself the right of governing the world, a right unknown to us, let it be our law of modesty and soberness to acquiesce in his supreme authority regarding his will as our only rule of justice, and the most perfect cause of all things,—not that absolute will, indeed, of which sophists prate, when by a profane and impious divorce, they separate his justice from his power, but that universal overruling Providence from which nothing flows that is not right, though the reasons thereof may be concealed.

3. Those who have learned this modesty will neither murmur against God for adversity in time past, nor charge him with the blame of their own wickedness, as Homer's Agamemnon does.— Εγω δ ' ουκ αιτιος ειμι, αλλα Ζευς και μοιρα. *"Blame not me, but Jupiter and fate."* On the other hand, they will note like the youth in Plautus, destroy themselves in despairs as if hurried away by the Fates. "Unstable is the condition of affairs; instead of doing as they list, men only fulfil their fate: I will hie me to a rock, and there end my fortune with my life." Nor will they, after the example of another, use the name of God as a cloak for their crimes. For in another comedy Lyconides thus expresses himself:—"God was the impeller: I believe the gods wished it. Did they not wish it, it would not be done, I know." They will rather inquire and learn from Scripture what is pleasing to God, and then, under the guidance of the Spirit, endeavour to attain it. Prepared to follow

whithersoever God may call, they will show by their example that nothing is more useful than the knowledge of this doctrine, which perverse men undeservedly assail, because it is sometimes wickedly abused. The profane make such a bluster with their foolish puerilities, that they almost, ac- cording to the expression, confound heaven and earth. If the Lord has marked the moment of our death, it cannot be escaped,—it is vain to toil and use precaution. Therefore, when one ventures not to travel on a road which he hears is infested by robbers; when another calls in the physician, and annoys himself with drugs, for the sake of his health; a third abstains from coarser food, that he may not injure a sickly constitution; and a fourth fears to dwell in a ruinous house; when all, in short, devise, and, with great eagerness of mind, strike out paths by which they may attain the objects of their desire; either these are all vain remedies, laid hold of to correct the will of God, or his certain decree does not fix the limits of life and death, health and sickness, peace and war, and other matters which men, according as they desire and hate, study by their own industry to secure or avoid. Nay, these trifles even infer, that the prayers of the faithful must be perverse, not to say superfluous, since they entreat the Lord to make a provision for things which he has decreed from eternity. And then, imputing whatever happens to the providence of God, they connive at the man who is known to have expressly designed it. Has an assassin slain an honest citizen? He has, say they, executed the counsel of God. Has some one committed theft or adultery? The deed having been provided and ordained by the Lord, he is the minister of his providence. Has a son waited with indifference for the death of his parent, without trying any remedy? He could not oppose God, who had so predetermined from eternity. Thus all crimes receive the name of virtues, as being in accordance with divine ordination.

4. As regards future events, Solomon easily reconciles human deliberation with divine providence. For while he derides the stupidity of those who presume to undertake anything without God, as if they were not ruled by his hand, he elsewhere thus expresses himself: "A man's heart deviseth his ways but the Lord directeth his steps," (Prov. 16:9); intimating, that the eternal decrees of God by no means prevent us from proceeding, under his will, to provide for ourselves, and arrange all our affairs. And the reason for this is clear. For he who has fixed the boundaries of our life, has at the same time entrusted us with the care of it, provided us with the means of preserving it, forewarned us of the dangers to which we are exposed, and supplied cautions and remedies, that we may not be overwhelmed unawares. Now, our duty is clear, namely, since the Lord has committed to us the defence of our life, —to defend it; since he offers assistance,—to use it; since he forewarns us of danger,—not to rush on heedless; since he supplies remedies,—not to neglect them. But it is said, a danger that is not fatal will not hurt us, and one that is fatal cannot be resisted by any precaution. But what if dangers are not fatal, merely because the Lord has furnished you with the means of warding them off, and surmounting them? See how far your reasoning accords with the order of divine procedure: You infer that danger is not to be guarded against, because, if it is not fatal, you shall escape without precaution; whereas the Lord enjoins you to guard against its just because he wills it not to be fatal. These insane cavillers overlook what is plainly before their eyes—viz. that the Lord has furnished men with the artful of deliberation and caution, that they may employ them in subservience to his providence, in the preservation of their life; while, on the contrary, by neglect and sloth, they bring upon themselves the evils which he has annexed to them. How comes it that a provident man, while he consults for his safety, disentangles himself from impending evils;

while a foolish man, through un- advised temerity, perishes, unless it be that prudence and folly are, in either case, instruments of divine dispensation? God has been pleased to conceal from us all future events that we may prepare for them as doubtful, and cease not to apply the provided remedies until they have either been overcome, or have proved too much for all our care. Hence, I formerly observed, that the Providence of God does not interpose simply; but, by employing means, assumes, as it were, a visible form.

5. By the same class of persons, past events are referred improperly and inconsiderately to simple providence. As all contingencies whatsoever depend on it, therefore, neither thefts nor adulteries, nor murders, are perpetrated without an interposition of the divine will. Why, then, they ask, should the thief be punished for robbing him whom the Lord chose to chastise with poverty? Why should the murderer be punished for slaying him whose life the Lord had terminated? If all such persons serve the will of God, why should they be punished? I deny that they serve the will of God. For we cannot say that he who is carried away by a wicked mind performs service on the order of God, when he is only following his own malignant desires. He obeys God, who, being instructed in his will, hastens in the direction in which God calls him. But how are we so instructed unless by his word? The will declared by his word is, therefore, that which we must keep in view in acting, God requires of us nothing but what he enjoins. If we design anything contrary to his precept, it is not obedience, but contumacy and transgression. But if he did not will it, we could not do it. I admit this. But do we act wickedly for the purpose of yielding obedience to him? This, assuredly, he does not command. Nay, rather we rush on, not thinking of what he wishes, but so inflamed by our own passionate lust, that, with destined purpose, we strive against him. And in this way, while acting wickedly, we

serve his righteous ordination, since in his boundless wisdom he well knows how to use bad instruments for good purposes. And see how absurd this mode of arguing is. They will have it that crimes ought not to be punished in their authors, because they are not committed without the dispensation of God. I concede more—that thieves and murderers, and other evil-doers, are instruments of Divine Providence, being employed by the Lord himself to execute the Judgments which he has resolved to inflict. But I deny that this forms any excuse for their misdeeds. For how? Will they implicate God in the same iniquity with themselves, or will they cloak their depravity by his righteousness? They cannot exculpate themselves, for their own conscience condemns them: they cannot charge God, since they perceive the whole wickedness in themselves, and nothing in Him save the legitimate use of their wickedness. But it is said he works by their means. And whence, I pray, the fœtid odour of a dead body, which has been unconfined and putrefied by the sun's heat? All see that it is excited by the rays of the sun, but no man therefore says that the fetid odour is in them. In the same way, while the matter and guilt of wickedness belongs to the wicked man, why should it be thought that God contracts any impurity in using it at pleasure as his instrument? Have done, then, with that dog-like petulance which may, indeed, bay from a distance at the justice of God, but cannot reach it!

6. These calumnies, or rather frenzied dreams, will easily be dispelled by a pure and holy meditation on Divine Providence, meditation such as piety enjoins, that we may thence derive the best and sweetest fruit. The Christian, then, being most fully persuaded, that all things come to pass by the dispensation of God, and that nothing happens fortuitously, will always direct his eye to him as the principal cause of events, at the same time paying due regard to inferior causes in their own place. Next, he will

have no doubt that a special providence is awake for his preservation, and will not suffer anything to happen that will not turn to his good and safety. But as its business is first with men and then with the other creatures, he will feel assured that the providence of God reigns over both. In regard to men, good as well as bad, he will acknowledge that their counsels, wishes, aims and faculties are so under his hand, that he has full power to turn them in whatever direction, and constrain them as often as he pleases. The fact that a special providence watches over the safety of believers, is attested by a vast number of the clearest promises. "Cast thy burden upon the Lord, and he shall sustain thee: he shall never suffer the righteous to be moved." "Casting all your care upon him: for he careth for you." "He that dwelleth in the secret place of the Most High, shall abide under the shadow of the Almighty." "He that toucheth you, toucheth the apple of mine eye." "We have a strong city: salvation will God appoint for walls and bulwarks." "Can a woman forget her sucking child, that she should not have compassion on the son of her womb? yea, they may forget, yet will I not forget thee." Nay, the chief aim of the historical books of Scripture is to show that the ways of his saints are so carefully guarded by the Lord, as to prevent them even from dashing their foot against a stone. Therefore, as we a little ago justly exploded the opinion of those who feign a universal providence, which does not condescend to take special care of every creature, so it is of the highest moment that we should specially recognise this care towards ourselves. Hence, our Saviour, after declaring that even a sparrow falls not to the ground without the will of his Father, immediately makes the application, that being more valuable than many sparrows, we ought to consider that God provides more carefully for us. He even extends this so far, as to assure us that the hairs of our head are all numbered. What more can we wish, if not even a hair of our head can fall, save in accordance with his will? I speak not merely of the human race in general. God having chosen the Church for his abode, there cannot be a doubt, that in governing it, he gives singular manifestations of his paternal care.

7. The servant of God being confirmed by these promises and examples, will add the passages which teach that all men are under his power, whether to conciliate their minds, or to curb their wickedness, and prevent it from doing harm. For it is the Lord who gives us favour, not only with those who wish us well, but also in the eyes of the Egyptians (Exod. 3:21), in various ways defeating the malice of our enemies. Sometimes he deprives them of all presence of mind, so that they cannot undertake anything soundly or soberly. In this ways he sends Satan to be a lie in the mouths of all the prophets in order to deceive Ahab (1 Kings 22:22), by the counsel of the young men he so infatuates Rehoboam, that his folly deprives him of his kingdom (1 Kings 12:10, 15). Sometimes when he leaves them in posses- sion of intellect, he so fills them with terror and dismays that they can neither will nor plan the execution of what they had designed. Sometimes, too, after permitting them to attempt what lust and rage suggested, he opportunely interrupts them in their career, and allows them not to conclude what they had begun. Thus the counsel of Ahithophel, which would have been fatal to David, was defeated before its time (2 Sam. 17:7, 14). Thus, for the good and safety of his people, he overrules all the creatures, even the devil himself who, we see, durst not attempt any thing against Job without his permission and command. This know- ledge is necessarily followed by gratitude in prosperity, patience in adversity, and incredible security for the time to come. Every thing, therefore, which turns out prosperous and ac- cording to his wish, the Christian will ascribe entirely to God, whether he has experienced his beneficence through the instrumentality of men, or been aided by inanimate creatures. For he will thus consider with

himself: Certainly it was the Lord that disposed the minds of these people in my favour, attaching them to me so as to make them the instruments of his kindness. In an abundant harvest he will think that it is the Lord who listens to the heaven, that the heaven may listen to the earth, and the earth herself to her own offspring; in other cases, he will have no doubt that he owes all his prosperity to the divine blessing, and, admonished by so many circumstances, will feel it impossible to be ungrateful.

8. If any thing adverse befalls him, he will forthwith raise his mind to God, whose hand is most effectual in impressing us with patience and placid moderation of mind. Had Joseph kept his thoughts fixed on the treachery of his brethren, he never could have resumed fraternal affection for them. But turning toward the Lord, he forgot the injury, and was so inclined to mildness and mercy, that he even voluntarily comforts his brethren, telling them, "Be not grieved nor angry with yourselves that ye sold me hither; for God did send me before you to preserve life." "As for you, ye thought evil against me; but God meant it unto good," (Gen. 45:5; 50:20). Had Job turned to the Chaldees, by whom he was plundered, he should instantly have been fired with revenge, but recognising the work of the Lord, he solaces himself with this most beautiful sentiment: "The Lord gave, and the Lord has taken away; blessed be the name of the Lord," (Job 1:21). So when David was assailed by Shimei with stones and curses, had he immediately fixed his eyes on the man, he would have urged his people to retaliate the injury; but perceiving that he acts not without an impulse from the Lord, he rather calms them. "So let him curse," says he, "because the Lord has said unto him, Curse David." With the same bridle he elsewhere curbs the excess of his grief, "I was dumb, I opened not my mouth, because thou didst it," (Ps. 39:9). If there is no more effectual remedy for anger and impatience, he assuredly has not made little progress who has learned so to meditate on

Divine Providence, as to be able always to bring his mind to this, The Lord willed it, it must therefore be borne; not only because it is unlawful to strive with him, but because he wills nothing that is not just and befitting. The whole comes to this. When unjustly assailed by men, overlooking their malice (which could only aggravate our grief, and whet our minds for vengeance), let us remember to ascend to God, and learn to hold it for certain, that whatever an enemy wickedly committed against us was permitted, and sent by his righteous dispensation. Paul, in order to suppress our desire to retaliate in- juries, wisely reminds us that we wrestle not with flesh and blood, but with our spiritual enemy the devil, that we may prepare for the contest (Eph. 6:12). But to calm all the impulses of passion, the most useful consideration is, that God arms the devil, as well as all the wicked, for conflict, and sits as umpire, that he may exercise our patience. But if the disasters and miseries which press us happen without the agency of men, let us call to mind the doctrine of the Law (Deut. 28:1), that all prosperity has its source in the blessing of God, that all adversity is his curse. And let us tremble at the dreadful denunciation, "And if ye will not be reformed by these things, but will walk contrary unto me; then will I also walk contrary unto you," (Lev. 26:23, 24). These words condemn our torpor, when, according to our carnal sense, deeming that whatever happens in any way is fortuitous, we are neither animated by the kindness of God to worship him, nor by his scourge stimulated to repentance. And it is for this reason that Jeremiah (Lament. 3:38), and Amos (Amos 3:6), expostulated bitterly with the Jews, for not believing that good as well as evil was produced by the command of God. To the same effect are the words in Isaiah, "I form the light and create darkness: I make peace and create evil. I the Lord do all these things," (Is. 45:7).

9. At the same time, the Christian will not overlook inferior causes. For, while he regards those by whom he is

278

benefited as ministers of the divine goodness, he will not, therefore, pass them by, as if their kindness deserved no gratitude, but feeling sincerely obliged to them, will willingly confess the obligation, and endeavour, according to his ability, to return it. In fine, in the blessings which he receives, he will revere and extol God as the principal author, but will also honour men as his ministers, and perceive, as is the truth, that by the will of God he is under obligation to those, by whose hand God has been pleased to show him kindness. If he sustains any loss through negligence or imprudence, he will, indeed, believe that it was the Lord's will it should so be, but, at the same time, he will impute it to himself. If one for whom it was his duty to care, but whom he has treated with neglect, is carried off by disease, although aware that the person had reached a limit beyond which it was impossible to pass, he will not, therefore, extenuate his fault, but, as he had neglected to do his duty faithfully towards him, will feel as if he had perished by his guilty negligence. Far less where, in the case of theft or murder, fraud and preconceived malice have existed, will he palliate it under the pretext of Divine Providence, but in the same crime will distinctly recognise the justice of God, and the iniquity of man, as each is separately manifested. But in future events, especially, will he take account of such inferior causes. If he is not left destitute of human aid, which he can employ for his safety, he will set it down as a divine blessing; but he will not, therefore, be remiss in taking measures, or slow in employing the help of those whom he sees possessed of the means of assisting him. Regarding all the aids which the creatures can lend him, as hands offered him by the Lord, he will avail himself of them as the legitimate instruments of Divine Providence. And as he is uncertain what the result of any business in which he engages is to be (save that he knows, that in all things the Lord will provide for his good), he will zealously aim at what he deems for the best, so far as his abilities enable him. In adopting his measures, he will not be carried away by his own impressions, but will commit and resign himself to the wisdom of God, that under his guidance he may be led into the right path. However, his confidence in external aid will not be such that the presence of it will make him feel secure, the absence of it fill him with dismay, as if he were destitute. His mind will always be fixed on the Providence of God alone, and no consideration of present circumstances will be allowed to withdraw him from the steady contemplation of it. Thus Joab, while he acknowledges that the issue of the battle is entirely in the hand of God, does not therefore become inactive, but strenuously proceeds with what belongs to his proper calling, "Be of good courage," says he, "and let us play the men for our people, and for the cities of our God; and the Lord do that which seemeth him good," (2 Sam. 10:12). The same conviction keeping us free from rashness and false confidence, will stimulate us to constant prayer, while at the same time filling our minds with good hope, it will enable us to feel secure, and bid defiance to all the dangers by which we are surrounded.

10. Here we are forcibly reminded of the inestimable felicity of a pious mind. Innumerable are the ills which beset human life, and present death in as many different forms. Not to go beyond ourselves, since the body is a receptacle, nay the nurse, of a thousand diseases, a man cannot move without carrying along with him many forms of destruction. His life is in a manner interwoven with death. For what else can be said where heat and cold bring equal danger? Then, in what direction soever you turn, all surrounding objects not only may do harm, but almost openly threaten and seem to present immediate death. Go on board a ship, you are but a plank's breadth from death. Mount a horse, the stumbling of a foot endangers your life. Walk along the streets, every tile upon the roofs is a source

of danger. If a sharp instrument is in your own hand, or that of a friend, the possible harm is manifest. All the savage beasts you see are so many beings armed for your destruction. Even within a high walled garden, where everything ministers to delight, a serpent will sometimes lurk. Your house, constantly exposed to fire, threatens you with poverty by day, with destruction by night. Your fields, subject to hail, mildew, drought, and other injuries, denounce barrenness, and thereby famine. I say nothing of poison, treachery, robbery, some of which beset us at home, others follow us abroad. Amid these perils, must not man be very miserable, as one who, more dead than alive, with difficulty draws an anxious and feeble breath, just as if a drawn sword were constantly suspended over his neck? It may be said that these things happen seldom, at least not always, or to all, certainly never all at once. I admit it; but since we are reminded by the example of others, that they may also happen to us, and that our life is not an exception any more than theirs, it is impossible not to fear and dread as if they were to befall us. What can you imagine more grievous than such trepidation? Add that there is something like an insult to God when it is said, that man, the noblest of the creatures, stands exposed to every blind and random stroke of fortune. Here, however, we were only referring to the misery which man should feel, were he placed under the dominion of chance.

11. But when once the light of Divine Providence has illumined the believer's soul, he is relieved and set free, not only from the extreme fear and anxiety which formerly oppressed him, but from all care. For as he justly shudders at the idea of chance, so he can confidently commit himself to God. This, I say, is his comfort, that his heavenly Father so embraces all things under his power—so governs them at will by his nod—so regulates them by his wisdom, that nothing takes place save according to his appointment; that received into his favour, and entrusted to the care of his

angels neither fire, nor water, nor sword, can do him harm, except in so far as God their master is pleased to permit. For thus sings the Psalm, "Surely he shall deliver thee from the snare of the fowler, and from the noisome pestilence. He shall cover thee with his feathers, and under his wings shalt thou trust; his truth shall be thy shield and buckler. Thou shalt not be afraid for the terror by night; nor for the arrow that flieth by day; nor for the pestilence that walketh in darkness; nor for the destruction that wasteth at noonday" &c. (Ps. 91:2-6). Hence the exulting confidence of the saints, "The Lord is on my side; I will not fear: what can man do unto me? The Lord taketh my part with them that help me." "Though an host should encamp against me, my heart shall not fear." "Yea, though I walk through the valley of the shadow of death, I will fear no evil." (Ps. 118:6; 27:3; 23:4).

How comes it, I ask, that their confidence never fails, but just that while the world apparently revolves at random, they know that God is every where at work, and feel assured that his work will be their safety? When assailed by the devil and wicked men, were they not confirmed by remembering and meditating on Providence, they should, of necessity, forthwith despond. But when they call to mind that the devil, and the whole train of the ungodly, are, in all directions, held in by the hand of God as with a bridle, so that they can neither conceive any mischief, nor plan what they have conceived, nor how much soever they may have planned, move a single finger to perpetrate, unless in so far as he permits, nay, unless in so far as he commands; that they are not only bound by his fetters, but are even forced to do him service,—when the godly think of all these things they have ample sources of consolation. For, as it belongs to the lord to arm the fury of such foes and turn and destine it at pleasure, so it is his also to determine the measure and the end, so as to prevent them from breaking loose and wantoning as they list. Supported by this conviction, Paul, who had said in one place that his journey was hindered by Satan (1 Thess. 2:18), in another resolves, with the permission of God, to undertake it (1 Cor. 16:7). If he had only said that Satan was the obstacle, he might have seemed to give him too much power, as if he were able even to overturn the counsels of God; but now, when he makes God the disposer, on whose permission all journies depend, he shows, that however Satan may contrive, he can accomplish nothing except in so far as He pleases to give the word. For the same reason, David, considering the various turns which human life undergoes as it rolls, and in a manner whirls around, retakes himself to this asylum, "My times are in thy hand," (Ps. 31:15). He might have said the course of life or *time* in the singular number, but by *times* he meant to express, that how unstable soever the condition of man may be, the vicissitudes which are ever and anon taking place are under divine regulation. Hence Rezin and the king of Israel, after they had joined their forces for the destruction of Israel, and seemed torches which had been kindled to destroy and consume the land, are termed by the prophet "smoking fire brands." They could only emit a little smoke (Is. 7:4). So Pharaoh, when he was an object of dread to all by his wealth and strength, and the multitude of his troops, is compared to the largest of beasts, while his troops are compared to fishes; and God declares that he will take both leader and army with his hooks, and drag them whither he pleases (Ezek. 29:4). In one word, not to dwell longer on this, give heed, and you will at once perceive that ignorance of Providence is the greatest of all miseries, and the knowledge of it the highest happiness.

12. On the Providence of God, in so far as conducive to the solid instruction and consolation of believers (for, as to satisfying the curiosity of foolish men, it is a thing which cannot be done, and ought not to be attempted), enough would have been said, did not a few passages remain which

seem to insinuate, contrary to the view which we have expounded, that the counsel of God is not firm and stable, but varies with the changes of sublunary affairs. First, in reference to the Providence of God, it is said that he repented of having made man (Gen. 6:6), and of having raised Saul to the kingdom (1 Sam. 15:11), and that he will repent of the evil which he had resolved to inflict on his people as soon as he shall have perceived some amendment in them (Jer. 18:8). Secondly, his decrees are sometimes said to be annulled. He had by Jonah proclaimed to the Ninevites, "Yet forty days and Nineveh shall be over-thrown," but, immediately on their repentance, he inclined to a more merciful sentence (Jonah 3:4-10). After he had, by the mouth of Isaiah, given Hezekiah intimation of his death, he was moved by his tears and prayers to defer it (Is. 38:15; 2 Kings 20:15). Hence many argue that God has not fixed human affairs by an eternal decree, but according to the merits of each individual, and as he deems right and just, disposes of each single year, and day, and hour. As to repentance, we must hold that it can no more exist in God than ignorance, or error, or impotence. If no man knowingly or willingly reduces himself to the necessity of repentance, we cannot attribute repentance to God without saying either that he knows not what is to happen, or that he cannot evade it, or that he rushes precipitately and inconsiderately into a resolution, and then forthwith regrets it. But so far is this from the meaning of the Holy Spirit, that in the very mention of repentance he declares that God is not influenced by any feeling of regret, that he is not a man that he should repent. And it is to be observed, that, in the same chapter, both things are so conjoined, that a comparison of the passages admirably removes the appearance of contradiction. When it is said that God repented of having made Saul king, the term *change* is used figuratively. Shortly after, it is added, "The Strength of Israel will not lie nor repent; for he is not a man, that he should repent," (1 Sam. 15:29). In these words, his immutability is plainly asserted without figure. Wherefore it is certain that, in administering human affairs, the ordination of God is perpetual and superior to every thing like repentance. That there might be no doubt of his constancy, even his enemies are forced to bear testimony to it. For, Balaam, even against his will, behaved to break forth into this exclamation, "God is not a man, that he should lie; neither the son of man, that he should repent: has he said, and shall he not do it? or has he spoken, and shall he not make it good?" (Num. 23:19).

13. What then is meant by the term repentance? The very same that is meant by the other forms of expression, by which God is described to us humanly. Because our weakness cannot reach his height, any description which we receive of him must be lowered to our capacity in order to be intelligible. And the mode of lowering is to represent him not as he really is, but as we conceive of him. Though he is incapable of every feeling of perturbation, he declares that he is angry with the wicked. Wherefore, as when we hear that God is angry, we ought not to imagine that there is any emotion in him, but ought rather to consider the mode of speech accommodated to our sense, God appearing to us like one inflamed and irritated whenever he exercises Judgment, so we ought not to imagine any thing more under the term repentance than a change of action, men being wont to testify their dissatisfaction by such a change. Hence, because every change whatever among men is intended as a correction of what displeases, and the correction proceeds from repentance, the same term applied to God simply means that his procedure is changed. In the meantime, there is no inversion of his counsel or will, no change of his affection. What from eternity he had foreseen, approved, decreed, he prosecutes with unvarying uniformity, how sudden soever to the eye of man the variation may seem to be.

14. Nor does the Sacred History, while it relates that the destruction which had been proclaimed to the Ninevites was remitted, and the life of Hezekiah, after an intimation of death, prolonged, imply that the decrees of God were annulled. Those who think so labour under delusion as to the meaning of *threatenings*, which, though they affirm simply, nevertheless contain in them a tacit condition dependent on the result. Why did the Lord send Jonah to the Ninevites to predict the overthrow of their city? Why did he by Isaiah give Hezekiah intimation of his death? He might have destroyed both them and him without a message to announce the disaster. He had something else in view than to give them a warning of death, which might let them see it at a distance before it came. It was because he did not wish them destroyed but reformed, and thereby saved from destruction. When Jonah prophesies that in forty days Nineveh will be overthrown, he does it in order to prevent the overthrow. When Hezekiah is forbidden to hope for longer life, it is that he may obtain longer life. Who does not now see that, by threatening of this kind, God wished to arouse those to repentance whom he terrified, that they might escape the Judgment which their sins deserved? If this is so, the very nature of the case obliges us to supply a tacit condition in a simple denunciation. This is even confirmed by analogous cases. The Lord rebuking King Abimelech for having carried off the wife of Abraham, uses these words: "Behold, thou art but a dead man, for the woman which thou hast taken; for she is a man's wife." But, after Abimelech's excuse, he thus speaks: "Restore the man his wife, for he is a prophet, and he shall pray for thee, and thou shalt live; and if thou restore her not, know thou that thou shalt surely die, thou and all that art thine," (Gen. 20:3, 7). You see that, by the first announcement, he makes a deep impression on his mind, that he may render him eager to give satisfaction, and that by the second he clearly explains his will. Since the

other passages may be similarly explained, you must not infer from them that the Lord derogated in any respect from his former counsel, because he recalled what he had promulgated. When, by denouncing punishment, he admonishes to repentance those whom he wishes to spare, he paves the way for his eternal decree, instead of varying it one whit either in will or in language. The only difference is, that he does not express, in so many syllables, what is easily understood. The words of Isaiah must remain true, "The Lord of hosts has purposed, and who shall disannul it? And his hand is stretched out, and who shall turn it back?" (Isaiah 14:27).

CHAPTER 18.

THE INSTRUMENTALITY OF THE WICKED EMPLOYED BY GOD, WHILE HE CONTINUES FREE FROM EVERY TAINT.

This last chapter of the First Book consists of three parts: I. It having been said above that God bends all the reprobate, and even Satan himself, at his will, three objections are started. First, that this happens by the permission, not by the will of God. To this objection there is a twofold reply, the one, that angels and men, good and bad, do nothing but what is appointed by God; the second, that all movements are secretly directed to their end by the hidden inspiration of God, sec. 1, 2. II. A second objection is, that there are two contrary wills in God, if by a secret counsel he decrees what he openly prohibits by his law. This objection refuted, sec. 3. III. The third objection is, that God is made the author of all wickedness, when he is said not only to use the agency of the wicked, but also to govern their counsels and affections, and that therefore the wicked are unjustly punished. This objection refuted in the last section.

Sections.

1. The carnal mind the source of the objections which are raised against the Providence of God. A primary objection, making a distinction between the *permission* and the *will* of God, refuted. Angels and men, good and bad, do nought but what has been decreed by God. This proved by examples.

2. All hidden movements directed to their end by the unseen but righteous instigation of God. Examples, with answers to objections.

3. These objections originate in a spirit of pride and blasphemy. Objection, that there must be two contrary wills in God, refuted. Why the one simple will of God seems to us as if it were manifold.

4. Objection, that God is the author of sin, refuted by examples. Augustine's answer and admonition.

1. From other passages, in which God is said to draw or bend Satan himself, and all the reprobate, to his will, a more difficult question arises. For the carnal mind can scarcely comprehend how, when acting by their means, he contracts no taint from their impurity, nay, how, in a common operation, he is exempt from all guilt, and can justly condemn his own ministers. Hence a distinction has been invented between *doing* and *permitting* because to many it seemed altogether inexplicable how Satan and all the wicked are so under the hand and authority of God, that he directs their malice to whatever end he pleases, and employs their iniquities to execute his Judgments. The modesty of those who are thus alarmed at the appearance of absurdity might perhaps be excused, did they not endeavour to vindicate the justice of God from every semblance of stigma by defending an untruth. It seems absurd that man should be blinded by the will and command of God, and yet be forthwith punished for his blindness. Hence, recourse is had to the evasion that this is done only by the permission, and not also by the will of God. He himself, however, openly declaring that he *does* this, repudiates the evasion. That men do nothing save at the secret instigation of God, and do not discuss and deliberate on any thing but what he has previously decreed with himself and brings to pass by his secret direction, is proved by numberless clear passages of Scripture. What we formerly quoted from the Psalms, to the effect that he does whatever pleases him, certainly extends to all the actions of men. If God is the arbiter of peace and war, as is there said,

and that without any exception, who will venture to say that men are borne along at random with a blind impulse, while He is unconscious or quiescent? But the matter will be made clearer by special examples. From the first chapter of Job we learn that Satan appears in the presence of God to receive his orders, just as do the angels who obey spontaneously. The manner and the end are different, but still the fact is, that he cannot attempt anything without the will of God. But though afterwards his power to afflict the saint seems to be only a bare permission, yet as the sentiment is true, "The Lord gave, and the Lord has taken away; as it pleased the Lord, so it has been done," we infer that God was the author of that trial of which Satan and wicked robbers were merely the instruments. Satan's aim is to drive the saint to madness by despair. The Sabeans cruelly and wickedly make a sudden incursion to rob another of his goods. Job acknowledges that he was deprived of all his property, and brought to poverty, because such was the pleasure of God. Therefore, whatever men or Satan himself devise, God holds the helm, and makes all their efforts contribute to the execution of his Judgments. God wills that the perfidious Ahab should be deceived; the devil offers his agency for that purpose, and is sent with a definite command to be a lying spirit in the mouth of all the prophets (2 Kings 22:20). If the blinding and infatuation of Ahab is a Judgment from God, the fiction of bare permission is at an end; for it would be ridiculous for a judge only to permit, and not also to decree, what he wishes to be done at the very time that he commits the execution of it to his ministers. The Jews pur- posed to destroy Christ. Pilate and the soldiers indulged them in their fury; yet the disciples confess in solemn prayer that all the wicked did nothing but what the hand and counsel of God had decreed (Acts 4:28), just as Peter had previously said in his discourse, that Christ was delivered to death by the determinate counsel and foreknowledge of God (Acts

2:23); in other words, that God, to whom all things are known from the beginning, had determined what the Jews had executed. He repeats the same thing elsewhere, "Those things, which God before had showed by the mouth of all his prophets, that Christ should suffer, he has so fulfilled," (Acts 4:18). Absalom incestuously defiling his father's bed, perpetrates a detestable crime. God, however, declares that it was his work; for the words are, "Thou midst it secretly, but I will do this thing before all Israel, and before the sun." The cruelties of the Chaldeans in Judea are declared by Jeremiah to be the work of God. For which reason, Nebuchadnezzar is called the servant of God. God frequently exclaims, that by his hiss, by the clang of his trumpet, by his authority and command, the wicked are excited to war. He calls the Assyrian the rod of his anger, and the axe which he wields in his hand. The overthrow of the city and downfall of the temple, he calls his own work. David, not murmuring against God, but acknowledging him to be a just judge, confesses that the curses of Shimei are uttered by his orders. "The Lord," says he, "has bidden him curse." Often in sacred history whatever happens is said to proceed from the Lord, as the revolt of the ten tribes, the death of Eli's sons, and very many others of a similar description. Those who have a tolerable acquaintance with the Scriptures see that, with a view to brevity, I am only producing a few out of many passages, from which it is perfectly clear that it is the merest trifling to substitute a bare permission for the providence of God, as if he sat in a watch-tower waiting for fortuitous events, his Judgments meanwhile depending on the will of man.

2. With regard to secret movements, what Solomon says of the heart of a king, that it is turned hither and thither, as God sees meet, certainly applies to the whole human race, and has the same force as if he had said, that whatever we conceive in our minds is directed to its end by the secret inspiration of God. And certainly, did he not work

internally in the minds of men, it could not have been properly said, that he takes away the lip from the true, and prudence from the aged—takes away the heart from the princes of the earth, that they wander through devious paths. To the same effect, we often read that men are intimidated when He fills their hearts with terror. Thus David left the camp of Saul while none knew of its because a sleep from God had fallen upon all. But nothing can be clearer than the many passages which declare, that he blinds the minds of men, and smites them with giddiness, intoxicates them with a spirit of stupor, renders them infatuated, and hardens their hearts. Even these expressions many would confine to permissions as if, by deserting the reprobate, he allowed them to be blinded by Satan. But since the Holy Spirit distinctly says, that the blindness and infatuation are inflicted by the just Judgment of God, the solution is altogether inadmissible. He is said to have hardened the heart of Pharaoh, to have hardened it yet more, and confirmed it. Some evade these forms of expression by a silly cavil, because Pharaoh is elsewhere said to have hardened his own heart, thus making his will the cause of hardening it; as if the two things did not perfectly agree with each other, though in different senses —viz. that man, though acted upon by God, at the same time also acts. But I retort the objection on those who make it. If to harden means only bare permission, the contumacy will not properly belong to Pharaoh. Now, could any thing be more feeble and insipid than to interpret as if Pharaoh had only allowed himself to be hardened? We may add, that Scripture cuts off all handle for such cavils: "I," saith the Lord, "will harden his heart," (Exod. 4:21). So also, Moses says of the inhabitants of the land of Canaan, that they went forth to battle because the Lord had hardened their hearts (Josh. 11:20). The same thing is repeated by another prophet, "He turned their hearts to hate his people," (Psalm 105:25). In like manner, in Isaiah, he says of the Assyrian,

"I will send him against a hypocritical nation, and against the people of my wrath will I give him a charge to take the spoil, and to take the prey," (Isaiah 10:6); not that he intends to teach wicked and obstinate man to obey spontaneously, but because he bends them to execute his Judgments, just as if they carried their orders engraven on their minds. And hence it appears that they are impelled by the sure appointment of God. I admit, indeed, that God often acts in the reprobate by interposing the agency of Satan; but in such a manner, that Satan himself performs his part, just as he is impelled, and succeeds only in so far as he is permitted. The evil spirit that troubled Saul is said to be from the Lord (1 Sam. 16:14), to intimate that Saul's madness was a just punishment from God. Satan is also said to blind the minds of those who believe not (2 Cor. 4:4). But how so, unless that a spirit of error is sent from God himself, making those who refuse to obey the truth to believe a lie? According to the former view, it is said, "If the prophet be deceived when he has spoken a thing, I the Lord have deceived that prophet," (Ezek. 14:9). According to the latter view, he is said to have given men over to a reprobate mind (Rom. 1:28), because he is the special author of his own just vengeance; whereas Satan is only his minister (see Calv. in Ps. 141:4). But as in the Second Book (Chap. 4 sec. 3, 4), in discussing the question of man's freedom, this subject will again be considered, the little that has now been said seems to be all that the occasion requires. The sum of the whole is this,—since the will of God is said to be the cause of all things, all the counsels and actions of men must be held to be governed by his providence; so that he not only exerts his power in the elect, who are guided by the Holy Spirit, but also forces the reprobate to do him service.

3. As I have hitherto stated only what is plainly and unambiguously taught in Scripture, those who hesitate not to stigmatise what is thus taught by the sacred oracles, had

better beware what kind of censure they employ. If, under a pretence of ignorance, they seek the praise of modesty, what greater arrogance can be imagined than to utter one word in opposition to the authority of God—to say, for instance, "I think otherwise,"—"I would not have this subject touched?" But if they openly blaspheme, what will they gain by assaulting heaven? Such petulance, indeed, is not new. In all ages there have been wicked and profane men, who rabidly assailed this branch of doctrine. But what the Spirit declared of old by the mouth of David (Ps. 51:6), they will feel by experience to be true—God will overcome when he is judged. David indirectly rebukes the infatuation of those whose license is so unbridled, that from their grovelling spot of earth they not only plead against God, but arrogate to themselves the right of censuring him. At the same time, he briefly intimates that the blasphemies which they belch forth against heaven, instead of reaching God, only illustrate his justice, when the mists of their calumnies are dispersed. Even our faith, because founded on the sacred word of God, is superior to the whole world, and is able from its height to look down upon such mists.

Their first objection—that if nothing happens without the will of God, he must have two contrary wills, decreeing by a secret counsel what he has openly forbidden in his law —is easily disposed of. But before I reply to it, I would again remind my readers, that this cavil is directed not against me, but against the Holy Spirit, who certainly dictated this confession to that holy man Job, "The Lord gave, and the Lord has taken away," when, after being plundered by robbers, he acknowledges that their injustice and mischief was a just chastisement from God. And what says the Scripture elsewhere? The sons of Eli "hearkened not unto the voice of their father, because the Lord would slay them," (1 Sam. 2:25). Another prophet also exclaims, "Our God is in the heavens: he has done whatsoever he has pleased," (Ps. 115:3). I have already shown clearly enough that God is the author of all those things which, according to these objectors, happen only by his inactive permission. He testifies that he creates light and darkness, forms good and evil (Is. 45:7); that no evil happens which he has not done (Amos 3:6). Let them tell me whether God exercises his Judgments willingly or unwillingly. As Moses teaches that he who is accidentally killed by the blow of an axe, is delivered by God into the hand of him who smites him (Deut. 19:5), so the Gospel, by the mouth of Luke, declares, that Herod and Pontius Pilate conspired "to do whatsoever thy hand and thy counsel determined before to be done," (Acts 4:28). And, in truth, if Christ was not crucified by the will of God, where is our redemption? Still, however, the will of God is not at variance with itself. It undergoes no change. He makes no pretence of not willing what he wills, but while in himself the will is one and undivided, to us it appears manifold, because, from the feebleness of our intellect, we cannot comprehend how, though after a different manner, he wills and wills not the very same thing. Paul terms the calling of the Gentiles a hidden mystery, and shortly after adds, that therein was manifested the manifold wisdom of God (Eph. 3:10). Since, on account of the dullness of our sense, the wisdom of God seems manifold (or, as an old interpreter rendered it, multiform), are we, therefore, to dream of some variation in God, as if he either changed his counsel, or disagreed with himself? Nay, when we cannot comprehend how God can will that to be done which he forbids us to do, let us call to mind our imbecility, and remember that the light in which he dwells is not without cause termed inaccessible (1 Tim. 6:16), because shrouded in darkness. Hence, all pious and modest men will readily acquiesce in the sentiment of Augustine: "Man sometimes with a good will wishes something which God does not will, as when a good son wishes his father to live, while God wills him to die. Again, it may happen that man with a bad will wishes what God wills righteously, as when a bad son wishes his father to die, and God also wills it. The former wishes what God wills not, the latter wishes what God also wills. And yet the filial affection of the former is more consonant to the good will of God, though willing differently, than the unnatural affection of the latter, though willing the same thing; so much does approbation or condemnation depend on what it is befitting in man, and what in God to will, and to what end the will of each has respect. For the things which God rightly wills, he accomplishes by the evil wills of bad men,"—(*August. Enchirid. ad Laurent. cap.* 101). He had said a little before (cap. 100), that the apostate angels, by their revolt, and all the reprobate, as far as they themselves were concerned, did what God willed not; but, in regard to his omnipotence, it was impossible for them to do so: for, while they act against the will of God, his will is accomplished in them. Hence he exclaims, "Great is the work of God, exquisite in all he wills! so that, in a manner wondrous and ineffable, that is not done without his will which is done contrary to it, because it could not be done if he did not permit; nor does he permit it unwillingly, but willingly; nor would He who is good permit evil to be done, were he not omnipotent to bring good out of evil," (*Augustin. in* Ps. 111:2).

4. In the same way is solved, or rather spontaneously vanishes, another objection—viz. If God not only uses the agency of the wicked, but also governs their counsels and affections, he is the author of all their sins; and, therefore, men, in executing what God has decreed, are unjustly condemned, because they are obeying his will. Here *will* is improperly confounded with *precept*, though it is obvious, from innumerable examples, that there is the greatest difference between them. When Absalom defiled his father's bed, though God was pleased thus to avenge the adultery of David, he did not therefore enjoin an abandoned son to commit incest, unless, perhaps, in respect of David,

as David himself says of Shimei's curses. For, while he confesses that Shimei acts by the order of God, he by no means commends the obedience, as if that petulant dog had been yielding obedience to a divine command; but, recognising in his tongue the scourge of God, he submits patiently to be chastised. Thus we must hold, that while by means of the wicked God performs what he had secretly decreed, they are not excusable as if they were obeying his precept, which of set purpose they violate according to their lust.

How these things, which men do perversely, are of God, and are ruled by his secret providence, is strikingly shown in the election of King Jeroboam (1 Kings 12:20), in which the rashness and infatuation of the people are severely condemned for perverting the order sanctioned by God, and perfidiously revolting from the family of David. And yet we know it was God's will that Jeroboam should be anointed. Hence the apparent contradiction in the words of Hosea (Hosea 8:4; 13:11), because, while God complained that that kingdom was erected without his knowledge, and against his will, he elsewhere declares, that he had given King Jeroboam in his anger. How shall we reconcile the two things, — that Jeroboam's reign was not of God, and yet God appointed him king? In this way: The people could not revolt from the family of David without shaking off a yoke divinely imposed on them, and yet God himself was not deprived of the power of thus punishing the ingratitude of Solomon. We, therefore, see how God, while not willing treachery, with another view justly wills the revolt; and hence Jeroboam, by unexpectedly receiving the sacred unction, is urged to aspire to the kingdom. For this reason, the sacred history says, that God stirred up an enemy to deprive the son of Solomon of part of the kingdom (1 Kings 11:23). Let the reader diligently ponder both points: how, as it was the will of God that the people should be ruled by the hand of one king, their being rent into two parties was contrary to his will; and yet how this same will originated the revolt. For certainly, when Jeroboam, who had no such thought, is urged by the prophet verbally, and by the oil of unction, to hope for the kingdom, the thing was not done without the knowledge or against the will of God, who had expressly com- manded it; and yet the rebellion of the people is justly condemned, because it was against the will of God that they revolted from the posterity of David. For this reason, it is afterwards added, that when Rehoboam haughtily spurned the prayers of the people, "the cause was from the Lord, that he might perform his saying, which the Lord spake by Ahijah," (I Kings 12:15). See how sacred unity was violated against the will of God, while, at the same time, with his will the ten tribes were alienated from the son of Solomon. To this might be added another similar example—viz. the murder of the sons of Ahab, and the extermination of his whole progeny by the consent, or rather the active agency, of the people. Jehu says truly "There shall fall unto the earth nothing of the word of the Lord, which the Lord spake concerning the house of Ahab: for the Lord has done that which he spake by his servant Elijah," (2 Kings 10:10). And yet, with good reason, he upbraids the citizens of Samaria for having lent their assistance. "Ye be righteous: behold, I conspired against my master, and slew him, but who slew all these?"

If I mistake not, I have already shown clearly how the same act at once betrays the guilt of man, and manifests the righteousness of God. Modest minds will always be satisfied with Augustine's answer, "Since the Father delivered up the Son, Christ his own body, and Judas his Master, how in such a case is God just, and man guilty, but just because in the one act which they did, the reasons for which they did it are different?" (*August. Ep. 48, ad Vincentium*). If any are not perfectly satisfied with this explanation—viz. that there is no concurrence between God and man, when by His righteous impulse man does what he ought not to do, let them give heed to what Augustine elsewhere observes: "Who can refrain from trembling at those Judgments when God does according to his pleasure even in the hearts of the wicked, at the same time rendering to them according to their deeds?" (*De Grat. et lib. Arbit. ad Valent.* c. 20). And certainly, in regard to the treachery of Judas, there is just as little ground to throw the blame of the crime upon God, because He was both pleased that his ˙Son should be delivered up to death, and did deliver him, as to ascribe to Judas the praise of our redemption. Hence Augustine, in another place, truly observes, that when God makes his scrutiny, he looks not to what men could do, or to what they did, but to what they wished to do, thus taking account of their will and purpose. Those to whom this seems harsh had better consider how far their captiousness is entitled to any toleration, while, on the ground of its exceeding their capacity, they reject a matter which is clearly taught by Scripture, and complain of the enunciation of truths, which, if they were not useful to be known, God never would have ordered his prophets and apostles to teach. Our true wisdom is to embrace with meek docility, and without reservation, whatever the Holy Scriptures, have delivered. Those who indulge their petulance, a petulance manifestly directed against God, are undeserving of a longer refutation.

Printed in Great Britain
by Amazon